MANUFACTURING
URGENCY

MANUFACTURING

THE DEVELOPMENT INDUSTRY AND VIOLENCE AGAINST WOMEN

URGENCY

CORINNE L. MASON

University of Regina Press

Parts of chapter 1 were previously published in C.L. Mason, "Global Violence Against Women as a National Security 'Emergency,'" *Feminist Formations* 25(2): 55–80. Used with permission. Parts of chapter 2 were previously published in C.L. Mason, "'Cripping' the World Bank: Disability, Empowerment, and The Cost of Violence Against Women," *International Feminist Journal of Politics* 17(3): 435-453. Used with permission.

Printed and bound in Canada at Marquis. The text of this book is printed on 100% post-consumer recycled paper with earth-friendly vegetable-based inks.

Cover design: Duncan Campbell, University of Regina Press
Text design: John van der Woude, JVDW Designs
Copy editor: Dallas Harrison
Proofreader: Kristine Douaud
Indexer: Patricia Furdek
Cover art: "Rubber Awareness Bracelets" by C L 1 / Snapwire

Library and Archives Canada Cataloguing in Publication

Mason, Corinne L., 1986-, author
    Manufacturing urgency : the development industry and violence against women / Corinne L. Mason.

Includes bibliographical references and index. Issued in print and electronic formats. ISBN 978-0-88977-471-1 (softcover).--ISBN 978-0-88977-472-8 (PDF).--ISBN 978-0-88977-473-5 (HTML)

1. Women--Violence against. 2. International agencies. I. Title.

HV6250.4.W65M37 2017   362.88082   C2017-901025-5   C2017-901026-3

10 9 8 7 6 5 4 3 2 1

University of Regina Press, University of Regina
Regina, Saskatchewan, Canada, S4S 0A2
tel: (306) 585-4758 fax: (306) 585-4699
web: www.uofrpress.ca

U OF R PRESS

We acknowledge the support of the Canada Council for the Arts for our publishing program. We acknowledge the financial support of the Government of Canada. / Nous reconnaissons l'appui financier du gouvernement du Canada. This publication was made possible through Creative Saskatchewan's Creative Industries Production Grant Program.

Canada Council for the Arts   Conseil des Arts du Canada   Canada   creative SASKATCHEWAN

For Olive Frances

CONTENTS

IIIIIIIIIIIIIIIIIIIIIII

ACKNOWLEDGEMENTS

||||||||||||||||||||||||

I would like to thank the people who worked diligently helping me to shape this book: Kathryn Trevenen, Stephen Brown, Holly Johnson, Shoshana Magnet, Jaya Peruvmba, and Susan Ilcan. All of them provided tremendous support and encouragement in the earliest days of writing this book.

The book has been many years in the making, and I benefited from the love, support, kindness, and solidarity of my birth and chosen families, friends, feminist and queer communities, and generous colleagues at the University of Ottawa and Brandon University. You know who you are.

This book was not written in isolation. I tested ideas in a variety of settings, including conferences and workshops. I am very thankful for the feedback that I received from scholars, graduate students, and practitioners at Taking the Measure of Gender Workshop at Carleton University, *International Feminist Journal of Politics* annual conferences, and meetings of the National Women's Studies Association and Women's and Gender Studies et Recherches Feministes.

Thank you to Acquisitions Editor Karen Clark, the entire team at the University of Regina Press, and the anonymous reviewers, who helped me to publish this book in its best form.

The *International Feminist Journal of Politics* and *Feminist Formations* previously published some of this material. Thank you for granting me permission to reprint it here.

Thank you to those I interviewed: members of Gender Action, Meredith Turshen, Alys Willman, Todd Minerson, Jane Partpart, Eva Rathgeber, and Christina Finch.

Finally, the biggest and most love-filled thank you to my partner and best friend, Rune Breckon. We found love in a hopeless place.

This research was supported by the Social Sciences and Humanities Research Council of Canada.

ABBREVIATIONS

||||||||||||||||||||||||||

AIDS	acquired immune deficiency syndrome
DALYs	disability-adjusted life years
EPZs	export processing zones
FGM/C	female genital mutilation/cutting
GAD	gender and development
GAP	Gender Action Plan
HIV	human immunodeficiency virus
H1N1	strain of influenza popularly known as "swine flu"
I-VAWA	International Violence against Women Act
LGBT	lesbian, gay, bisexual, transgender
NGO	non-governmental organization
QDDR	Quadrennial Diplomacy and Development Review
UN	United Nations
USAID	United States Agency for International Development
WAD	women and development
WID	women in development

INTRODUCTION

||||||||||||||||||||||

The mass media serve as a system for communicating
messages and symbols to the general populace....In a world
of concentrated wealth and major conflicts of class interest,
to fulfill this role requires systematic propaganda.
—Edward S. Herman and Noam Chomsky,
Manufacturing Consent

The development industry cares about violence against women. A myriad of campaigns, documents, policies, checklists, statements, and action plans concerning gender issues—and specifically global violence against women—exists out there. Organizations are doing plenty of work on this issue, and with good reason. Across the world, 35 per cent of women have experienced physical or sexual violence, according to a United Nations (UN) study completed in 2013 (UN Women 2014). When the government of Canada last counted women's lifetime experience of violence in 1993, half of all women in Canada said that they had experienced at least one incident of physical or sexual violence since the age of sixteen (Canadian Women's Foundation 2015). Of course, issues involved in collecting information and reporting on violence against women—women not being believed by police, misgendering of transgender women during investigations, and lack of resources to collect data—skew the accuracy of these statistics. These numbers alone tell us that violence against women matters.

During the UN Decade for Women (1975–85), violence against women was continuously on conference agendas. Women around the world prioritized the issue in conference dialogues. However, it was rarely highlighted as the most important or urgent concern in official reports and action plans.[1] Thirty years later, violence against women emerged as *the* "priority issue" of the UN Commission for the Status of Women in 2013. The UN secretary-general supported an "in-depth study on all forms of violence against women" published in 2006, and the United Nations released its most comprehensive global campaign to end violence against women—UNiTE to End Violence against Women— in 2012 (UN 2006, 2012a). The World Bank, an organization known for its primary interest in economic growth, published new research and developed a new mantra on the cost of violence against women for the economy (2009a). The United States became adamant that ending violence against women was central to its foreign aid policy under the leadership of Hillary Clinton as secretary of state during her 2009–13 tenure. The U.S. Agency for International Development (USAID) and the State Department of Defense now collectively communicate the urgency to end violence against women as a national security concern.

What has changed in thirty years? Although violence against women has surely manifested itself in various new and insidious forms since 1985, gendered violence itself has not become more significant. Violence against women has always been an imperative issue for survivors, feminist activists, and concerned academics. Why has this issue come to matter to the development industry now? Why has it become urgent?

The primary aim of *Manufacturing Urgency: The Development Industry and Violence against Women* is to answer these questions through an analysis of some of the most hegemonic rhetoric on violence against women stemming from the most well-known and powerful institutions and actors in the world that make up the development-industrial complex. Specifically, I focus on leaders, financiers, and agenda setters: the World Bank, the United Nations, and American foreign policy. Through an analysis of research, documents, campaigns, and reports,

---

1   According to Jutta M. Joachim (2007), it was not until feminists made connections between violence against women and established and popular development discourses of the 1990s—namely human rights and economic development—that anti-violence initiatives in development policy and programs were secured. Feminists working with the development industry both externally and internally set the global agenda by communicating the importance of the issue as it connects to other development concerns.

and through interviews with gender advocates working in the development industry, I argue that violence against women matters because it is now rhetorically connected to the most important development objectives of the day.

According to global public health policy expert Meredith Turshen, whom I interviewed in 2012, development concerns too often reflect the "flavour of the day" and do not necessarily lead to increased budgets and resources. In fact, many of the announcements and research reports, and much of the foreign aid rhetoric, about violence against women do not lead to funding allocations, and if they do they are a "drop in the bucket" for industry heavyweights such as the World Bank. Although tracking funding and tangible outcomes of anti–violence against women rhetoric in the development community would make for an interesting book, I restrict my analysis to how this issue has become a flavour of the day and which kinds of discursive framings are necessary to create urgency around it in the development industry.

My focus on transnational rhetoric is designed to unravel and understand how violence against women is discursively manufactured as an urgent concern by development experts in order to fulfill other development objectives, including security concerns, economic growth schemes, and feel-good aid. I argue that this creation of urgency generates narrow understandings of this multifaceted issue that obscure its complexities and narrow its solutions. The rhetoric on urgency at the transnational level provides a justification for top-down, swift solutions that foreclose, or at least obscure, alternative organizing to end violence against women. Although the effort to end this violence seems like a change in direction, or even a feminist leap, for some organizations and actors in the development industry, my research shows that violence against women as the urgent issue for development reproduces the status quo more than it changes relations of power. I maintain that, whether violence against women—like any other human rights issue—is a fleeting flavour of the day or a calculated and enduring interest in the development industry, mapping and critically analyzing how the issue is represented as urgent is essential to better understanding how the development industry operates, at least discursively.

The title *Manufacturing Urgency* plays, of course, on Herman and Chomsky's *Manufacturing Consent: The Political Economy of the Mass*

Media, originally published in 1988. In it, the authors borrow from Walter Lippmann's phrase "the manufacture of consent" from his book *Public Opinion* published in 1922. His work on propaganda in the context of democracies influenced Herman and Chomsky's criticism of the media—namely his "propaganda model" that they used to analyze the U.S. media in terms of structure and performance. Ultimately, they argued that the U.S. media manufacture consent (and content) to reflect corporate investor interests and media profiteering by avoiding "flak" and adhering to an anti-communist agenda (which has largely been replaced by a "war on terror" rhetoric today). *Manufacturing Urgency* and *Manufacturing Consent* are very different studies, but ultimately they share a similar aim: to uncover the labour behind the scenes of public rhetoric and to provoke thought about how discourse functions to serve an industry's objectives. Like Herman and Chomsky's study of media, this book is not devoted to conspiracy theories or claims of a monolithic industry; rather, its aim is to demonstrate how the development industry and the institutions within it "serve as a system for communicating messages and symbols to the general populace." As Herman and Chomsky argue, "in a world of concentrated wealth and major conflicts of class interest, to fulfill this role requires systematic propaganda" (2002, 1). For example, in 2016 the International Monetary Fund finally admitted that neo-liberal austerity measures might be doing more bad than good in struggling economies, yet the organization also claimed to be at the forefront of the new agenda of "reconsideration" and its economists (who have clearly made "mistakes" and are responsible for burying economies in debt) were cited by the media as experts in this paradigm shift (Elliot 2016; Ostry, Loungani, and Furceri 2016). Herman and Chomsky might call this a "necessary illusion" used to divert the general populace away from a political process to overthrow the power of the organization or to imagine alternatives.

Manufacturing Urgency is concerned primarily with how the expertise of the development industry is maintained and strengthened even as cracks, inconsistencies, mistakes, and harms are uncovered. The book asks, after decades of ignoring violence against women, or at least not prioritizing the issue: which discourses have to be manufactured to ensure that the development industry emerges as the solution? When an issue becomes urgent, how do organizations in the industry rise up as experts, and which stories do they tell about taking the issue seriously? Discourses of urgency are about manufacturing an issue that needs to be dealt with *now*, and focusing on this discursive moment allows one to see the processes behind the project of what I call "making urgent." Urgency to end violence against women can reflect the reality of the issue as a pressing concern, but urgency is also a discursive and affective production. It does not merely exist; rather, it is designated. In fact, the line between urgent and non-urgent issues is drawn and redrawn in various contexts. Ultimately, for women who experience violence transnationally, this manufactured sense of urgency is insufficient, but it does work to maintain the power of the development industry.

Each chapter of this book labours at a different theoretical intersection to demonstrate the ways in which urgency is differently—yet similarly—manufactured. The first chapter examines the connections between violence against women and security agendas in development; the second connects disability and crip theory to the study of global violence against women; and the third weaves together affect theory and cultural studies of emotion with violence against women. My intention is to use these three case studies, three theoretical foci, and three representations of global violence against women to illustrate the varying impacts of manufacturing urgency around the issue of violence against women in the development industry. I am interested in how texts show up and circulate within these contexts and histories, and the structural apparatuses of the institutions that publish them.

What connects these three case studies are critical responses to discourses of urgency. Each chapter engages with a diversity of theories, many of which are rarely employed in development studies, not only to introduce new ways of critically engaging with the development industry, but also to demonstrate the need for multiple, varied, non-standardized, and at times deviating approaches to understanding the complexities of gender-based violence and proposed solutions to it. Although at times it might seem like this book veers in unexpected directions—imperialism, disability, and emotions—it does so because violence against women, and its representations, can only be understood through deep, transnational, and intersectional theoretical analyses.

Using both discursive analysis of documents and interviews with development experts, this book works toward decolonizing and critically evaluating representations of violence against women. In other words, it aims to unravel the historical, political, and cultural constructions of definitions and to provide solutions to global violence against women. Using transnational feminism as a theoretical frame and methodological entry point, decolonizing the project of making urgent reveals how concern in the development industry for violence against women is embedded within oppressive structures of power. In particular, this book investigates how neo-liberal, imperial, and neo-colonial development outcomes of anti-violence strategies are obscured by a seemingly moral and innocent call to end violence against women globally. Ultimately, I argue that the need for top-down development is secured by the role of the development industry in the project of making urgent. In other words, this project creates a space for this industry to become a leader in addressing global violence against women as a development "problem." It is in the interests of development experts to lead the charge on this issue because revealing it as a systemic global issue that interlocks with systems of gendered, racialized, classed, ableist, heterosexist/homophobic power, and other relations of rule would question development itself as a moral and political project.

Understanding how urgency functions discursively exposes how global systems of oppression are not undone but reinforced by the development industry in its attempt to eliminate violence against women. Importantly, the industry secures a sense of urgency on this issue by also requiring development expertise, and thus structures of uneven global power produced by development itself, while ignoring women's organizations already successfully mobilizing around the issue transnationally.

URGENCY

By using the term "urgency" as a framework in this book, I aim to suggest that there is a sudden and intensified interest in ending violence against women *now* among powerful actors in the development industry. The *Oxford English Dictionary* (2013b) defines the word *urgency* as "importance requiring swift action; an earnest and persistent quality; insistence." According to popular organizational leadership theorist John Kotter (2008, 23), "any effort to make changes of any magnitude" begins with a "sense of urgency." He argues that one must create this sense to encourage people to move in new directions.[2] He claims that opposition to a "true sense of urgency" is both complacency and false urgency (x). For Kotter, complacency requires only that the status quo be reproduced. A false sense of urgency can mean that real solutions to real problems cannot be found. This sense of urgency is frantic, uncoordinated, anxiety-producing, and dysfunctional. In contrast, a true sense of urgency focuses only on critical issues. It is his conception of *created* urgency, or what I call *manufactured* urgency, that is most pertinent to my analysis.

In communication studies and cultural studies, theorists have investigated conceptions of urgency, especially in relation to global health. For example, Penelope Ironstone-Catterall (2011) has argued that constructions of risk and uncertainty have affective dimensions and circulate discursively in relation to HIV/AIDS. She analyzes the communication of risk in everyday life. Focusing on industrial meat production and consumption, social hygiene related to contagions such as influenza, and the popularity of worst-case-scenario guidelines, she suggests that there is much at stake in understanding how a sense of urgency circulates within risk communication.

In *The Republic of Therapy: Triage and Sovereignty in West Africa's Time of AIDS*, anthropologist and medical practitioner Vinh-Kim Nguyen (2010) addresses urgency within the context of triage decisions in West Africa in the face of scarce access to retroviral therapies. Nguyen argues that the moral and political economy of "triage" creates possibilities for the practice of affective testimonials of seropositivity and immediate need in the context of prioritizing medical care. Using the term "therapeutic citizenship," Nguyen suggests that confessional technologies were central to staying alive because they were often deployed to communicate people's most urgent needs for medical care. Triage patients often created a sense of urgency with personal testimonies and performances of the most "needy" subjects for humanitarian intervention.

Urgency can be understood through its discursive circulation. For example, narratives regarding the risk of infection are communicated

---

2   For Kotter (2008), the business world has changed under globalization, in which there are new and always changing urgencies related to competition in a liberalized economy and in turbulent political crises.

as urgent through public health announcements that ask the populace to stay alert, to wash their hands, to receive anti-viral shots, or to seek medical attention *before* they become infected. Infection is often communicated as imminent, and the action on, or reaction to, a potential contagion is communicated as pressing. Urgency is also affective in nature. That is, it makes a sensory impact on people's bodies. In the language of affect and emotion theory, a sense of risk, anxiety, tension, or need can be described or coded as urgent (Ahmed 2004a, b; Massumi 2002). Discourses of urgency manufacture temporal anxieties. Although not all issues and concerns are distinctively and explicitly *described* as urgent, narratives of urgency can be produced through the discursive circulation of an issue *as* urgent by other standards or means. For example, that one needs a vaccination *now* might be immediately related not to one's own health but to stop the potential spread of a virus.

Unsurprisingly, to communicate the importance of working to end violence against women, the issue is often described popularly and in scholarly writing as "epidemic in proportion" or as a "global pandemic." Not only does this language imply the urgency of the issue, but also it is discursively prescriptive. As Soraya Chemaly asks, "violence against women is a global pandemic? Like H1N1? Like in *Contagion*? No way. *Think of your instinctive response to the idea of a worldwide bio-terror— that's what your response should be to the normalized level of violence against women around the world*" (2011; emphasis added). The grammar of urgency is prescriptive in that it requires *swift solutions*. Under the mounting pressure of a pandemic, one must think quickly, respond instantly, and act immediately to an issue *already* out of control.

In feminist international relations theory, which has heavily influenced my writing here, Cynthia Enloe and Ruth Jacobson use the concept of urgency and the phrase "tyranny of urgency" to describe how some issues are understood as urgent while others are seen as low priorities. In *The Curious Feminist: Searching for Women in a New Age of Empire*, Enloe argues that "'later' is a patriarchal time zone" (2004, 215). She suggests that feminist, or even women-centred, issues are not often made urgent; they can be left to "later." Her conceptualization of a patriarchal time zone is useful for international relations theorists in understanding the lack of integration of gender concerns in post-conflict and postwar transitions in which national unity, neo-liberal economic reform, and military or peacekeeping operations take precedence over feminist "distractions" (Jacobson 2013). Once national machineries, for example, deal with the most important issues first, gender questions can then be answered. Jacobson argues that the "tyranny of the urgent" is "an acknowledgement of the *barriers to integrating any kind of longer-term perspectives under the pressure of the hour-by-hour-demands*" (221; emphasis added). As I illustrate in this book, there are global cases of violence against women that must be dealt with now, and ordinary crises, or ongoing crises, of violence can be left for later.

In many ways, violence against women is an ordinary issue that is both systemic and structural. Generally, it is not dealt with as a pressing issue unless it is individualized. In North America, for example, with the exception of the criminalization of individual perpetrators of violence, there is no clear, obvious, or quick solution to violence against women, especially when the complexity of the political, cultural, economic, and social climate, which secures women's vulnerability to violence, is taken seriously. When it is understood as an individual or interpersonal issue, and especially a cultural one, makeshift solutions are presented as possible answers.

For example, in Canada violence against women is structural and systemic. At the intersection of colonization, racism, and misogyny, Indigenous women and girls are particularly vulnerable to violence. In 2014, the Royal Canadian Mounted Police counted over 1,200 Indigenous women who had been murdered or gone missing. Over 200 of these cases remain unsolved (RCMP 2014). Violence against Indigenous women is an urgent issue, yet it remains an ordinary and ongoing crisis in that, aside from rare and individualized responses that seek to criminalize perpetrators, it continues to be an issue slated for remedy later. The issue has not been enveloped by discourses of urgency. It is too complicated for *now*.

As I will demonstrate throughout this book, feminist language is often used to manufacture urgency to intervene in women's lives now, while a feminist politic that interlocks women's lived realities of systemic and structural oppression is left to what Enloe (2004) calls the "patriarchal time zone." For example, I argue elsewhere that the Canadian government's attention to the issue of sex-selective abortions (targeting girls) as "femicide" or "gendercide" obscures the real issue of murdered Indigenous women (Mason 2016). The moral panic about and subsequent attempts to change the legal right of Canadians to access abortion services by way of (ultimately failed) motions such as Motion 408 (to condemn discrimination against females occurring through sex-selective pregnancy termination) stemmed from a single *Canadian Medical Association Journal* editorial. This study, which manufactured urgency around the issue, extrapolated data from a small qualitative study in the United States on Indian women who had explicitly sought sex-selective abortions. The study, and the media coverage that followed it, led to the attempt to develop new regulations on access to reproductive health services. A temporal anxiety had been manufactured through discourses of urgency and without empirical evidence of sex-selective abortions actually taking place in Canada. While members of Parliament debated abortion access under the guise of protecting women and girls, and wielding the terms "femicide" and "gendercide" to do so, the really pressing issue of violence against Indigenous women and girls, and the targeting of racialized women as sexist and untrustworthy in their reproductive autonomy, continued to be questions left for later.

In so-called urgent moments, thinking critically about how urgency is produced and sustained, where emphasis is placed and where it is not, is of utmost importance. As Paula Treichler (1999, 1) argues in *How to Have a Theory in an Epidemic: Cultural Chronicles of AIDS*, scholars must "think carefully about ideas in the midst of a crisis": "[We must] use our intelligence and critical faculties to *consider theoretical problems*, develop policy, and articulate long-term social needs *even as we acknowledge the urgency* of the AIDS crisis and try to satisfy its relentless demand for immediate action" (emphasis added). In her work on HIV/AIDS, she maintains that there is a parallel "epidemic" worthy of study. She maintains that the circulation of default representations and hegemonic discursive devices to explain HIV/AIDS has created an "epidemic of signification" for over two decades (11). Analyzing both texts and images, she maintains that scholars and advocates must trace the cultural evolution of HIV/AIDS to make sense of the represented reality of the pandemic and the articulation of one's experience of it. Similar to the HIV/AIDS crisis, the global "epidemic" of violence against women has a parallel "epidemic of signification."

I maintain that the crisis of violence against women globally demands immediate action, but it is also important to trace the cultural production of its urgency and to critically analyze the representations of violence against women at the transnational level. This book is concerned with thinking through how we understand global violence against women as urgent through its signification, and it investigates which ideas of gender, race, class, sexuality, and disability are communicated through discourses of urgency established by experts in the development industry.

THEORETICAL FRAMEWORK

TRANSNATIONAL FEMINISM

This book builds upon a sophisticated body of transnational feminist theory. Drawing on Inderpal Grewal and Caren Kaplan's (1994) and Richa Nagar and Amanda Lock Swarr's (2010) conceptions of transnational feminism, it explores the relationship of representations of violence against women to "scattered hegemonies" or the interconnected webs of various sites and operations of power that affect, and are affected by, the reality of women's lives. As Grewal and Kaplan (1994) outline, tracing the interconnections among scattered hegemonies, including global economic structures, patriarchal nationalisms, "authentic" forms of "tradition," and other insidious structures of domination, is central to the field of transnational feminist inquiry. Borrowing from transnational feminist theories (Alexander and Mohanty 2010; Mohanty 2003) in particular, this book grapples with questions of power and representation. As Nagar and Swarr (2010) point out, transnational feminist theory has grown out of two interconnected dialogues in the field of feminist studies. It has been used by those seeking to question globalization, neo-liberalism, and social justice issues, and it has been used in debates since the 1980s on issues of voice, authority, identity, and representation in regard to the production of knowledge across borders. Transnational feminism is often misunderstood as a subfield of feminist theory with shared values, meanings, ideas, and languages (Nagar and Swarr 2010, 3). Instead, transnational feminism is a diverse field of study with porous boundaries in which theorists have intervened differently in a variety of questions pertaining to gender issues. Transnational feminism is an unstable field critical of its own definitions and practices. Such self-critique is politically useful in working toward cross-border solidarities while remaining accountable to asymmetrical "national and transnational processes [that] are mutually, though unequally, imbricated" (Alexander 2005, 183).

In practice, transnational feminism is conceptualized as an alternative to "global feminism" that has come to dominate Western feminist interventions in issues related to globalization (Desai 2005; Mohanty 2003). Since most Western feminist discourses rely on either a universalizing model of human rights or a cultural relativist approach, transnational feminists propose an alternative feminist vision of scholarship and practice that addresses women's relationships to multiple patriarchies and economic hegemonies. In *Feminism without Borders: Decolonizing Theory, Practicing Solidarity*, Chandra Talpade Mohanty (2003) sets out a framework for transnational feminism as a project of discursive "decolonization" in the name of cross-border solidarity. In particular, she challenges how Third World women have historically been represented in Western feminist scholarship as similarly oppressed. This way of making women visible is ineffectual in designing strategies to combat oppression globally. For Mohanty, "communities of resistance" are created through the ongoing discursive decolonization of Western feminist discourses.

Similarly, for Nagar and Swarr (2010, 5), transnational feminism is a three-pronged project:

> [It is] an intersectional set of understandings, tools, and practices that can: (a) attend to racialized, classed, masculinized, and heteronormative logics and practices of globalization and capitalist patriarchies, and the multiple ways in which they (re)structure colonial and neocolonial relations of domination and subordination; (b) grapple with the complex and contradictory ways in which these processes both inform and are shaped by a range of subjectivities and understandings of individual and collective agency; and (c) interweave critiques, actions, and self-reflexivity so as to resist a priori predictions of what might constitute feminist politics in a given place and time.

Using transnational feminism as a theoretical point of entry, I am particularly cautious of reading development discourse as hegemonic. Although the development industry has the power to shape discourse, feminists and social justice advocates also resist and reformulate this "expertise" to their own ends. The development industry is the focus of this book, and thus I centre the voices of the "experts," but this project is aimed at decolonizing development thought as one stage of a multi-stage project of resistance. Rather than conceptualize grand theories of hegemonic domination of the development industry, I use transnational feminist theory to consider how violence against women is made urgent in different ways in distinct but interconnected development discourses.

CRITICAL RACE THEORY

Although transnational feminist theory emerged out of theories from women of colour feminisms, Third World feminisms, multicultural feminisms, and international feminisms, different deployments of transnational feminism both continue to follow and depart from critical feminist political legacies and intellectual histories. Keeping this in mind, my theoretical framework borrows from theories of transnational feminism while remaining strongly connected to Canadian critical race feminism. In particular, my work is grounded by Sherene Razack's (1998) conceptualization of an interlocking analysis.[3] Razack argues that feminist analyses that focus on the intersections of matrices of power often ignore how systems of domination *require and secure one another*. That is, race, gender, class, sexuality, and disability, situated within projects of neo-colonization, imperialism, and/or transnational neo-liberal capitalism, not only intersect to produce women's subjectivities but also operate together as inextricable systems of oppression. Although Grewal and Kaplan's (1994) term "scattered hegemonies" suggests that women's subjectivities are produced through multiple and intersecting global powers, I am specifically concerned with mapping "the lines

---

3   My research is also influenced by Canadian critical race feminist work on violence against women, especially Yasmin Jiwani's (2006) work on violence against immigrant women and women of colour in Canada. I agree with Jiwani that violence against women must be defined in ways that "encapsulate the complex dynamics of interlocking forms of oppression" (3).

cutting across them" to understand how scattered hegemonies inter-lock and secure one another (13). In particular, my concern with how development discourses of eradicating violence against women secure a sense of urgency for development expertise, and even development itself, led me to analyze discourses of violence against women as they interlock with global systemic hierarchies of race, gender, class, sex-uality, and disability. They also interlock with structural oppressions, including uneven global systems of economic restructuring, military conquests, neo-colonial occupations, and donor-structured develop-ment operations that refuse global solidarity and cross-border feminist organizing. I therefore consider my research as contributing to transna-tional critical race and anti-capitalist feminism.

POST-DEVELOPMENT THINKING

Although transnational feminist theory pays attention to how develop-ment expertise flows from North to South, my research is also framed by post-development thinking. In particular, this book begins from the understanding that the development industry functions to secure the unidirectional flow of ideas, resources, and mobilizations from experts to development subjects or clients, even as Third World people are con-sidered "partners." Borrowing from post-development and feminist development scholars, I understand the need for expertise on issues of development such as poverty, hunger, HIV/AIDS, and gender equality to be the industry's central axis of control. Although the term "partnership" has become part of the development lexicon, it remains a buzzword with little substantive meaning (Cornwall and Eade 2010). For development, partnership is imposed and relies on a history of colonial rule and a neo-colonial mastery of knowledge and resources that secures the need for development assistance. Not only do these powerful institutions define the issues of development, but also they provide the solutions and the resources. As post-development scholar Arturo Escobar (1995) reveals in *Encountering Development: The Making and Unmaking of the Third World*, what are understood to be the "problem" of poverty and the "clientalization" of subjects for development interventions rely on the production of knowledge about both the causes of and the solutions to what are conceptualized as *development issues*.

Production of the ongoing need for development funding and expertise cannot be overstated. As critical development, post-development, and postcolonial scholars maintain, the production of development knowledge is an essential site of study (Crush 1995; Escobar 1995; Kapoor 2008). In particular, the "cultural assumptions, power implications, and hegemonic politics" of development discourse and the production of knowledge for development are important sites of investigation (Kapoor 2008, xiii).

In *The Postcolonial Politics of Development*, Ilan Kapoor (2008, xv) defines the "discourse of development" as "the dominant representations and institutional practices that structure the relationships between West and Third World." Kapoor claims that discourse is always bound up within institutions, and thus development discourse is not only about issues of representation but also about how discursive frameworks are materialized through institutional policy making and programming (xv). In *The Power of Development*, Jonathan Crush (1995, 6) claims that "development discourse is constituted and reproduced within a set of material relationships, activities and powers—social, cultural and geopolitical." Discourses of development are established and circulated within and through a knowledge-power nexus often called the "development industry" (5).

My research is influenced by post-development theory because it emerged alongside the integration of feminist and cultural studies into the development field and was contingent on the cultural or textual turn in the social sciences. Once reliant on modernization theory (or a catch-up approach), some development scholars turned away from economic models and growth narratives to focus on "the conventions of writing and representation by which Western disciplines and institutions 'make sense' of the world" (Crush 1995, 3). The integration of postmodern, postcolonial, and feminist thought into development thinking, or thinking about development, fuels my critique of development expertise as objective and my ongoing concern with claims to truth and representation in the development industry and in the academy.

Borrowing from Escobar's (1995) Foucauldian and Deleuzian mapping of power and knowledge in development discourses, I maintain that the circulation of representations, descriptors, categories, languages, and claims to truth are about "disciplining difference" (Munck 1999,

205). In other words, I follow Escobar's argument that development has not vastly improved the living conditions of people in the Third World; rather, those considered "undeveloped" have been recolonized by development and its discourses. Drawing on postcolonial scholar Edward Said's *Orientalism* (1978), Homi Bhahba's (1984) definition of colonial discourse, and feminist Chandra Talpade Mohanty's (1991) critiques of the representation of Third World women, Escobar's post-development theory outlines how development representations are discursive dominations of "others" that have real material consequences. Escobar provides a powerful challenge to the "discovery" of poverty, the "developmentalization" or "clientalization" of women and environmental issues, and the mythical tales of economic growth and overpopulation. For post-development theorists, development, both in text and in practice, is inherently problematic. Regardless of the changing languages, strategies, and practices of development (e.g., modernization, gender inclusive, rights based, participatory, or sustainable), development discourse must be decolonized. That is, post-development theorists argue that their work is a necessary "form of criticism or deconstructive practice" (Saunders 2002, 20). Put bluntly, there are no alternative development strategies, only alternatives to development.

||||||||||||||||||||||

These three theoretical fields are important to my work and how I approached both the research and the writing of this book. I hold together transnational feminism, critical race theory, and post-development thinking to thoroughly and thoughtfully investigate development discourses of violence against women. In seeking to understand how violence against women has become an urgent concern for the development industry, I use tenets of post-development scholarship to map the circulation of representations, grammars, and logics that secure the need for development itself while simultaneously creating and sustaining difference and inequality. Paying specific attention to how discourses of violence against women are gendered, racialized, classed, sexualized, and ableist, I use critical race feminism to wrestle with processes and relations of domination and control that interlock to inform and shape a range of subjectivities and discourses. Finally, using transnational feminism as praxis, my research aims to provide critiques of development discourses in the name of critically informed and reflexive mobilizations in opposition to violence against women in all of its manifestations across borders and outside the development-industrial complex that obscures transnational feminist and grassroots resistance.

METHODOLOGY

TRANSNATIONAL FEMINISM

My research methodology is also shaped by transnational feminist thought. The research questions that fuelled this book were geopolitically broad and interdisciplinary and thus required both a flexible scope and a broad set of data. An investigation of how discourses of development aid in manufacturing urgency around the issue of violence against women led me to adopt a transnational feminist methodology. It is indebted to Minoo Moallem, who conceptualizes a "transnational methodology" as an approach to collecting and analyzing "a wide range of discursive and visual cultural productions that circulate both nationally and internationally" (2005, 26). In other words, she works to collect text, talk, and image from a variety of spaces and places, and by bringing them together she can map similar, and sometimes disjunctive, flows of culture and knowledge. This methodological approach allows her "to analyze historical, discursive, and media productions at both the macro and [the] micro levels and to bring the past and the present, the global and the local, and the national and the transnational into the same frame of reference" (25). Taking her approach, I investigate international and national development documents and policies, laws, popular images in campaigns, and media releases that circulate nationally and transnationally in the same frame of reference. Although transnational feminist methodologies might seem too broad, or too all-encompassing, the scope of my research is limited by my focus on circulating discourses produced in three sites where violence against women is considered a development concern: the United Nations, the World Bank, and American foreign policy.

Importantly, a transnational methodology allows me to "assemble" cultural texts with interviews in a non-linear and interdisciplinary fashion. Following the methodological approach set out by Jasbir K. Puar in *Terrorist Assemblages: Homonationalism in Queer Times*, my research objectives require the assemblage of "varied and often disjunctive primary sources" (2007, xv). In many ways, my three case studies are varied and seemingly disjunctive. Yet, by placing them alongside one another I can show how the discourses emanating from the three sites function to garner a sense of urgency around violence against women, even if they use different discourses, justifications, and languages to do so. By assembling various cultural texts in a transnational frame, I can discursively analyze the hegemonic, or most powerful, narratives of violence against women while also investigating what Puar calls "the unexpected, the unplanned irruptions, the lines of flight" (xv).

Although unreferenced, Gilles Deleuze and Félix Guattari's (2004) conception of the "rhizome" undoubtedly inspired Puar's (2007) notion of the "assemblage." In *A Thousand Plateaus*, originally published in 1998, Deleuze and Guattari describe a typical writing method as a "root" as singular points are plotted in a fixed and linear order. In a rhizomatic method, in contrast, "any point...can be connected to anything other, and must be" (7). Even "the lines of flight" ultimately lead back to the rhizome. Thus, there cannot be any dualism or binary logic because all lines tie back into one another. Ultimately, a rhizomatic method is best described as a mapping. According to Deleuze and Guattari, a "map is open and connectable in all of its dimensions," is always open to modification, and has multiple entryways (13–14). Such practices of mapping are central to transnational feminist praxis.

For transnational feminists, assemblages (Puar 2007), cartographies (Mohanty 2003), topographies (Katz 2001), and even kaleidoscopes (Shohat 2002) are used to describe research methodologies that resemble Deleuze and Guattari's (2004) rhizomatic method.[4] Using a transnational

---

4   Mohanty (2003) argues that cartographies of struggle are necessary conceptual maps with which to understand race, gender, colonialism, and their ongoing shifts (45). In "On the Grounds of Globalization: A Topography for Feminist Political Engagement," Cindi Katz (2001) argues that feminists must not rely on victimized notions of place or locality under globalization, but excavate geopolitical layers that produce particular places to reveal intersections of domination and resistance at other scales of analysis. Katz argues that feminists must follow contour lines that connect subjects to understand social relations of power and production. In "Area Studies, Gender Studies, and the...

feminist methodology in this book, I have assembled various cultural texts with concern for interlocking lines that connect "scattered hegemonies," or interspersed operations of power, rather than seek singular points of power or control or binary positions (Grewal and Kaplan 1994). In other words, these assemblages, cartographies, topographies, and kaleidoscopes are all invested in mapping the operations and flows of powers rather than in pinpointing moments, spaces, actors, or institutions as having or wielding power.

My transnational feminism methodology allows me to follow multiple historical and contemporary narratives in various different, and often disjunctive, directions theoretically and thematically, and ultimately to analyze them in the same frame of reference to emphasize linked ideas, communicative strategies, cultural productions, and transnational discursive systems that allow for, and help to produce, the idea that violence against women is an urgent concern for development and that the development industry has solutions to stop it. Inspired by Rebecca Dingo's (2012) *Networking Arguments: Rhetoric, Transnational Feminism, and Public Policy Writing*, this book traces how anti–violence against women narratives show up similarly across texts, campaigns, documents, and policies even as they engage "different arguments," justifications, examples, and exceptions, and thus, as I show, these discourses have distinct but connected effects and affects (19).

CASE STUDIES

Although my research is wide ranging, it is structured around a specific conceptualization of discourses of development (Escobar 1995; Kapoor 2008). I understand such discourses to be comprised of dominant representational and institutional practices of transnational actors in the field (Kapoor 2008, xv). Although discourses of development are fractured, and contested from both inside and outside the industry, I am interested in the knowledge produced about violence against women from international institutions and powerful actors in the field. Specifically,

---

...Cartographies of Knowledge," Ella Shohat (2002, 70) argues that a transnational feminist approach is concerned with mapping genders, sexualities, races, classes, nations, and even continents as "interwoven and relationalist."

I aim to decolonize discourses of development by analyzing how the development industry communicates knowledge about subjectivities of women, practices of violence, and solutions to both underdevelopment and gender inequality.[5] Although many international campaigns to end violence against women would provide interesting material through which to understand how women's issues are made visible on the international stage, here I limit my scope to understanding how solutions to this problem are promoted in and through development assistance and expertise. That is, I focus on national and international development institutions that offer assistance in the form of knowledge, expertise, donor relations, and foreign aid.

I have chosen to analyze U.S. foreign policy, the World Bank, and the United Nations for their particular roles as agenda setters, knowledge makers, and influential donors of foreign aid. I have chosen these cases because of their different mandates, inner workings, members, and levels of operation. I have collected documents, images, media reports, and interviews associated with these cases, focused specifically on recent policies, campaigns, and laws that communicate the urgency of ending violence against women transnationally. Using transnational feminism as a methodology, I trace narratives of gender, race, class, sexuality, and disability across multiple scales and sites.

This method provides an opportunity for intensive analysis of details associated with single cases. In many ways, I treat my sites of study as individual cases. In fact, each chapter can stand on its own as a deep and concentrated analysis of specificity in particular sites of the development industry. Yet my aim in assembling three case studies is to think about the larger contexts in which the cases exist. As defined by Matthew B. Miles and A. Michael Huberman (1994, 25), a case can be defined as "a phenomenon of some sort occurring in a bounded context." Instead of focusing on the circumscribed context, sociologist John Gerring (2004) maintains that case studies focus on specifics to point to phenomena larger than the cases themselves. I follow his conceptualization

---

5   Here I use the term "underdevelopment," borrowing from Walter Rodney's (1972) *How Europe Underdeveloped Africa*. Whereas development scholars often use the term "undeveloped," I want to highlight the project of *actively* underdeveloping nations by means of colonialism, economic restructuring, uneven global capitalism, and neo-liberal development models.

in assembling the cases studied here, very different in terms of sites, scales, topics, and concepts; and my theoretical archive ranges from studies of security, to crip theory and disability, to affect theory. In resisting the employment of case study research as a way to build singular and specific analyses in one site, my aim in building and connecting the three case studies here, and reading them "sideways" following Puar (2007), is to provide an archive that allows for generalizability. I thus build a complex theory of urgency that exposes the larger and broader function of development discourses, specifically about how women's rights are harnessed to a variety of development projects.

Although this book is about violence against women, it is also about the circulation and impact of texts, campaigns, rhetoric, policies, and images that make up development discourses. It aims to push readers to think critically about deployment of the issue of violence against women for other objectives and to remain curious about how projects of gender equality are harnessed to development.

My first site of study is recent American foreign policy. I focus on how Hillary Clinton, acting as secretary of state (2009–13), made violence against women a central concern of American foreign policy by describing the issue as a security and development concern. In this case study, I investigate circulating discourses about violence against women emerging from the United States. Clinton is not a traditional development actor in the way that I conceptualize the United Nations and World Bank in this book. However, the United States is a nation with powerful and influential bilateral development aid programs and global power in framing discourses of development. Additionally, as security concerns become incorporated into, if not come to dominate, the development industry, sites of critical inquiry of development are also shifting. As Mark Duffield (2007, 2) notes, there is a new "moral logic [that connects] development and security" in the "post-9/11" era.[6] Because development is understood to reduce poverty, and thus

---

6   I use the term "post-9/11" here to denote how the "pre-" and "post-" 9/11 periods are discursively imagined and demarcated as separated by the terrorist attacks on the United States of September 11, 2001. Using the term "post-9/11" troubles this imagining and calls for a contextual account of simultaneously linked and disjunctive systems of power present along a historical continuum of the "pre-" and "post-" 9/11 periods.

instability, it also aims to improve security. U.S. foreign relations, including aid transfers, in the post-9/11 period are fuelled by concerns about national security. Seemingly counter-intuitive, foreign aid has become focused on "home." As Duffield maintains, development is concerned more with techniques of securing the Western way of life than with interventions for improving other lives abroad (2). In this case study, I investigate the focus on violence against women in American foreign policy between 2009 and 2013, with Clinton at the helm, to map how violence against women is problematized as an urgent development and security concern.

My second case study is the World Bank, a large and complicated institution. As Kate Bedford (2009, xxv) points out, there are methodological hurdles associated with studying the World Bank. Because of the size and complexity of the organization, researchers can rarely confirm or deny almost any hypothesis about it (Miller-Adams 1999, xi). In terms of gender analyses, researchers and evaluators from within the institution itself have experienced difficulty in ascertaining the effects of gender policy trajectories on actual lending and investments. According to Bedford (2009), researchers of the World Bank constantly worry that their results will be invalid a month after completing a project because of the constant turbulence within the organization. According to Graham Harrison (2001, 529), the World Bank has trouble sticking to its convictions for more than a presidential term. However, investigating its role as a producer of knowledge and powerful framer of development policy remains crucial. Citing Karin Schoenpflug (2006), Bedford argues that "what the Bank says about gender matters, because its policy discourses help legitimize specific ways of perceiving reality and exclude others" (2009, xxv). Borrowing from Escobar (1995), Bedford suggests that policies are productive instruments that result in concrete practices of thinking and acting (xxiv). Although research and policy texts might not comprise the determining factors for the lending practices of the World Bank or its employees on the ground, they remain knowledge-producing mechanisms that both help to make meaning of gender issues in the wider development industry and, at the least, reflect the institutional narratives that communicate the mandate of the World Bank to itself and its members. In other words, policy and research outline the ideologies and practices of the World Bank as the leader in the industry and, importantly, to employees, many of whom enact loans, grants, and programs of assistance in Third World countries (xxvii).

Given the complexity of the organization, I have limited my investigation to a World Bank report entitled *The Cost of Violence* (2009a). I contextualize my analysis of this report within an exploration of both historical World Bank–funded research and policy reports on women's empowerment and gender equality and feminist and critical economist accounts of the track record of the bank on women's issues. Although I do not make grand claims about its *actual* investment in the issue of violence against women, I analyze the report as an attempt to manufacture urgency around the issue by gender advocates within the organization and as a representation of gender ideologies circulating there at the time.

For my third site of study, I have chosen the United Nations because, in the field of gender and development, it has been an agenda setter and continues to set the trajectory of gender equality strategies in the development industry. According to Manisha Desai (2005) and Jutta M. Joachim (2007), the United Nations has been the site at which non-governmental organizations (NGOs) and feminist activists have mobilized around the issue of violence against women. In her extensive study of the United Nations, Joachim considers the relationship between the mobilization of NGOs and other activists and the UN agenda and reveals how the "proper framing" of issues by external and internal mobilizers has shaped that agenda.

Of course, the United Nations is also a complicated site of study given its sheer size and the multiplicity of internal agendas, concerns, and divisions. Because of the impossibility of studying the entire organization, I focus on the UN secretary-general's campaign entitled UNiTE to End Violence against Women and its complementary Say NO campaign. These campaigns reflect not only the trajectories of the organization on gender issues but also internal and external pressures by feminist mobilizers to take gender issues seriously (Joachim 2007; Miller and Razavi 1998). Although violence against women is a major area of focus for the UN Development Fund for Women, now incorporated within UN Women (the entity for gender equality and women's empowerment), the fact that the UNiTE campaign is housed within the secretary-general's office suggests that there is a sense of urgency around the issue at the highest level. Although I am particularly interested in framing the issue in the

UNiTE to End Violence against Women and Say NO campaigns, this case study draws on a long history of feminist and anti-violence mobilization at the United Nations to provide context for these campaigns.

INTERVIEWS

I recognize that a singular focus on text and image would be insufficient to answer my research questions about the discursive construction of urgency around the issue of violence against women. To avoid what David Mosse (2005, 15) calls "discursive determinism," or linking discourse directly with practice, I complement my analysis of text and image with interviews from gender and development experts. In 2012, I conducted semi-structured interviews with twelve gender experts and development practitioners, in person in Ottawa or over the phone through a snowballing technique. Some participants allowed me to publish their names and workplaces, while others requested anonymity. I interviewed those who could be considered "femocrats" in the development industry. I specifically sought gender advocates who work, or have worked, within the development industry to better comprehend the inner workings of the field. My interviews focused on how campaigns, policies, laws, and research texts on violence against women are created and disseminated within development institutions to understand better how feminists working inside and outside them understand transnational violence against women.

To plan my interviews, I turned to Carol Miller and Shahra Razavi (1998), whose work on femocrats in development institutions reveals that feminists mobilize successfully both outside and inside the constraints of such institutions. Using the phrase "missionaries and mandarins," they suggest that feminists "on the inside" work for change but also have to deal with the regulations imposed on them (vii). "Missionaries" work for change from within institutions, whereas "mandarins" adapt to the constraints of regulatory bureaucracies in large development organizations. Gender experts who speak the language of institutions often shape descriptions of and solutions to women's inequalities from within development institutions. These descriptions and languages circulate with power to shape larger discourse in the development industry because they originate from, or are supported by, some of the most powerful institutions in the field.

While conducting the interviews, I had not yet developed a theory of urgency, and I was trying to make sense of a multitude of campaign images, documents, policies, laws, and media reports regarding violence against women. Through these interviews, I realized that there was nothing new about the urgency of gender-based violence; rather, communicating their concerns about violence against women was a way for the development industry to justify its expertise on gender, even as decades of development had yet to solve major obstacles to equality.

Here I use discourse analyses of some of the interviews with development practitioners to better understand the intentions behind creating and circulating narratives of urgency and to thoroughly investigate urgent responses to violence against women as a development concern. This multi-method approach is necessary to overcome methodological obstacles associated with research on development organizations and actors, as I have outlined above. Although I maintain that visual and textual representations of the issue of violence against women greatly influence development interventions in the issue, it is equally important to recognize the relationship between text and practice. Development documents "spell out the common sense of the development community" (Williams 1995, 175), and ultimately shape practices of thinking and acting, but I am also aware that the "burden of proof" is on critical scholars to map the links, and especially the breaks, between texts and development outcomes (Bedford 2009, xxviii).

A NOTE ON TERMINOLOGY

Throughout this book, I employ the term "violence against women" instead of "domestic violence," "intimate partner violence," "partner abuse," or "gender-based violence" for a variety of reasons. First, the term "violence against women" is used overwhelmingly in literature, campaigns, and policy discourses in the development industry. Following the 1993 Declaration on the Elimination of Violence against Women, most development institutions, including those that I focus on in this book, have used that term. The declaration defines violence against women as "any act of gender-based violence that results in, or is likely to result in, physical, sexual or psychological harm or suffering to women, including threats of such acts, coercion or arbitrary deprivation of liberty, whether occurring in public or in private life" (UN 1993). I thus use the term, the most popular in the field of development, to remain consistent with the texts that I investigate. However, because I critique discourses of development in this book, and am critical of the deployment of concerns about women's lives in the development industry, I use the term with a more nuanced and politicized meaning. Additionally, my definition of the term is more expansive than that of the UN declaration.

With a concern about how the term "violence against women" is defined in development discourses, I interviewed former and current femocrats about meaning-making practices around it. According to Eva Rathgeber, a consultant for development organizations, "violence against women" is often used as a "watered-down" and "mechanistic" term, with the exception of UN Women, which has a more sophisticated understanding of the issue. Yet she claims that UN Women is an organization housed in a complicated and large institution, which means that "they will always be somewhat more conservative in what they can do, as opposed to the more progressive NGOs" (personal communication, 2012). Mirroring this view, Jane Parpart claims that the term is used "technically in order to request monies from hostile audiences" and requires a promise of plausible solutions that requires a less complex and nuanced definition of the issue (personal communication, 2012). In her extensive work with the United Nations and World Health Organization, Meredith Turshen found that the term was narrowly defined. She recalled that collecting information about violence against women meant collecting statistics to gain the attention of funders, with too little interest in "violent economies" and too much interest in sexual violence as only "wartime violence" at the expense of intersectional, historical, and transnational accounts of the "continuums" of violence that affect women disproportionately (personal communication, 2012).

According to my interviewees, "violence against women" is a term that circulates with little concern for or attention to feminist debates about how to define violence or the use of "woman" as a universalizing category of analysis. Women are too often assumed to be equally vulnerable to violence by men because of their assigned sex as female, and therefore solutions to such violence are a model of "global sisterhood" (Mohanty 2003). In the development industry, "violence against women" is a term that circulates with the assumption that cisgender women experience violence by cisgender men, leaving out the question of violence against transgender women and collapsing the complexities between sex and gender. Most often, violence against women is reduced to physical harm to the (assigned) female body, especially sexual violence such as rape. Of course, violence against women is often perpetrated by cisgender men and often does result in harm to the body, but "violence against women" as a term used in development discourses does little to connect the issue to gender identity and expression. According to Parpart, the development industry has yet to produce a nuanced analysis of gender, and this is reflected in how the industry deals with violence against women. Although it might speak the feminist language of "masculinities" and "femininities," gender continues to be mapped onto sexed bodies in heteronormative and cisgendered ways. Parpart suggests that "gender experts" in many development organizations actually "have little understanding of the functions of gender and pay no attention to intersectionality or performativity" (personal communication, 2012). In practice, this means that development organizations are concerned with only some women's well-being.

Violence against women circulates in development discourses as a concept that excludes transgender individuals and others who experience both patriarchal violence for failing to live up to gender norms and the violence of being overwhelmingly ignored by or shunned from anti–violence against women initiatives. Even in critical and feminist development scholarship, transgender and queer bodies are rarely represented or included (for two exceptions, see Bedford 2009; Lind 2009).

Although I use the term "violence against women" in this book to remain consistent with the term used by the development industry, I do so unfaithfully. I use the term as defined by critical race scholars, including Andrea Smith and the INCITE! Women of Colour against Violence collective. I understand practices of violence to be intimately linked to and sustained by other axioms of domination, including institutional racism, homophobia, transphobia, classism, ableism, and neo-colonialism (hooks 2000; INCITE! 2006; Razack 2004). As INCITE! argues, definition of the term "violence against women" must be broadened to include "attacks on immigrants' rights and Indian treaty rights, the proliferation of prisons, militarism, attacks on the reproductive rights of women of color, medical experimentation on communities of color, homophobia/heterosexism and hate crimes against lesbians of color, economic neo-colonialism, and institutional racism" (2006, 2). Such a definition is highly nuanced and sophisticated. However, I would expand it to include impacts of the development project on women. Development might be included in the phrase "economic neo-colonialism," but this book demonstrates how the development industry, specifically the "developmentalization" of women and gender issues, is a process of ongoing discursive and material colonization that must be challenged as a form of violence. According to Patricia Hill Collins, "definitions of violence lie not in acts themselves but in *how groups controlling positions of authority conceptualize such acts*" (1998, 922; emphasis added). Thus, a thorough definition of the term "violence against women" must consider the violence of discursive colonization of the term within the development industry.

OUTLINE OF THE BOOK

In the first chapter, I consider the urgency of anti–violence against women strategies embedded in the "development and in/security" nexus (Duffield 2010). In the post-9/11 era, women's issues, including violence against women, have become central in American foreign aid and policy objectives. I investigate the implications of state actors, including Hillary Clinton as the secretary of state from 2009 to 2013, communicating the importance of ending violence against women as a means to eradicate national security threats such as terrorism. Focusing on discourses of urgency around ending the "culture of violence against women," as phrased by Clinton, I investigate possible passing of the International Violence against Women Act that would centre anti-violence strategies in American foreign policy. Assembling a multiplicity of texts to analyze interconnections among security, development, and anti-violence initiatives, I take seriously the impact of urgent post-9/11 responses to security and development as a global strategy to end violence against women. I consider insecurity and security and use the term "in/security" to draw attention to how the American security agenda in particular claims to make the world more secure but actually creates insecurity in the lives of the most marginal.

In Chapter 2, I investigate the World Bank report *The Cost of Violence* (2009a). Arguing that ending violence against women is an urgent concern for development because it is inefficient, gender advocates at the World Bank use a measurement called disability-adjusted life years (DALYs) to measure the economic costs associated with violence against women. I use crip theory (McRuer 2006) to investigate the framing of violence against women as an issue of ability, empowerment, and productivity. Given the World Bank's historical emphasis on women's empowerment through economic engagements, I consider the repercussions of promoting workplace empowerment as a scheme of prevention and response, with little attention paid to economic violence.

The focus of the first two chapters is on how violence against women is represented as urgent in development discourses. In the third chapter, I switch gears to investigate how anti–violence against women strategies are *felt*, or manufactured to be felt, as urgent. In other words, I investigate affective discourses of urgency. Focusing on the UN UNiTE to End Violence against Women and Say NO campaigns, I explore the possibilities for certain "political feelings" about violence against women when it is presented as an urgent concern (Gould 2009). I examine how the urgency of eliminating violence against women globally is affectively communicated and how these affective capacities operate to influence how people feel about, and act upon, the problem.

Throughout *Manufacturing Urgency* is a consideration of both the discursive nature and the affective nature of urgency. As Kotter (2008) points out, a sense of urgency must be created. By investigating how the United Nations, World Bank, and American foreign policy makers communicate the importance of ending violence against women, I aim to reveal how the issue becomes important when connected to what I consider the most important development flavours of the day: national security, neo-liberal economic growth, and feel-good aid. I also reveal which questions and concerns are left for later. These development concerns fuel a sense of urgency around the issue of global violence against women at the expense of more suitable strategies to end violent practices. I argue that a sense of urgency created around the issue obscures a more nuanced understanding of it and other mobilizations against violence happening around the world. As development experts mobilize feminist languages, concepts, and strategies, and as their campaigns, policies, and laws open up possibilities for swift solutions, I maintain that a manufactured urgency positions the development industry as a leader in ending global violence against women at the expense of women's well-being.

CHAPTER 1
HILLARY CLINTON CARES ABOUT VIOLENCE AGAINST WOMEN

IIIIIIIIIIIIIIIIIIIIIIIII

This is a big deal for American values and for American foreign
policy and our interests, but it is also a big deal for our security,
because where women are disempowered and dehumanized,
you are more likely to see not just antidemocratic forces,
but extremism that leads to security challenges for us.
—Hillary Clinton, cited in Tzemach Lemmon,
"The Hillary Doctrine"

According to Hillary Clinton, former U.S. secretary of state (2009–13), violence against women must end if the Third World is to develop and modernize.[1] In an official address to women's rights advocates during a trip to Papua New Guinea as secretary of state, Clinton claimed that "no country in the 21st century can advance when

---

1   Although there are problems with use of the term "Third World," I have chosen to use it in this book for a number of reasons. Following Chandra Talpade Mohanty's (2003) conceptualization of the term, I agree that "Third World" suggests a quick erasure of the multiple political, economic, and cultural differences within and between countries that make up this space. I also agree with Mohanty that using "North/South" or "developed/developing" as an alternative term lacks the explanatory power to theorize about colonial legacies and neo-colonial processes (227). So I use the term to mark the ongoing discursive and material construction of the Third World to point out how its spaces are understood and represented regardless of changes in terminology.

half its population is left behind" (qtd. in Lee 2010).[2] According to Clinton, women and girls should be at the centre of all future American foreign policy objectives because violence against women is an urgent issue for the United States (Clinton 2010; Iannotti 2011; Tzemach Lemmon 2011). Claiming that the international interests and national security of the United States *depended* on the extension of women's equality across the globe, Clinton committed to promoting women's rights during her tenure. She was the most-travelled secretary of state in American history, visiting 112 countries during her four-year tenure and crossing 956,733 miles, enough to span the globe more than thirty-eight times (Davidson 2013). Branding her promotion of women's rights on the road "The Hillary Doctrine," journalist Gayle Tzemach Lemmon (2011) of *Newsweek* named the secretary of state "the advocate in chief for women worldwide."

Clinton called violence against women a real and urgent problem: "Give women equal rights, and entire nations are more stable and secure. Deny women equal rights, and the instability of nations is almost certain. The subjugation of women is, therefore, a threat to the common security of our world and to the national security of our country" (TED blog 2010).

Clinton's 2011 speech, and subsequent media coverage, mobilized discourses of gender and sexual exceptionalism, or the temporality of notions of backwardness and tradition in opposition to modernity and progress, to create a *"frenzied mode of emergency,"* the urgent need for the United States to spread human rights manufactured on the ground

---

2   Clinton made these comments in November 2010 on a visit to Papua New Guinea, the first for a secretary of state in the previous twelve years (U.S. News 2010). Her visit there to speak about human rights issues also marked the unveiling of a U.S. and ExxonMobil–partnered $15 billion gas project due to begin in 2014 (Lee 2010; Reuters 2011). The United States is simultaneously partnering with ExxonMobil for a mentoring project to "end the culture of violence against women and girls in Papua New Guinea" (Lee 2010). According to Clinton, maintaining U.S. power over global competitors such as China requires that the nation capitalize on both opening new markets to the global economy through infrastructure investments and promoting a human rights agenda. Speaking against a Republican-proposed budget cut of 16 per cent to U.S. diplomacy and foreign assistance spending, Clinton "put aside the moral, humanitarian do-good side" and spoke "straight Realpolitik," claiming that such a cut to spending would cause U.S. strategic interests and global influence to falter (Reuters 2011).

of moral superiority (Puar 2007, 9; emphasis added). As this chapter demonstrates, modes of emergency allow for rearticulations of global gender, sexual, and racial logics and permit "genderwashing" to be mobilized at these urgent moments. Borrowing from Jasbir K. Puar's (2007) work on "pinkwashing," I use the term "genderwashing" to denote how feminist and liberal concerns about equality and women's rights are harnessed for imperial projects. Here genderwashing signifies that discourses of "being good on women's issues" obscure gender inequalities at home by highlighting and targeting those abroad as urgent concerns.

I argue that the Hillary Doctrine should be understood as a particular brand of U.S. state feminism, focused on women's rights around the world, that intersects with national security discourses and ongoing global militarization of women's rights. The Hillary Doctrine discursively maintains that global violence against women is a pressing national security issue for the United States by suggesting that a nation's instability is causally related to poverty and gender inequality. Put simply, countries where violence against women is rampant are fragile states and thus breeding grounds for terrorism and threats to the United States. According to the authors of *The Hillary Doctrine: Sex and American Foreign Policy* (Hudson and Leidl 2015), though American practices of implementing the doctrine are uneven at best, Clinton's call to action has fundamentally changed American foreign policy, even if only in rhetoric.

During her tenure as secretary of state, women's rights were placed at the forefront of U.S. foreign policy. In 2010, the inaugural Quadrennial Diplomacy and Development Review (QDDR) was released in an effort to make a sweeping reform of the U.S. State Department and the U.S. Agency for International Development to encourage offices for development and security to work more closely together. The QDDR maintains that alienation, marginalization, and resentment caused by underdevelopment are risks to American security that can be mitigated through development aid. The QDDR claims that changing negative attitudes about the United States around the world will be central to new foreign relations, which include "softer" politics such as promoting women's rights (QDDR 2010, i). In the report, violence against women is presented as *the* gender issue to be tackled by future development and security initiatives.

During Clinton's tenure, proposed legislation entitled the International Violence against Women Act (I-VAWA) was first deliberated in Congress. I-VAWA is supported by Amnesty International (2010), Women Thrive WorldWide (2010), and a coalition of 200 women's organizations. Upon its introduction to the 111th Congress, one-third of the House and Senate co-sponsored the bill. The Senate Foreign Relations Committee also approved it. According to my interview with Christina Finch in 2013, a women's program associate at Amnesty International USA, I-VAWA was set to be reintroduced in the 113th Congress, and she expected that it would have considerable bipartisan support in both the House and the Senate at that time. The appointment of John Kerry to succeed Clinton as secretary of state gave Finch and her team hope for the continued commitment of the administration to pass the legislation, given his leadership on the Senate Foreign Relations Committee for four years and his long-time support of the bill. As of March 2015, I-VAWA was reintroduced in the House during 114th Congress without amendments from earlier versions.

Similar to the Hillary Doctrine, I-VAWA links development with U.S. national security in the name of women's rights. Although I-VAWA and the Hillary Doctrine are separate agendas since Clinton is not directly connected to the bill, they are discursively similar. That is, both define violence against women as a national security issue and generate a sense of urgency around the issue by using already circulating discourses of safety and security in a post-9/11 world. Both I-VAWA and the Hillary Doctrine claim that ending violence against women globally will protect the United States from external threats. Furthermore, both outline how ending violence against women is tied to strengthening global security by reducing social tensions. And both link security issues to the need for development assistance in countries with high rates of violence against women. To be sure, according to Senator Benjamin Cardin, an original co-sponsor of I-VAWA, "one of the most effective forces for defeating extremism is female safety....Violence against women undermines the effectiveness of existing U.S. investments in global development and stability" (qtd. in Aroon 2010).

In the context of a recent emphasis on centring women and girls within American foreign policy objectives under the leadership of Clinton, I analyze here how violence against women is manufactured as an urgent concern to serve national security objectives. I assemble critical race theory, security studies, and feminist anti-imperial scholarship to analyze popular media texts and U.S. laws that contribute to the manufacturing of urgency around the issue of global violence against women. Specifically, I analyze popular media accounts of the Hillary Doctrine and I-VAWA "sideways" (Puar 2007, 117). That is, reading I-VAWA alongside articulations of anti-violence rhetoric emerging from several media sites in the United States, I assemble a multiplicity of texts to explore the interconnections of security, development, and anti-violence initiatives and what is communicated about them to the American public.

By analyzing the International Violence against Women Act in connection with circulation of the Hillary Doctrine, I unravel how a concern for women's rights links development and in/security in American foreign policy priorities. In other words, when presented as a security and development issue, ending global violence against women invites securitized and militarized strategies and interventions but ignores how they are inherently violent. Additionally, by demonstrating how the Hillary Doctrine approach toward violence against women uses the language of criminality in an effort to move away from speaking about violence as cultural, I outline American strategies to end violence against women globally and specifically how they are informed by domestic criminalization of this type of violence. I explicitly connect the discipline and punishment of communities of colour at home and the management of Third World bodies abroad, an important piece of the development and in/security puzzle often missed by critical scholars. I maintain that criminalization of violence against women at home informs securitization of it abroad and actually fails to protect women from violence. I-VAWA's investment in police, military, and peacekeeping forces to prevent or respond to violence against women abroad marks an increasingly militarized response from the United States, where militarized policing is rampant. Ultimately, the creation of urgency around violence against women in American foreign policy creates a context in which failed responses to it at home are exported and intensified at the expense of more suitable anti-violence initiatives that respond to interpersonal, state-sponsored, and imperial violence simultaneously.

FEMINIST MOBILIZATIONS AT THE STATE LEVEL

The Hillary Doctrine and I-VAWA mark the tenacity and power of human rights and feminist organizations and individuals within the U.S. government, such as Clinton herself, who genuinely care about women's well-being globally and who push for change in the development industry. In my interviews with gender advocates from Amnesty International USA about I-VAWA, for example, I found that femocrats are working extremely effectively under tight constraints and with hope that state feminism, embodied by Clinton and proposed laws such as I-VAWA, will have positive impacts globally. It is difficult to critique such innovative approaches to ending violence against women, especially those developed by advocates working on the ground for women's rights. Surely, ending violence globally is a priority for all feminists and anti-violence advocates. To this end, the analysis that follows should not be read as an all-embracing disapproval of state feminism or a criticism of femocrats. However, I do illustrate how the Hillary Doctrine and I-VAWA are embedded within the development and in/security nexus and can easily be used as tools to justify global interventions on the ground of U.S. national security. Ultimately, I am concerned with how the Hillary Doctrine and I-VAWA communicate the urgency of violence against women while maintaining systems of imperial domination at the expense of more complex and nuanced strategies to end this violence transnationally.

In the first section of this chapter, I expand Mark Duffield's (2010) conceptualization of "the development and security nexus" to understand the intertwining of U.S. foreign aid and security interests. By analyzing the inaugural Quadrennial Diplomacy and Development Review (QDDR 2010), I unravel the intertwining of development and in/security and the increasing focus on women's issues. I consider the biopolitical and necropolitical nature of what I call "the development and in/security nexus" as a frame within which to understand how violence against women is used to shore up support for interventions into international spaces marked as underdeveloped and thus demarcated as breeding grounds for terrorism.

Returning to the Hillary Doctrine in the second section, I consider how the ubiquitous phrase "it's not cultural; it's criminal" spoken by Clinton all over the world regarding violence against women has been used to bypass feminist and critical race debates on how to intervene in women's issues abroad. Focusing on domestic responses to violence against women that centre on the criminal justice system, I interrogate best practices exported by the United States. I provide context for analyzing the proposed I-VAWA alongside the Hillary Doctrine by outlining domestic anti-violence strategies and consider the implication of marking violence as criminal and relying on criminalized and militarized responses.

In the third section, I consider the potential implications of passing I-VAWA. In particular, I consider whether the investments in police, military, and peacekeeping forces are appropriate in prevention of and response to gendered violence. By investigating some of the human rights abuses committed by U.S. forces in Iraq and sexual abuses within their own ranks, I interrogate how U.S. political interests are pursued at the expense of suitable anti-violence initiatives and thus reveal how an urgent concern for the issue of violence against women is highly manufactured. I maintain that, by linking this issue to underdevelopment and security issues such as terrorism, the increased attention paid to women's rights marks a genderwashing of American foreign interests.

THE DEVELOPMENT AND IN/SECURITY NEXUS IN THE QDDR

In 2010, the inaugural QDDR was released in an effort to make a sweeping reform of the U.S. State Department and U.S. Agency for International Development. Signed-off by Secretary of State Hillary Clinton, the report is meant to help the American development and in/security industries to "get the most of every dollar from its investors." Comparing development and foreign relations to any other business venture, the QDDR begins thus:

> Somewhere in the world today, a jeep winds its way through a remote region of a developing country. Inside are a State Department diplomat with deep knowledge of the area's different ethnic groups and a USAID development expert with long experience helping communities lift themselves out of poverty. They are on their way to talk with local councils about a range of projects—a new water filtration system,

new ways to elevate the role of women in the community,
and so on—that could make life better for thousands of people *while improving local attitudes toward the United States.*
(i; emphasis added)

Merging development goals and American interests, the QDDR follows in the footsteps of four quadrennial defence reviews published
in 1997, 2001, 2006, and 2010 by the Departments of Defense and
Homeland Security that aim to improve resource efficiency. As pre-emp-
tive defences against security threats, development and diplomacy are
ushered in to improve the reputation of the United States around the
world. As the QDDR states, "for the United States, development is a
strategic, economic, and moral imperative—as central to our foreign
policy as diplomacy and defense" (ix). The advice of the QDDR is that
the State Department will work under the guidance of National Security
Department staff to respond to security crises, while USAID will focus on
humanitarian crises (xiii). Of particular interest, the QDDR announced
expansion of International Security Affairs by establishing a new Bureau
for Arms Control, Verification, and Compliance and working with
Congress to establish a Bureau for Counterterrorism. In the nexus of
development and in/security, the QDDR positions an assemblage of
institutions as needing to respond to the excess of underdevelopment.

Alienation, marginalization, and resentment caused by underdevelopment are conceptualized in the QDDR as risks to U.S. security that can
be mitigated through the securitization of development: changing negative attitudes about the United States is central to new foreign relations
(QDDR 2010, i). Development is presented as a moral approach to military and imperial efforts. As Duffield (2010, 60) reminds us, it was not
the "war on terror" that was the first to aim at the "hearts and minds"
of "hateful" Muslim terrorists through development initiatives, but the
British in newly independent Malaya in 1951 who first coined the term.

Following this legacy, we must understand Clinton's "smart power"
not as a new concept but as a re-presentation of old colonial logic.
Although her approach, or the interlacing of hard military power with
soft economic, development, and technological power, has changed the
American foreign policy landscape, the Hillary Doctrine also solidifies
the most dominant conceptualizations of in/security and development

in the post-9/11 period. In my reading, Clinton's tenure as secretary of state reflects the most hegemonic rhetoric of the development and in/ security nexus, even though one might assume that Clinton's feminism disrupted the status quo.

Informed by feminist international relations and feminist security studies,[3] my conceptualization of in/security builds on Duffield's (2010) approach to thinking about human security and his foundational work at the intersection of development and security studies. By focusing on security and development as a nexus, or a "constellation of institutions, practices, and beliefs," Duffield claims that securitization can best be understood through the ways that discourse, ideology, and praxis circulate among an assemblage of stakeholders (56). That is, there are not only state actors or international organizations in the nexus but also a variety of influencers and sites of power. One might imagine this nexus as a puzzle that scholars like Duffield are trying to put together piece by piece to better understand its functioning.

According to Duffield's (2010) theory of the development and security nexus, the move from solely economistic conceptions of development to more people-centred approaches in the 1990s was coupled with a new understanding of security as being about interpersonal social relations rather than only political relations between states (55). Duffield claims that biopolitical management of life emerged as central in development aid and became increasingly connected to security, thereby creating a strong nexus of development and security. He argues that neither development nor security can be delivered without understanding the importance of "containment of the human manifestations of underdevelopment" (63). Both geopolitical control of migration, especially the containment of Third World bodies, and governing of individual bodies to be self-reliant and manage the risks associated with underdevelopment

---

3   Scholars in these fields conceptualize security and securitization in various and sophisticated ways. For example, Ann Tickner was one of the first to argue that international relations issues were profoundly gendered and called for studies of human security instead of only state-based analyses. Feminist international relations scholars (e.g., Cohn 1987; Enloe 1989, 2007; Peterson 2007; Sjoberg 2010; Tickner 1992) have broadened the definitions of security and insecurity in their approaches to analyzing gendered experiences of war, occupation, imperialism, and militarization.

are representative of a "new spatial configuration" of the development and security nexus (63).[4] In other words, the excess of underdevelopment, or that which leaks from its containment, poses a security concern. One only has to read news on migrant deaths in Turkey, Greece, Austria, and Libya, especially the deaths of migrants travelling from war-torn Syria through the British Channel, to understand how insecurity and under-development are conceptualized as threats to the West.

Although Duffield's (2010) focus on biopolitical management of the Third World is important, it is also necessary to understand the func-tioning of necropolitics within the development and in/security nexus. For Achille Mbembe (2003), necropower produces geopolitical, tem-poral, and spatial relations whereby people are daily confronted with the possibility of death. Again one might consider the increased toll of migrant deaths, where the possibility of death in travelling by water out of warn-torn countries such as Syria is just as real a possibility as death on land. Indebted to Giorgio Agamben's (1998) theory of the state of exception, necropower can be defined as the suspension of guarantees of social order and law so that violence can operate in the service of civilization. Mbembe (2003, 24) asserts that during colonization colo-nies could be ruled through absolute lawlessness by regimes because of the racialized denial of a common bond between "the conqueror and the native." In the eyes of the conqueror, the division between life and "savage life" or another form of "animal life" relied on racial logic. For example, in regard to post-9/11 Islamophobia in Canada, Sherene Razack (2008) uses the notion of the colour line (Du Bois 1903) to theo-rize the divide between those with "the right to have rights" and those living in "camps" to describe the establishment of post-9/11 security certificates that justify the incarceration of individuals perceived as security threats, often without evidence. Focusing on both the apartheid

---

4   For Marianne H. Marchand (2008), people migrate for a variety of reasons related to underdevelopment, such as poverty, lack of secure employment opportunities, and violence. In her work on Mexican immigrants to the United States and Canada, she claims that insecurity must be understood as part of the process of migration for those who attempt to permeate borders as well as those who work to secure them. For Marchand, the "migration and insecurities nexus" would better reflect these issues than do current migration and security studies. It is from her use of "insecurities" that I have devised the term "development and in/security nexus."

of South Africa and the occupation of Palestine, Mbembe (2003, 40) argues that in the state of exception, or camp, people live in a liminal space between life and death, a place of the decaying living and the slowly dying: "In our contemporary world, weapons are deployed in the interest of maximum destruction of persons and the creation of death-worlds, new and unique forms of social existence in which vast populations are subjected to conditions of life conferring upon them the status of living dead." According to Lauren Berlant (2007, 760), slow death, in particular, can be understood as the ongoing, the getting by, and it includes those "populations marked out for wearing out." That is, structural inequalities make it such that those slowly dying are not intensifying the death drive but doing the "ordinary work of living on" under conditions in which they are faced with the indifference of death (761). Responding to the way in which Michel Foucault's biopower focuses on the privatization (or individualization) of death in the quest to optimize some lives, Mbembe's (2003) necropolitics conceptualizes power to lie within the capacity to decide who matters and who does not. In other words, necropower slates some for life (West) and others for death (underdeveloped world).

Absorbed with birth rates, health and education statistics, labour opportunities, and living standards, the development industry concerns itself with biopolitical management. Yet we can understand necropolitics as essential to the practice of development since the economic models, and neo-liberal economic restructuring in particular, that aim to manage life are also nonchalant about death even as global managers deploy the technologies that ensure it. While development focuses explicitly on life in terms of quality and quantity, it creates and supports the Third World as a geopolitical death-world. One need look no further than the devastating consequences of structural adjustment programs of the 1980s and 1990s and the subsequent forms of neo-liberal prescriptions that have resulted in the intensification of poverty, the lack of access to private health care in the midst of a growing HIV/AIDS epidemic, food insecurity and famine, migration, and patterns of precarious employment to understand how development biopolitics and necropolitics fold into one another.

To incorporate both necropolitics and biopolitics into conceptions of development and security, I find it more useful to think of the development and in/security nexus to draw attention to insecurity as not only the motive for securitization but also the outcome of its proliferation. I do not merely invert the binary of security/insecurity; rather, I use the development and in/security nexus to account for the insecurity of those who find themselves on the other side of "the global life-chance divide," as Duffield (2010) describes it. Importantly, such a rearticulation of the development and in/security nexus prohibits the characterization of insecurity as the imposition of want and fear and the response as protection and empowerment. In other words, "insecurity" and "security" cannot be understood as antagonistic terms in which the latter is understood as being able to solve the former. Instead, a development and in/security nexus positions protection (read security) and empowerment (read development) as equally implicated in the imposition of insecurity across the Third World with specific impacts on women.

For some scholars of development, the use of foreign aid expertise and funds has been wrongfully diverted from poverty-reduction strategies to post-9/11 security tactics. For others, the security and development discourse has provided unbridled, and questionable, support for new foreign relations. According to Jane Parpart (2010, 88), "the association of underdevelopment with a high risk of conflict (and insecurity) has provided a renewed purpose for development agencies, whose role in addressing global under-development has become in many ways *a new form of riot control, offering solace to those who blame current conflicts on poverty and globalization*" (emphasis added). Although the extent to which energy and money are diverted from traditional development initiatives to purely security-based projects can be debated, in the discursive realm security and development have become inextricably intertwined. As Björn Hettne (2010, 34) asserts, "indeed, in current policy, the 'inextricable links' between security and development are repeated like a mantra, and encompass vast arrays of problems and policy goals." That is, development and security are coupled discursively, often emerging together in post-9/11 agendas that seek to make urgent the connection between "doing" development and "protecting" against security threats.

In the QDDR (2010), underdevelopment is rediscovered as a security threat, and violence against women is presented as an urgent security issue. Important here is that gender inequality, illustrated by violence against women, is discovered as an archetypal excess of underdevelopment and a priority focus because it is said to lead to conflict. Where violence against women is rampant, states are understood to be fragile and prone to conflict. The QDDR report maintains that intervening in issues of gender inequality is indispensable to secure American interests both abroad and at home. Given the leadership of Clinton, the focus on women and girls in the report is not surprising, yet their centrality functions in an important way in the development and in/security nexus. The claim that gender inequality is both a development and a national security issue might change how the United States "does" security and development.

The connection between development and security is present not only in American foreign policy discourses, including the QDDR, but also at the highest levels of international organizations. In the report of the High-Level Panel on Threats, Challenges, and Change (UN 2004, 2), UN Secretary-General Kofi Annan claimed that development and security are major priorities: "Development has to be the first line of defense for a collective security system that takes prevention seriously. Combating poverty will not only save millions of lives but also strengthen States' capacity to combat terrorism, organized crime and proliferation. *Development makes everyone more secure*" (emphasis added). Citing biological security (associated with the spread of HIV/AIDS), organized terrorism, and interstate conflict, as well as the proliferation of nuclear weapons, the UN expert panel claimed that a "UN for the 21st Century" necessarily includes a more tenacious focus on security and development (5).

Quoting President Barack Obama's National Security Strategy, the QDDR (2010, 23) claims that "countries are more peaceful and prosperous when women are accorded full and equal rights and opportunit[ies]. When those rights and opportunities are denied, countries lag behind." As I explore in Chapter 2, the urgency to end violence against women is also constructed through economic discourses in the development industry. For now, it is important to flag the coupling of security and economic growth narratives, suggesting that these two development objectives can be done simultaneously. Encouraging gender issues to be mainstreamed into all areas of development, defence, and diplomacy at the State Department and USAID, the "status of the world's women" is presented as a matter not only of morality but also of national security

(23). This connection to national security manufactures violence against women as an urgent concern.

For the sake of peace and prosperity, American foreign relations rely heavily on women's equality as a common-sense approach to doing security and development. As a well-known, and undercriticized, buzzword, *gender* is heavily circulated in the development community. According to Andrea Cornwall and Deborah Eade (2010, 1–2), buzzwords in development discourses sustain the "model, myths, and passions" of development praxis and are "sprinkled liberally" in funding proposals, promotional material, and policy. Although some buzzwords dip in and out of fashion in the development lexicon, gender has remained an important language component since the 1980s. Ines Smyth (2010) argues that instead of feminist languages and concepts, often introduced through external activism, most development institutions adopted the term "gender" in the 1980s as a depoliticized and catchall term to denote the focus on gender, violence against women, and empowerment as a human rights and social development objective.

It is necessary to flag the use of "gender" and women's rights as discursive manoeuvres in the QDDR (2010) report. In circulating in development discourses, gender is "common sense" in that it is used to make sense of the development and in/security agenda. Indebted to Stuart Hall's (1990) work on the media, Yasmin Jiwani (2006) claims that institutions often use common-sense knowledge, or a historical archive of circulating ideologies, to explain new phenomena through dominant ways of knowing. In development discourse, gender functions as a narrative that "makes sense." Communicated as a moral imperative of development, a social aspect of growth schemes, gender functions as common-sense knowledge in that it does not dislodge development expertise or models of assistance. It functions as a common-sense approach and a moral interlocutor between doing development for the sake of the poor globally and doing security for the sake of those at home.

The development and in/security nexus requires a bonding agent. That is, to communicate the importance of both development and security, in U.S. foreign relations an adhesive is required to communicate its dual and simultaneous importance. Ending violence against women emerges as *the* urgent motive to support the new direction of U.S. foreign relations. Ending violence against women is an innocent and "do-good" deed. As I explore in Chapter 3, "feel-good" concerns also manufacture urgency to eliminate violence against women. Importantly, since gender equality functions uncontroversially, it becomes the moral glue that attaches the issue of underdevelopment to the security-based imperative to intervene. Linking security and development by way of anti–violence against women discourses marks a genderwashing. The United States positions itself as threatened by the leakage of gender inequality into its national spaces, as if the issue does not exist there already, and as a benevolent actor willing to intervene in the name of both security and development.

Since the U.S. war on Afghanistan in 2001, and its subsequent invasion of Iraq in 2003, feminist theorizing about women and war has increased dramatically. In fact, how feminist values and women's rights have been used to justify the war on terror has literally dragged feminism into the field of war in the post-9/11 era. Of course, it is not only since the 9/11 attacks that feminists have been thinking about gender and conflict.[5] Although the deployment of feminism in the Afghanistan war is often understood as an exceptional case, Puar (2007) reveals how the manufacturing of 9/11 as an event has obscured similar historical operations. A project of urgency has facilitated the perception of 9/11 as merely a moment, or "flashpoint," and it has been viewed in visual and discursive "snapshots." These images of 9/11 disconnect it from pre-9/11 foreign policy and warmaking. As Puar notes, this "event-ness...blinds the past even as it spotlights the present" (xviii). Such conceptions of temporality are especially important to the study of so-called post-9/11 security initiatives. According to Malinda Smith (2010), both popular discourse and scholarly literature overwhelmingly refer to pre- and post-9/11. She argues that its repetition and circulation function to "bring into being a perception of a radical historical discontinuity, a watershed between a known past and an unknown future" (3). In fact, the hegemony of 9/11 event-ness has meant that critical analysis of the attacks too often begins with the "moment" of 9/11 and traces the trajectory of wars and invasions that followed it, but leaves context and history behind.

The war on terror is not a new war but a different militarized mobilization of old racialized and gendered logics and lexicons: "What becomes

---

5   See, for example, Enloe (1988, 1989).

immediately apparent is that U.S. militarization has meant a new mobilization of historically embedded colonial practice[s] and rhetorics of male superiority and white supremacy; of female vulnerability, inadequacy, and inferiority; and of subjugation of oppressed masculinities of men of color" (Mohanty, Pratt, and Riley 2008, 3). A plethora of feminist research has emerged on the "civilizing" and "saving" mission of the war on terror, often expanding on Gayatri Spivak's (1988, 297) famous phrase regarding "white men saving brown women from brown men," which originally spoke to the mobilization of gendered and racialized language during the British colonial occupation of India.[6] Undoubtedly, orientalist grammars have historically demarcated the "colour line" during conflicts.[7] In current Canadian critical race feminism, Razack's (2008) *Casting Out: The Eviction of Muslims from Western Law and Politics* has emerged as a key intervention in understanding representations of Muslim men as dangerous and Muslim women as imperilled in the post-9/11 period. Concerned with the "culturalization of racism" that has disproportionately targeted Muslim and Arab men and women in the post-9/11 period, Razack claims that white liberal feminists are too often heralded as experts on cultural difference, liberation, and civility (85). Arguing that "modern" women functioned as the more progressive sisters of "backward" women, imperialist Western feminism has become central war rhetoric. From Yasmin Jiwani's (2010) examination of how Afghan women become "worthy victims" of U.S. aid only when unveiled and modernized to Lila Abu-Lughod's (2002) response to the unveiling of Muslim women as a "saving" tactic, it has become clear to critical race feminists that this "clash of civilizations" (Huntington 1993) is being fought on the bodies of women.

Of course, debates about modernity have often occurred on women's bodies. For Partha Chatterjee (1993), postcolonial nationalist disputes

---

6   See, for example, Abu-Lughod (2002); Bhattacharyya (2008); and Razack (2008).

7   Razack (2004, 4, 9) suggests that Du Bois's (1903) concept of the colour line is particularly useful for understanding racial hierarchies. Focusing on peacekeeping initiatives in Somalia, she claims that Canadians consider themselves to be fair, rational, and saviours by being on the right (read white) side of the colour line. As Ghassan J. Hage (2000) suggests, whiteness is a regime of accumulation so that, even when peacekeepers are people of colour, the global colour line ensures that they come to know themselves as being on the right (white) side.

about modernity and tradition in India were focused on women's role as protectors of culture, and thus women were often read by colonizers as signifiers of "backwardness." Moreover, as Meyda Yeğenoğlu's (1998) feminist reading of Edward Said's (1978) *Orientalism* reveals, making women's bodies visible has always been central to colonial terrorization and control. In regard to colonialism, territory was often feminized, and both land and women were perceived as needing protection from dangerous men even while being violated (McClintock 1995; Peterson 2007). However, Indigenous women were not slated for protection but routinely violated under colonial regimes (Smith 2005). Thus, a concern for some women's rights is not specifically a post-9/11 security issue, though it is presented as such. The history of saving and civilizing "backward" countries has habitually relied on women's bodies.

Rather than trace the events of 9/11 to newly emerging security and development initiatives in the name of women's rights, I begin from the premise that the event-ness of 9/11 has obscured other wars, imperialisms, apartheids, and colonialisms and has used feminist, queer, and liberal language and rights to justify intervention.[8] This chapter, then, is palimpsestic: it aims to retrace the erased or obscured history and present of development and security discourses. Thus, my response to anti-violence initiatives emerging in the popularly demarcated post-9/11 period should be read not as an urgent or expedient response to an exceptional problematic, but as the continuation of feminist theorizing and activism on the subject.

Given that the war on terror was launched fifteen years ago, it is unsurprising that both gender and race logics of U.S. imperialism are similarly mobilized, yet have also changed course. As cultural theorist Stuart Hall (1990) asserts, new representations of racialized groups always bear the traces of past articulations. Although the discourse of saving Muslim women through "unveiling" no longer takes precedence in the popular media that it did in early coverage of the war on terror, what Cynthia Enloe (2007) has described as the militarization of "everyday life" has occurred and means that war objectives and discourses are widely integrated into national and local narratives.

---

8   For example, see Abu-Lughod (2002); the edited collection on feminism and war by Mohanty, Pratt, and Riley (2008); and Puar (2007).

One of the most concerning discourses that has remained in the so-called postwar period is that of national security. While American and Canadian troops disengage from Iraq and Afghanistan, respectively, security forces and development experts remain to make the transition "smoother." The urgency with which the United States surveils, militarizes, and protects its borders from threats has not decreased but in fact increased. According to Shoshana A. Magnet (2011), there is a new multi-billion-dollar industry forming around technological interventions that aim objectively to read and code bodies to contain perceived threats as new ones emerge (e.g., ISIS). Both at home and abroad, the United States is determined to defend itself in the name of national security. From borders to bodies, security remains a primary agenda in the post-9/11 era.

Clinton's quest to end global violence against women on the ground of security marks a representation of genderwashing. That is, the Hillary Doctrine, and the anti-violence discourse that circulated during her tenure as secretary of state, borrow from discourses already circulating in rhetoric on the war on terror at home and abroad. Here genderwashing functions to disavow the failure of the United States to "save" Afghan women (Abu-Lughod 2002; Jiwani 2006; Razack 2008), and feminist research reveals that women in Iraq are actually worse off economically, socially, and politically than before the U.S. invasion, which aimed to empower them (Zangana 2007). Despite these failures, Clinton, as the unofficial U.S. ambassador for women and girls, has made it clear that the country will continue on the trajectory begun in the war on terror, albeit through the development and in/security nexus, employing discursive and material practices that include criminalization.

"IT'S NOT CULTURAL; IT'S CRIMINAL"

The Hillary Doctrine also has a component of criminalization. This is an important part of the discursive strategy to manufacture violence against women as an urgent concern because it allows the doctrine to promote the United States as a global leader through exporting best practices. These practices are described through discourses of criminalization and bolster support for militarized and securitized responses to violence against women.

In 2010, Clinton claimed that there was a "culture of violence against women" in Papua New Guinea (U.S. News 2010) and that there was a "traditional" foundation for "female genital mutilation/cutting," among other violent practices (Clinton 2012). She also asserted that violence against women is not a cultural issue but a criminal one. Although this distinction seems to be contradictory, I intend to demonstrate how it is, in fact, complementary. Clinton originally used the phrase "it's not cultural; it's criminal" in 2009 at a UN Security Council meeting in regard to security issues related to sexual violence during conflicts. In 2011, Clinton used the same phrase in regard to the beating of female Egyptian protesters in the "post-revolution" state (qtd. in Telegraph 2011). She also used the phrase that year to communicate the importance of working to end violence against both women and LGBT individuals globally (Clinton 2011). "It's not cultural; it's criminal" is a powerful discursive manoeuvre to proactively side-step criticism from those concerned with both the universalism of human rights agendas and cultural relativism.

CULTURAL RELATIVISM VERSUS UNIVERSALISM

In anti-violence theory focused at the level of the transnational, the debate between universalism and cultural relativism is well known. This debate is often conducted on the bodies of women, on which manifestations of gender inequality are often marked as culturally based (Abu-Lughod 2002; Razack 2008). Here women's bodies are used as a tool of measurement to locate nations within or outside modernity, in which "traditional" practices (e.g., veiling) are understood as oppressive to women in contrast to their modern and uncovered "sisters" in the West. Moreover, focusing on violent practices, especially exoticized, fetishized, and culturalized violence such as female genital mutilation/cutting, honour killing, and dowry murder, proponents of women's rights as human rights aim their criticism on cultural relativists who argue for the autonomy and sovereignty of communities to shape their own social relations based upon localized cultural traditions. In feminist and development theory, questions of how, when, and if to intervene in women's issues are controversial.

Emerging alongside a human rights paradigm in the development mainstream, debates about cultural relativism and universalism have preoccupied the field of feminist studies (Kapoor 2008; Mohanty 2003; Nussbaum and Glover 1995; Spivak 2004). According to Ilan Kapoor (2008, 34), development proponents of universalism argue for the general application of Western laws on the basis of a universal "essence" or global "human nature"; human rights in particular are drafted by transnational elites who imagine themselves to be producing laws and not culture but rely on a particular tradition of law and a system of politics that granted rights to property owners and thus denied rights to women, people of colour, and men without property (see also Mills 1997; and Patemen 1988). Although rights have been extended in the contemporary period, human rights are based upon a system of state sovereignty under which non-citizens (refugees, "illegal" immigrants, temporary workers) and original occupiers of land (Indigenous people) are not recognized (Kapoor 2008, 34–35). One significant criticism of the universalist position is that it locates the West as the site of progress and dismisses local culture as always already backward and patriarchal.

For example, critical universalist Martha Nussbaum argues for a socially constructed view of transnational laws, including human rights treaties. In *Women, Culture, and Development: A Study of Human Capabilities* (Nussbaum and Glover 1995), she suggests that cultural relativist positions are too focused on difference and place feminists in a position that disallows both concerns and calls for justice in the name of oppressed women. Arguing that it is "impossible to deny that traditions perpetuate injustice against women in many fundamental ways," she is also concerned with the "morally retrograde" judgments against cultural traditions (1). She suggests that the impasse between universalism and cultural relativism is most problematic: "To say that a practice is all right wherever local tradition endorses it as right and good is to risk erring by withholding critical judgment where real evil and real oppression are surely present. To avoid the whole issue because the matter of proper judgment is so fiendishly difficult is tempting, but perhaps the worst option of all" (2). Erring on the side of universalism, while adopting a critical approach, Nussbaum is concerned with the customs that intensify Third World women's experiences of extreme poverty and oppression (3). Although she might be well intentioned in her concern for women, she utilizes "authentic" stories of Third World women to shore up what she claims is the best possible theory to suit her purpose as a "morally outraged top-drawer activist" interested in international intervention (Spivak 2004, 566). Suggesting that Nussbaum is merely "bringing the other into the self," Spivak is critical of how she discovers her philosophical argument for universalism on the bodies of the Indian women whom she interviewed (566).

Although feminists criticize universalism, those concerned with Western cultural imperialism too often rely on cultural relativism as an antidote. Communities in the Third World are cast as being either culturally different from or fundamentally similar to the West, albeit requiring education to catch up to First World standards on the treatment of women. Concerned with how both universal sameness and cultural difference have been wielded in colonial and imperial dialogues and projects, Uma Narayan (2000) suggests that cultural relativism is a dangerous tool. For example, when a community claims that violent practices are "cultural issues" or based upon "traditional" gender relations, anti-violence organizing becomes nearly impossible for the women most affected by the practices. The issue also becomes untouchable for those working against violence externally. Moreover, cultural essentialist claims about gender inequalities are often used by Western feminists and imperial powers to mark others as essentially different (Narayan 2000, 104; see also Abu-Lughod 2002; and Razack 2008). Claims to authentic cultures, traditions, and values emerging from within communities as distinct from the West are frequently wielded to defend against Western intervention and are as dangerous as universalism for women. According to Narayan (2000, 95), "many versions of relativism rely on a picture of 'cultures' that I previously criticized as culturally essentialist, a picture in which cultures appear neatly, pre-discursively, individuated from each other; in which the insistence of 'Difference' that accompanies that 'production' of distinct 'cultures' appears unproblematic; and the central or constitutive components of a 'culture' are assumed to be 'unchanging givens.'" Furthermore, Kapoor (2008, 34) claims that cultural relativist arguments are just as caught up in the same traditional-modern dualism as universalism by only inverting the good/bad binary between natural law and communitarian rights. Both Kapoor and Narayan suggest that feminists and development scholars should interrogate narratives of cultural difference as well as claims of universalism. In particular, Narayan (2000, 97) calls on feminists to consider the empirical accuracy, political utility, and dangerous nature of any generalizable argument about women's inequality or standardized solution (97).

CRIMINALIZATION AS A UNIVERSALISM

Hillary Clinton's claim that violence is not cultural but criminal marks a robust effort to move beyond (or around) the debate about cultural relativism and universalism as I have explored above. To make the issue urgent, the Hillary Doctrine *both* operationalizes a human rights discourse and argues that there is a "culture of violence" in underdeveloped nations. The suggestion that violence against women is a crime offers a new set of ideologies and strategies for development and in/security interventions that helps to frame the issue as particularly pressing. Moving away from complicated dialogues about culture in particular, Clinton's effort to address the urgency of violence against women is communicated through a distinctive universalism. Both national law and international law are constructions of supposedly agreed upon ideas on law and lawlessness based upon a European historical archive of philosophical theory. The standardization of agreed-upon crimes, and the required responses to crimes, are positioned as universally accepted ideas, even though, as Bernard Schissel and Carolyn Brooks (2008, 6) maintain, "definitions of and prohibitions for crime change over time and across social groups as societies, with little consensus around just what criminal behaviour is." Criminal law is not "culture free." Claiming to see crime only in the midst of culture is what Audrey Macklin (2002, 88) calls "looking at culture through the lens of law." Significantly, crime and culture "do not occupy different conceptual spaces" (97). By suggesting that crime, or the criminalization of certain behaviours and actions, is a concept that "we" can agree on, the Hillary Doctrine not only sets out an innovative justification for intervention in the name of security but also assumes chaos and lawlessness in the places marked as negligent in regard to criminalizing violence against women.

It also directly links responses to emergencies at home to responses to urgent issues abroad. Understanding violence as criminal invokes the idea that 911 must be called. Violence against women is treated as an emergency in which emergency services must be called. In the post-9/11 era, calling on 9/11 creates a sense of emergency that requires an urgent response. Importantly, this manufacturing of urgency through criminalized discourses relies on failed strategies in the United States and disavows alternative and non-state strategies to eliminate violence against women.

As feminist criminologists, prison abolitionists, and anti-violence activists have exposed, the criminalization of violence against women has failed systemically in the United States (Davis 2005; INCITE! 2006; Smith 2005). In penal abolition literature, scholars and activists, including Angela Davis (2003), argue that too often it is taken for granted that someone who commits a crime should be incarcerated. For many anti-violence advocates, the assumption that incarcerating individuals who commit crimes against women will actually reduce gendered violence is unfounded. In fact, penal abolition scholars show how the criminalization of violence against women further entrenches systems of oppression, including racism, sexism, and classism, that contribute to violence against women. Although the anti-violence movement in the United States began by correlating violence with systemic gender inequality, the criminalization of violence against women imposed gender-neutral legal language and individualistic responses, including the incarceration of perpetrators (Erwin 2006; INCITE! 2006). Alternative approaches to preventing violence exist, as do resistances to the criminal system, but the overwhelming emphasis on "best practice" approaches is centred on law enforcement and penal system reform (Erwin 2006).

In the United States, the domestic Violence against Women Act (VAWA) outlines the federal response to violence against women. VAWA, introduced in 1994, exists within the Violent Crime Control and Law Enforcement Act (otherwise known as the crime bill). Lobbied for by over 1,000 organizations beginning in the 1990s, VAWA was a landmark piece of federal legislation recognizing the public and political nature of violence against women. It primarily addressed the physical and sexual assault of women in public, at home, and in the courts. Importantly, a requirement of VAWA was education of the courts and law enforcement agencies as well as inclusion of women and their advocates in policy implementation. It also included a national study of domestic and sexual violence to gather statistical information (Meyer-Emerick 2001, 4–5).

Motivated by electoral support, members of Congress and senators were originally driven to pass VAWA by political circumstances external

to it (Brooks 1997, 81), and they continue to be committed to the legislation or its amendments through their constituents' support.[9] Although
women's organizations were invited to the table in the early 1990s when
the legislation was drafted, significant trade-offs were made while negotiating with the state. For Brooks, negotiating with the state meant that
some significant feminist intentions for VAWA were compromised. For
example, for feminists supporting VAWA, issues surrounding the death
penalty and sentencing requirements in the crime bill were problematic, and the idea that VAWA would be incorporated into such a bill was
disappointing, to say the least. As Brooks argues, "by associating domestic violence against women with other criminal acts the state can ignore
the many other roots of this violence" (79). Quickly, VAWA changed from
a bill with educational and awareness components to crime legislation
meant to incarcerate perpetrators of violence.[10]

In 1994, VAWA passed as part of the larger Violent Crime Control and
Law Enforcement Act with $33 billion devoted to crime measures, only
$1.62 billion of which was dedicated to ending violence against women.
According to Brooks (1997, 76–77), a majority of this allocation to VAWA
was provided to law enforcement training, mandatory arrest programs,
and (a small amount) women's shelters. Actual investment in education
and awareness was low. Brooks also argues that feminists lobbying for
VAWA were forced to choose between race and gender justice since the

9   According to the thorough research of Rachelle Brooks (1997) on VAWA,
     debates on the bill being consolidated into a crime bill, removal of the Racial
     Justice Act, and inclusion of a civil rights provision were divisive for Democrats
     and Republicans. In 2012, inclusion of rights for immigrant women,
     Indigenous women, and victims of same-sex violence in intimate partner
     relationships was the subject of major debate before VAWA eventually passed
     in 2013. Debates on VAWA, especially in regard to who should be protected and
     appropriate responses to violence, have been embedded in larger concerns
     over issues of race, class, sexuality, and citizenship, and members of both
     Congress and the Senate have historically voted in line with their party's
     ideology, regardless of its affect on women.
10   When sent to the House, the crime bill (which contained VAWA) included a
     separate provision to allow death row inmates to make an appeal on the basis
     of a racially discriminatory sentencing, known as the Racial Justice Act. It also
     included a ban on assault weapons. Republicans opposed both provisions. The
     Racial Justice Act and assault weapon ban caused heated debate in Congress in
     1994, so it took much political negotiation for the crime bill, and thus VAWA,
     to pass. Ultimately, the Racial Justice Act did not pass.

passing of VAWA occurred without the Racial Justice Act, also proposed within the crime bill and a major source of political contention between Democrats and Republicans. For Brooks, feminists implicitly endorsed removal of the Racial Justice Act: "Domestic violence and racial justice issues became competing policies rather than complementary ones, thus exemplifying the frequent inability of the state to address women's and feminists' multiple allegiances and identities....By ignoring the specificity of women's circumstances, the Act itself creates gaps through which many women will fall" (80). VAWA was reauthorized in 2000, 2005, and 2013. Most recently, in 2012 and 2013, the act became a partisan legislation with the inclusion of protections for same-sex partnerships and both "legal" and "illegal" immigrants, creating further tension among Republicans and Democrats (Bendery 2012).

According to INCITE! (2006, 1), working with the state rather than against it has meant that approaches to eradicating violence are often shaped by state and federal funding. As we can see with the example of VAWA, federal funding tied to the law specifically supported criminalized responses to violence against women, and VAWA has had a number of unintended consequences for the anti-violence movement, including the vulnerability of survivors to violence by both abusers and law enforcement personnel. The INCITE! collective maintains that criminalization of violence against women has not been successful in the United States. For example, mandatory arrest policies, which ensure that both abuser and victim are apprehended, have not helped to decrease the number of batterers who kill their partners, though they have led to a decrease in the number of abused women who kill their abusers in self-defence (223). This provision actually protects the abuser rather than the victim. Moreover, Andrea Ritchie (2006, 142), in agreement with the Audre Lorde Project, asserts that law enforcement agencies and courts "enforce societies' raced, gendered, and class[ed] structures, conventional notions of 'morality,' and social norms established by dominant groups." Thus, individuals who transgress these boundaries in terms of conduct, expression, or even existence, including transgender individuals, are monitored, harassed, wilfully ignored, or punished by the system. Ritchie maintains that the fear of police violence because of institutionalized racism, and inappropriate responses to violent situations by law enforcement personnel, such as mandatory arrest policies, have left women of colour, Indigenous women, poor women, queer and transgender women, women with disabilities, and immigrant women particularly vulnerable (151). Connecting the "war on crime," the "war on drugs," and the "war on terror," Ritchie reveals how "tough on crime" legislation, such as the crime bill, passed alongside VAWA in 1994, has negatively affected those most in need of protection. For example, though VAWA introduced in 1994 and 2000 visas for battered immigrant women, many women were not made aware of the act's provision or were unable to meet eligibility criteria that relied on evidence of abuse (INCITE! 2006, 300). For example, Patricia E. Erwin (2006) claims that an immigrant woman can apply for immigrant status without a husband if she can prove abuse. Yet, for non-status immigrants, filing a police report to prove abuse is inherently dangerous. Under mandatory arrest policies, immigrant women could find themselves vulnerable to deportation. The protections for immigrant women continue to be troublesome for survivors and anti-violence advocates, as the heated debate in 2012–13 revealed (Stahl 2012).

The passing of VAWA domestically sheds light on the impact of the potential passing of the International Violence against Women Act, which was introduced during Clinton's tenure and reflects her assertion that violence against women is a crime and an urgent global issue. Although the two sets of legislation are not the same, they are similar in that, by my reading, the individual and criminal components of I-VAWA reflect those of the domestic VAWA. Discourses of criminality are coupled with security discourses in I-VAWA, and though police and military are separate institutions, both VAWA and I-VAWA position state authorities as experts in responding to violence against women, even as evidence of their inability to comprehend the complexities of such violence comes to light.

EXPORTING BEST PRACTICES

When Hillary Clinton urgently claimed that violence against women is not cultural but criminal, she laid the groundwork for foreign policy to mirror domestic legislation. At the level of U.S. foreign relations, Erwin (2006) claims that there is a perplexing mix of international human rights discourses and "best practice" approaches that privilege legal reforms. In the United States, the legal system, law enforcement, and police protection have comprised the dominant response to the problem of violence against women. From mandatory arrest policies that place both parties under arrest in police responses to domestic violence, to obligatory batterer intervention counselling supervised by a parole officer, these policies increase surveillance measures. Such best practice approaches are heavily reliant on the criminal legal system (Erwin 2006; INCITE! 2006). At home, human rights discourses have rarely been integrated into mainstream anti-violence initiatives, even while they are promoted abroad. That is, human rights are not domestic issues but issues for "others" abroad. As a federally mandated legislation, VAWA represents the current best practice approach to ending violence against women. It is not clear that all American-informed strategies are being exported with current development projects that focus on violence against women, but penal reform and law enforcement measures are understood to be best practice approaches (Erwin 2006). Under the pressure of urgency, already established responses to violence against women will be exported, even when they are failed strategies. A mode of urgency created by discourses of security disallows alternative strategies from taking shape.

As I have explored above, critical scholars have maintained that the criminalization of violence against women has intensified the surveillance and incarceration of members of poor communities and communities of colour (INCITE! 2006, 223–24). Although criminal responses to violence are successful in terms of holding individuals culpable for their crimes, they have failed the most marginalized members of society. Since VAWA has been successfully used as a "tough on crime" policy, it has bolstered the prison-industrial complex. According to Davis (2003), the export of criminal justice responses by the United States is consistent with expansions of and relations between the prison-industrial complex and the military-industrial complex. Calling these complexes "symbiotic," Davis suggests that military and domestic prisons share the same technologies of punishment as well as mutually support and promote one another (88). Pointing to the connections between prison and military industrial complexes globally, Davis (2003, 2005) maintain that the global economy depends on prisoners for a range of profit-driven activities, from medical experiments to manufacturing labourers. Davis (2005, 72–73) claims that prisons, both domestic and military, are conceived of as solutions to the problems that capitalism creates but cannot solve. Pointing to human rights violations at Abu Ghraib and Guantánamo Bay, along with the proliferation of detention centres and military prisons in the war on terror, Davis warns of the racist ideologies institutionalized in U.S. domestic and exported penal systems in the targeting of security threats. Given the framing of eradicating violence against women as a security objective, it is necessary to consider the connection between U.S. criminal justice and the military.

According to Stephen M. Hill , Randall R. Beger, and John M. Zanetti (2007), security studies and criminology have too long been divided by disciplinary boundaries and thus have habitually misunderstood the connection between paramilitary policing at home and abroad. Paramilitary police are those that receive quasi-military training, equipment, and philosophy (306). The military training of foreign police, and the increasing militarization of police at home, have meant that racialized and other marginalized individuals, including the unemployed and political dissidents, are targeted as "the enemy" (304). Military methods bolster state protectionism at the expense of the rights of citizens. Militarized police tactics also depend on a type of "warrior culture" that equates combat readiness with law enforcement and causes citizens to be less inclined to report crimes (305). In Cuba, Nicaragua, Panama, Haiti, the Dominican Republic, Puerto Rico, and the Philippines, the U.S. military has trained police forces used to enforce political suppression or undertake coups d'état (308). Guided by U.S. political and economic investments, the training of foreign police forces has "plugged a security gap" in peacekeeping, military, and humanitarian interventions, with few signs of slowing down. Of the 7,160 police personnel deployed in UN peace-support missions at the end of 2005, almost half were paramilitary police officers. Known for working outside the normal frameworks of accountability and for using excessive force, foreign police forces trained by the military are concerning (312–13).

IMPLICATIONS FOR CRIMINALIZING VIOLENCE AGAINST WOMEN

For communities of colour at home, criminalizing violence against women has meant vulnerability to state-sponsored violence. For Third

World bodies abroad, the exportation of U.S. best practices inevitably employs ideologies already present in the U.S. system, including sexism, racism, classism, homophobia, and transphobia. This is what is at stake in discourses of urgency—too many important issues are earmarked for later or not considered at all. Since criminal justice responses further entrench already existing inequalities, exporting best practices in an expedient manner that already fails marginalized communities in the United States will have detrimental impacts globally. As Narayan (2000, 97) reminds feminists, it is important to consider the empirical accuracy, political utility, and dangerous nature of any generalizable strategy in regard to women's issues.

The manufacturing of urgency around violence against women abroad using criminalized rhetoric permits the exportation of best practices, which means, ultimately, imposing failed approaches and further criminalizing and securitizing racialized others always already understood as irrationally violent and dangerous. Furthermore, the exportation of U.S. best practices will likely involve the restructuring of already established community, customary, and state responses to violence against women. For example, police training offered by the United States is a top-down approach that ignores the grassroots mobilization of women's organizations. In an interview with an international training coordinator, Erwin (2006, 202) found that approaches to criminal justice reform failed when an agenda was imposed on the local community. Furthermore, as Erwin notes, the best practice approaches that the United States has exported focus too heavily on first-generation human rights issues, such as legal reform, and often ignore second-level human rights, such as employment, housing, and community development (200).

To recapitulate, Hillary Clinton's statement "it's not cultural; it's criminal" is important insofar as it moves away from narratives that culturalize and exoticize violence against Third World women. However, the standardization of a criminal justice approach is equally dangerous. When Clinton asserts that violence against women is not cultural but criminal, the systemic nature of such violence in its various manifestations is understood to be individualistic. In this definition, violence against women is narrowed down to conflicts in interpersonal gender relations and ignores how violent practices are perpetuated by geopolitical relations, imperialism, uneven globalization, immigration and displacement, the securitization of borders, occupation and ongoing colonization, and state-sanctioned and militarized violence. A criminological approach to violence against women globally prohibits such an expansive definition of violence against women and, I argue, does not provide appropriate strategies to oppose it.

Clinton's statement revealing or "discovering" the criminal nature of violence against women in the Third World assumes a correlation between earlier forms of organizing around violence against women in North America and what is happening in "backward" Third World communities today. Pointing to the need to criminalize, or take seriously, violence against women, the Hillary Doctrine represents the Third World as lagging behind the First World. Not only is solving this backwardness considered a development project, of which the United States has expertise to share, but also it is understood to be a new and urgent security concern. The so-called backwardness of the Third World is an excess of underdevelopment that must be contained. As Clinton aims to amp up interventions in violence against women around the globe, the assumption that, without the United States as a role model, Third World countries will be left to chaos and lawlessness continues to rely on a racial grammar that posits the West as superior, rational, and orderly in contrast to irrational and dangerous others who threaten the country's security.

Within the Hillary Doctrine, the claim that violence is not cultural but criminal relies on best practice approaches to anti-violence developed in the United States. Contingent on anti-violence strategies that have failed, even as they are successful in expanding the prison and military industrial complexes, U.S. criminal approaches centre security of the populace as having primary importance over the insecurity of others. As a development and in/security issue, violence against women gains increasing attention as an urgent concern. In this context, the proposed International Violence against Women Act can be read as the expansion and solidification of exporting failed best practices to eradicate violence against women.

THE INTERNATIONAL VIOLENCE AGAINST WOMEN ACT

In the context of the Hillary Doctrine circulating in the United States, it comes as no surprise that legislation entitled the International Violence against Women Act emerged. If passed by Congress, I-VAWA would effectively centre the issue of violence against women in all U.S. foreign relations, undoubtedly making the issue urgent. As a bill, its aim is to communicate the urgency of eradicating violence against women transnationally. According to Amnesty International (2010), I-VAWA is a concerted effort to eliminate violence against women internationally. I-VAWA "contains best practice provisions for preventing and responding to violence" developed by Amnesty International USA, Family Violence Prevention Fund, and Women Thrive Worldwide in conjunction with 150 other U.S. organizations and forty international experts (Amnesty International 2010). On June 3, 2015, I-VAWA was reintroduced in the 114th Congress.[11] According to Christina Finch, policy and advocacy director for women's human rights at Amnesty International USA, I-VAWA presents the most "comprehensive and holistic" response to violence against women at the international level (personal communication, 2012). Proponents suggest that the door has been opened to the passing of I-VAWA in the near future since the Obama administration has already developed new policy on strategies to end violence against women. For example, in 2012, Obama introduced a "Strategy to Prevent and Respond to Gender-Based Violence Globally." In both this strategy paper and I-VAWA, violence against women is identified as a national security concern and a foreign policy priority. For the champions of I-VAWA, such as Amnesty International USA, this new legislation marks an important step in the right direction (Finch, personal communication, 2013). Although I-VAWA has yet to pass in Congress, it must be taken seriously as one insidious piece of legislation that codifies militarized and imperial acts in the name of women's rights. It does so by manufacturing urgency about ending violence against women.

I-VAWA has surfaced within a larger nexus of institutional, discursive, and ideological arrangements that privileges the securitization of violence against women above all else. It has emerged within discourses of urgency that present violence against women as a pressing concern for security. In a press release, former Chairman of the United States Senate Committee

---

11 I-VAWA was reintroduced at the 112th Congress but did not pass because of time constraints and bipartisanship on this and other issues, including the domestic Violence against Women Act.

on Foreign Relations and current Secretary of State Senator John Kerry claimed that "the bill will protect women everywhere, and it turns out that championing these values is also an extremely effective and cost-efficient strategy to advance America's foreign assistance goals and strengthen our national security" (qtd. in Amnesty International 2010). Arguments about the urgency to end violence against women as a cost-efficient measure are not new. As I explore in Chapter 2, the World Bank also argues that ending violence against women is an efficient use of resources. Yet strengthening national security remains the central tenet of American discourse on the issue. In a press release by the Senate Committee on Foreign Relations (2010) in support of I-VAWA, subtitled "Strengthening National Security by Ending Violence against Women," Senator Dulahunt claimed that countries with the worst track records on violence against women were breeding grounds for terrorism and that it was necessary for the national security of the United States to be a global leader in ending such violence. By this logic, if violence against women is not eliminated, then terrorists are sure to strike the United States. Senator Collins added that he had "long been concerned about the treatment of women and girls all over the world, especially in Afghanistan." Furthermore, Senator Poe claimed that it was essential that the United States not only lead by example but also educate other countries on how to fight violence against women.

In 2012, when the bill was first read in the House, there were two major co-sponsors, Jane Schakosky and Ted Poe. In 2015, the bill was sponsored by Schakosky. According to his website, Poe is a conservative congress-man who unwaveringly supports the state of Israel and is behind the National Guard Border Enforcement Act, which would require the secre-tary of defence to deploy 10,000 National Guard troops to the U.S.-Mexico and U.S.-Canada borders to maintain control over "illegal" immigrants. He has also promoted the National Defense (SEND) Act, which would equip border guards with surplus defence weapons from Iraq, and he has supported various anti-abortion bills, including the No Taxpayer Funding for Abortion and Abortion Insurance Full Disclosure Act of 2015 and the Pain-Capable Unborn Child Protection Act (Poe 2015). Given his support of I-VAWA, it is clear that Poe has a narrow definition of violence against women and does not consider anti-reproductive health laws, occupation, border securitization, and anti-immigration as practices of violence that affect women's autonomy, empowerment, and human rights.

In an interview with the *Houston Chronicle* regarding his work on I-VAWA, Poe (2010) asserted that "we have to teach women that it is not culturally acceptable for men to abuse them, and that it is not acceptable to resolve conflict with violence....The women are so beat down culturally, they assume they are property." Citing Iran and the Taliban as the worst abusers of women, Poe used his thirty years as a criminal judge and prosecutor to reflect on the importance of the bill:

> Poe: After 22 years on the bench, I've seen it all. I remember I had a Middle Eastern man in my courtroom who actually said, 'In my culture, it's OK to beat her up.' That's exactly what he said. He said it was OK in his culture. He needed someone to teach him that it is not acceptable in anyone's culture to abuse a woman.
>
> Q: And did you teach him?
>
> Poe: Oh, yeah (laughing).

Responding to a case of violence against a woman in Houston, Poe stated, "I say get a rope," an undeniable reference to lynching. Given the connections that critical race scholars have made between the history of lynching in the United States and the torture at Abu Ghraib, such statements should be taken seriously.[12] And given the questionable motivations of co-sponsor Poe in supporting I-VAWA, which clearly targets other cultures as backward and exceptionally gender inequitable, it is troubling that Amnesty International USA has declared its unwavering support of the bill, especially when Poe was its co-sponsor.

According to Christina Finch from Amnesty International USA, I-VAWA has not received much critical attention from the public or academic sphere (personal communication, 2012). However, I found

---

12   Razack (2005) argues that the torture at Abu Ghraib can be understood as racialized and sexualized violence to strip Iraqi men of their humanity by undermining their masculinity. She suggests that Abu Ghraib should not be understood as an exceptional event but as racialized and sexualized violence connected to the castration of black men in historical lynching practices in the United States. For Razack, lynching is about maintaining the colour line. Poe's reference to lynching to respond to men's violence against women should be read along this historical continuum of racialized and sexualized violence.

that men's rights groups oppose the bill. For example, such groups in the United States have targeted it as a feminist bill and argued that it ignores research claiming that women are more likely than men to instigate partner violence and arguing that men, not women, are ignored in development programs (Rogers 2010). Additionally, the Save Indian Family Foundation (2010), also a men's rights group, has met staff from the U.S. Senate and House about anti-male laws in India. Specifically, the foundation claims that Indian laws protect women in the case of divorce and treat men like "ATM machines" when a dowry is involved. The foundation suggests that misandry is alive and well in India and that feminists and other powerful women, including union activists and politicians, discriminate against men. It also claims that UNICEF, the United Nations, USAID, and OXFAM are "organisations [that] strongly believe in unscientific feminist theories and they have no concerns for the conditions of millions of men, especially poor men in this country." Of course, I-VAWA could have a variety of unintended implications for local legal proceedings on cases of violence against women, including in the case of divorce. However, the concerns of misogynist men's rights groups are not concerns for the well-being of women.

In a different vein entirely, I am concerned about I-VAWA and the American track record of promoting women's rights globally. Although little has been written on the bill in the academy, Nissa Thompson (2008, 1) responded to an earlier version of it in a commentary in the *Berkeley Journal of Gender, Law, and Justice*, questioning whether it "is just another way that the U.S. government could craft justifications for interventions into foreign countries' politics with potentially harmful consequences for women." Although Thompson cautiously reads I-VAWA as a potentially positive response to harsh criticism of the American "liberation" of women in Afghanistan and Iraq, I suggest that I-VAWA can also be read as a new foreign policy discourse on the same continuum of war on terror rhetoric. Under the Obama administration, which focused on "softer" and "smarter" development and security approaches, especially under Clinton's leadership, I-VAWA might be a response to the Bush era, but when you look closely, it is not a response that drastically alters from early post-9/11 rhetoric.

In the unprecedented address by former First Lady Laura Bush in 2001, the liberation of Afghan women from Islamic fundamentalism was centralized as a tool to tame the dangerous powers of terrorist men. In 2016, I-VAWA, and the discourse surrounding its promotion, continues to represent gender equality as connected to fundamentalism and extremism. Again, women's rights are used to "civilize and save" others. In I-VAWA, violence against women is said to exist at a broader and more insidious scale in nations understood to be fragile or underdeveloped, and such violence is utilized as a signifier to mark geopolitically the breeding grounds of terrorism. Given the emphasis on security concerns within I-VAWA, risks and threats will be met with military, police, and security services, and securitization and militarization will likely be the primary responses to the crime of violence against women globally.

Although arguably overcited in critical feminist literature on the war on terror (given that there are many more organizations in Afghanistan that receive little Western feminist attention), it bears repeating that criticisms from organizations such as the Revolutionary Association of the Women of Afghanistan (2013) will once again be ignored if I-VAWA passes. Even if it marks a new way of softly or smartly intervening, intervention remains an issue. "Saving" women in countries marked by the high incidence of violence against women, and thus eliminating terrorism (to use American logic), remain the urgent concerns of I-VAWA. Importantly, the Revolutionary Association of the Women of Afghanistan and other organizations on the ground in Afghanistan are simultaneously organizing against violence within their communities and *violence committed against their communities* by imperial powers. Discourses of urgency ensure that criticisms of intervention and imperial violence go unheard, even while the United States seems to respond to critiques of the hard power of war.

Significantly, only "eligible" countries will be subject to I-VAWA if passed, meaning that only some manifestations of violence against women are urgent. Fortifying the coupling of development with security, the act defines eligibility based upon the most current World Development Report published by the World Bank at the time of passing. Countries classified as high income will not be subject to the new American foreign policy (I-VAWA 2010, 6). According to the strategy, from five to twenty countries that have "severe levels of violence against women" will be eligible according to the extent to which "violence against women and girls in each country is negatively affecting the achievement of United States development and security goals" (17). Clearly, the "development and security goals" of the United States, and not women's lives, comprise the real urgent issue here.

Passing of the bill would establish a new Office for Global Women's Issues within the Department of State and the Office of the U.S. Ambassador-at-Large, which would coordinate and advise on activities, policies, and funding related to women's programs for the Department of State and direct American foreign policy to integrate women's issues, especially responding to violence against women. Additionally, the ambassador-at-large would coordinate with USAID, the Millennium Challenge Corporation, and the Office of the Global AIDS Coordinator. I-VAWA allocates $10 million for each fiscal year between 2011 and 2015 to the development and management of this office (I-VAWA 2010, 12). An Office for Women's Global Development housed at USAID would also be established by I-VAWA and allocated $15 million for each fiscal year between 2011 and 2015 (subject to its passing) (15). I-VAWA legislates that the secretary of state and the ambassador-at-large for the Office of Global Women's Issues will be responsible for identifying "a critical outbreak of violence against women" and advise on appropriate responses (42). Mirroring the priorities of the inaugural Quadrennial Diplomacy and Development Review (2010), I-VAWA will legislate the coupling of security and development at the federal level, with a focus on the issue of violence against women, in particular, at the core.

Under the title of "Strategy, Policy, and Programs" in the 2010 version of I-VAWA (which remained unchanged as of September 2015), the objectives of the bill are outlined; they include ensuring the accountability of the United States in ending violence against women internationally and enhancing U.S. training of foreign military units, police forces, and judicial offices for responding to violence against women (2). I-VAWA also includes privately contracted military personnel required to respond to violence against women internationally (6). Although the bill outlines a more holistic approach to responding to violence against women, including awareness campaigns, working with men and boys, and microeconomic opportunities, it centres on criminal and legal protections. The Hillary Doctrine's "it's not cultural; it's criminal" is mirrored in this legislation. I-VAWA outlines the training of police officers, prosecutors, lawyers, corrections officers, judges, and traditional authorities as key responders to the crime of violence against women (21–22). In the bill, the president, secretary of state, and secretary of defence are established as the directors of both military and police responses to violence against women. Whereas other policies and programs have funding caps, as much money as deemed necessary is allotted to military and police training. The vague provision of funds for military and police anti-violence initiatives suggests that security strategies will be given primary importance, especially since eligible countries must correspond to U.S. security interests (17).

In my view, I-VAWA is entrenched in the development and in/security nexus to the point that it allows for the genderwashing of imperial relations. In other words, it is one of many development and security couplings emerging in American foreign policy, and as it circulates it strengthens the Hillary Doctrine, using women's rights as a guise for imperialism. That is why I use the term "genderwash." It is difficult to unravel the complexities of I-VAWA, especially since the Hillary Doctrine provides convincing justification for state feminism. Yet, if we thoroughly engage with what the bill is saying, and what it proposes to do, and contrast it with women's well-being, then we can see how the urgency to pass new legislation relies on disparate definitions of gender equality.

Again, though I-VAWA has not been studied extensively by scholars, Thompson (2008) provides a great initial analysis of it using assessment criteria outlined by Haifa Zangana (2007) in *City of Widows: An Iraqi Woman's Account of War and Resistance*. Thompson, expanding Zangana's work, evaluates the first version of I-VAWA by whether (1) it will decrease or increase local NGO dependency on USAID; (2) it prioritizes the "indoctrination of democracy" rather than meets women's needs; (3) it divorces political diplomacy from women's rights; and (4) it addresses the role of the United States in perpetrating international violence against women. Although I believe that these four sets of criteria are not the only ways in which I-VAWA must be analyzed, it is worth briefly outlining them here and providing a critical response to Thompson's foundational work on this topic.

Thompson (2008) is critical of I-VAWA as a bill that does little more than reproduce failed attempts at saving women in the war on terror. However, she also outlines the positive aspects of the bill. According to her, it would funnel millions of dollars into NGOs and international organizations for work in ending violence against women. Thompson also argues that I-VAWA should be applauded for its focus on women's needs, rather than on lofty empowerment and democracy initiatives, including training police officers and judicial system workers to better respond to violence against women. Yet top-down reforms of legal systems might not actually reflect women's needs, nor does I-VAWA consider what kind of organizing is already happening on the ground by women's organizations.

Thompson (2008) maintains that it is important to acknowledge how the United States is complicit in violence against women internationally. However, in my analysis of I-VAWA, I found that statements about accountability are both swift and vague. The bill does include a section to enhance a "zero tolerance policy for sexual exploitation and abuse in United Nations peacekeeping and humanitarian operations" (I-VAWA 2010, 50). Although Thompson (2008, 16) considers the acknowledgement that "American personnel and service people can and do perpetrate violence against women abroad" a step in the right direction, the bill does not legislate an explicitly zero tolerance policy on abuse by civilian police, paramilitary police, and other law authorities trained by American personnel or contracted private police services, on which the United States relies heavily. Moreover, there is awareness of the need to hold individual UN peacekeepers and military personnel accountable for perpetrating acts of violence, yet I-VAWA continues to rely on foreign humanitarian and military personnel to respond when women and girls allege that they have experienced violence, even at the hands of military, peacekeeping, and humanitarian workers. Such anti-violence strategies ignore how those supposed to protect women from violence often impose insecurity when victims seek judicial justice.

Strangely, I-VAWA entrusts military and police institutions to prevent violence against women and girls even though there is a high rate of violence against female civilians and military personnel perpetrated by male military and peacekeeping personnel.[13] Such feminist concerns do not make it to the table when discourses of urgency frame the issue. Given the record of human rights abuses perpetrated by the U.S. military and its associated personnel, it is clear that this institution will not be

---

13   See, for example, Alison (2007); Puar (2007); and Savage and Bumiller (2012).

successful in delivering an anti-violence message overseas. To analyze I-VAWA thoroughly, it is important to connect its promotion of militarized responses to violence against women abroad and the pervasiveness of violence, including gendered violence, within the U.S. military.

VIOLENCE AGAINST WOMEN AND THE MILITARY

The military is an inherently violent institution. Trained for war, soldiers are combatants and fighters, and they symbolize the sovereignty and security of nation-states. For theorists of masculinity, the military is understood to produce a certain type of "hegemonic masculinity" (Connell and Messerschmidt 2005). A singular hegemonic militarized masculinity does not exist globally, yet certain qualities of masculinity are promoted through military and militarized institutions all over the world. In her work on militarized masculinities, Sandra Whitworth (2005, 91) cites Major R. W. J. Wenek as stating in 1984 that "the defining role of any military force is the *management of violence by violence*, so that individual aggressiveness is, or should be, a fundamental characteristic of occupational fitness in combat units" (emphasis added). "Premised on violence and aggression, institutional unity and hierarchy, 'aggressive heterosexism and homophobia,' as well as misogyny and racism," Whitworth notes (91), the creation of soldiers involves the trained embodiment and performance of ideal militarized masculine qualities.

As Parpart (2010, 86) argues, "the business of explaining and managing international security" is a very masculine affair. Problematically, international relations experts regularly ignore gender, and studies of masculinities in particular are often sidestepped in analyses of conflict and the practices and spaces of violence. Feminist investigations have demonstrated that in war, but also in the military, peacekeeping operations, and guerrilla forces, violence against women is devastating. According to Miranda H. Alison (2007, 84), in the former Yugoslavia over 20,000 women were raped during the conflict in 1993. The United Nations estimated that somewhere between 250,000 and 350,000 women were raped during the Rwandan genocide in 1994 (Alison 2007, 87). The British Broadcasting Corporation (2009) reported that sexual assaults perpetrated by U.S. military personnel against both fellow troops and civilians in Iraq and Afghanistan rose by 8 per cent in 2008 to 2,923. Of reported attacks, 63 per cent were rape or aggravated assault. Given the fear, stigma, and trauma associated with reporting such violence, this statistic is believed to be lower than the actual number of violent acts committed by members of the U.S. military in Iraq. Such staggering statistics of rape in war suggest that violence against women, perpetrated by all sides, is central to acts of war.[14]

Although I-VAWA would establish the training of U.S. military personnel, contractors, and peacekeepers, it is doubtful that military personnel trained for combat would easily transition into prevention of and response to violence against women. In fact, it is unclear how the United States has come to promote military personnel as the best fit for the job. When military officers are trained for combat and are then responsible for softer jobs, it is often challenging for soldiers and civilians alike. According to Robert Daniel Wallace's (2010) research on the implications of using U.S. armed forces as nation builders in post-conflict Afghanistan and Iraq, the "mismatch between military resources and government expectations" is the result of using trained "warriors" as diplomats (114). Moreover, Ruth Blakeley (2006, 1140) maintains that the training that American military personnel have received on human rights has been ineffective. After U.S. troops killed twenty-four civilian Iraqis, including women and children, in Haditha in 2005 (Savage and Bumiller 2012), U.S. forces were obliged to take a course in battlefield ethics.[15] From the torture of Iraqi prisoners at Abu Ghraib (Puar 2007; Razack 2008), to American Marines urinating on dead Afghan bodies and laughing, to the use of waterboarding and other methods of torture of alleged terrorists held at Guantánamo Bay (McGreal 2012), it is clear that human rights training, where it exists, has done little to change the actions of military personnel on the ground.

---

14   See Alison (2007) and Price (2001) for discussions of rape, masculinities, and war; see Puar (2004) for a discussion of queer(ing) masculinities, sexual violence, and imperialism.

15   In 2012, the case against seven U.S. Marines failed in the courts. According to the military court, finding evidence and witnesses was too difficult. Additionally, the Marines claimed that they believed themselves to be in danger following the chaos of a combat operation, known as a "fog-of-war" defence. According to Stephen Saltzburg, cited in the *New York Times*, the acquittal rate of military personnel for murder and manslaughter is more than twice as high as it is in civilian criminal cases (Savage and Bumiller 2012).

In 1993, the murder of a Somali teenager and the shooting of two Somali men by Canadian soldiers of the elite Airborne Regiment in Belet Huen during a peacekeeping operation revealed the misplacement of military officers as peacebuilders. Given the socialization of individuals into warriors, the protector and peacebuilder role is difficult for military personnel. Joining the army to become soldiers, those in the Canadian Airborne Regiment thought that their peacekeeping mission would be boring. When the peacekeeping in Somalia was given a Chapter 7 designation by the United Nations (which allows for UN forces to enforce peace), soldiers were amped up about more active peacemaking opportunities (Whitworth 2005, 100–01). When the regiment arrived in Belet Huen, it was clear that it was not a war zone, and Whitworth suggests that when the soldiers were convinced that they would "die for nothing" their violence began (101). Given the number of known racists and neo-Nazis in the regiment, it came as no surprise that part of their operation was termed "Operation Snatch Niggers" and that soldiers thought of Somali men as lazy, ungrateful, backward homosexuals who deserved to be killed (103–04).

Soldiering requires violence: it is at the centre of military operations. Whitworth (2005, 105) argues that a change of mission cannot undo the training and socialization that go into creating a soldier, and "the skills of war are often at odds with those required for peace operations." More generally, training military personnel in enforcing human rights, peacekeeping, or (in the case of I-VAWA) preventing violence against women will not be enough to undo the violence inherent in military culture and the socialization of soldiers. As those who inflict violence and deploy technologies of death on others in the name of security, military personnel are not the people in whom to invest anti-violence strategies.

HIRING WOMEN IN THE U.S. MILITARY

I-VAWA (2010) outlines the roles that women are to play in joining and leading forces internationally. I-VAWA legislates staffing goals for women as military and police peacekeepers as well as the deployment of civilian women to all levels of service in peacekeeping operations (39). As an anti-violence strategy, the employment of women might be an effort to neutralize military masculinities, to demonstrate and export gender equality in the United States, or to provide a "soft" face in "hard" times. According to Zillah Eisenstein (2004, 16), female military officers are often used to "humanize and democratize war-making." Of course, women join the military (or other armed forces, including those state sanctioned and unsanctioned) for a variety of personal, political, and economic reasons. However, at a symbolic level in the United States, women are habitually used to signify the humanity and progressiveness of military actions (though represented differently along lines of race, class, and sexuality). As Eisenstein reveals in her book *Against Empire: Feminisms, Racism, and the West*, "gender" operates to soften both acts of aggression and foreign policy in the United States. She cites Nicholas Kristof of the *New York Times* as claiming that a female soldier is one of the best weapons of our time because "wom[e]n holding guns" make "Iraq soldiers squeamish" (17). In Islamic countries in particular, Kristof believes, "foreign chauvinism" would work to the benefit of the United States. Such statements both demonize all Muslim men as inherently misogynist and esteem the gender equity said to exist in the United States and its military. According to Eisenstein, Kristof suggests that co-ed units would help the U.S. military look less like "rapists who will do harm to civilians" (17). I maintain that such genderwashing would do little to change the masculine culture of the institution. Hiring female soldiers as a gender equality initiative obscures sexist violence within military ranks, and racialized and sexualized violence during missions, but does little to actually change cultures of racism and misogyny in military institutions. Given the horrific acts of physical and sexual violence perpetrated against civilians and colleagues by personnel of the U.S. military and its associates, the objective to look less like rapists is predictable. Yet, because of the high incidence of violence perpetrated by male U.S. soldiers against female soldiers, it is unclear that including more women in the military will solve the issue of violence against women at home or abroad.

As Eisenstein (2004, 19) reveals, in 2003 over fifty women came forward to speak publicly about their experiences of violence in the U.S. Air Force. According to former Congresswoman Jane Harman (2008) in the *Huffington Post*, "women serving in the U.S. military are more likely to be raped by a fellow soldier than killed by enemy fire in Iraq." Indeed, "in the case of sexual assault and rape, the enemy eats across the table at the mess hall, shares a vehicle on patrol, and bandages wounds inflicted on the battlefield. As the old Pogo cartoon says, '*We have met the enemy and he is us*'" (emphasis added). According to the documentary *The Invisible War: The Battleground Is in Your Barracks*, an Oscar-nominated film by Kirby Dick and Amy Ziering (2012), there is systemic violence against women in the U.S. military, which includes negligent investigations and explicit cover-ups of abuses against female military members. In the United States, only 8 per cent of sexual assaults are prosecuted in the military, and only 2 per cent result in convictions (Dick and Ziering 2012). A Pentagon report released in 2013 estimates that as many as 26,000 military members were sexually assaulted in 2012, and thousands of victims are unwilling to report these assaults (Canadian Broadcasting Corporation 2013). Furthermore, a U.S. Air Force officer who headed a sexual assault prevention office was himself arrested on charges of "abusive sexual contact," which both reveals the depth of the problem of violence against women in the military and throws into question the institution's ability to promote anti-violence anywhere (Burns 2013). As American foreign policy sets its sights on using military operations to eradicate violence against women in the name of security, it is essential that these stories of the insecurity of female members of the military, as well as those marginalized on the grounds of gender identity and expression, sexuality, race, and class, are made invisible. As Puar (2007) asserts, gender exceptionalism at the international level requires a smoke-and-mirrors approach to self-representation by contrasting the self as benevolent with others perceived to be far worse abusers of women's rights. Investing in military, police, and peacekeeping forces not only to promote and model anti-violence strategies but also to respond to anti-violence is a misplaced target of I-VAWA. Although creating legislation acknowledging that U.S. military personnel commit acts of violence against women while abroad should be heralded, police, military, and peacekeeping forces are not the appropriate bodies to do the work of preventing and responding to gendered violence when it is so rampant within their own ranks.

I-VAWA emerges within the development and in/security nexus that communicates eliminating violence against women as an urgent concern. Although ending this violence globally is urgent, it is manufactured as such through the genderwashing of American security interests. I-VAWA does invest in local NGOs and international institutions that have experience in anti-violence initiatives. Instead, it explicitly centralizes U.S. development and security interests since the bill can only be used to intervene in certain "eligible" countries. It also suggests that police, military, and peacekeeping operations will be at the forefront of responding to violence against women internationally since intervention must correlate with security. Given that violence against women is represented as urgent, emergency forces are offered as key responders to the issue, which effectively obscures the roots of violence in these forces.

QUEERING URGENCY AND INSECURITY

The Hillary Doctrine has changed since the end of Clinton's tenure as secretary of state. Although Clinton is no longer in charge of American foreign policy, her brand of smart power has had a lasting impact on development, in/security, and violence and how they intersect discursively in U.S. national security rhetoric. Theorizing the incorporation of LGBT rights, in addition to gender issues, into the development and in/security nexus is an essential site of study, which I will briefly outline here and return to in the conclusion of this book.

As queer theorists in particular entered the dialogue on the war on terror, it became clear that justifying invasion not only depends on saving imperilled women but also relies on the recuperation of homonormativity at home (Duggan 2004). The feminization and sexualization of racialized men is now understood as an intersectional mobilization in war on terror discourses (Puar 2004, 2007). According to Puar (2007), the war on terror has relied on the production of specifically "perverse" queer bodies as opposed to "properly" queer subjects. As homonationalists, or (white) queer patriots, are swept up into the American national imaginary, Muslim sexualities are further orientalized. What Jiwani (2006) has called a "doubling discourse" Puar (2007, xxv) describes as the simultaneous deployment of Mbembe's (2003) necropolitics and Foucault's (2003) biopolitics, in which Arab/Muslim terrorists are understood sexually as both excessive and repressive, emasculated and monstrous, and ultimately slated for death since a U.S. national "sexual exceptionalism" allows homonormative citizens to be folded into a politics of life. In other words, though the United States has emerged as "good on gays" in the post-9/11 period, it has required a homophobic Muslim counterpart, a new justification for warmaking and imperial practices.

Given the interconnected workings of gender and sexual exceptionalism in the post-9/11 moment, it is unsurprising that the Hillary Doctrine has extended its concern for women's rights and set out to promote LGBT rights globally. In official remarks for the Recognition of International Human Rights Day, Clinton (2011) made an explicit connection between ending violence against women globally and the American promotion of LGBT rights abroad. The secretary of state claimed that, like violence against women, discrimination and violence against LGBT individuals would not be tolerated, and the United States was prepared to put $3 million into a new Global Equality Fund in an effort to make gay rights central in foreign policy objectives. Such an announcement from the level of the Office of the Secretary of State marks a significant success in queer activism, yet Clinton's announcement problematically relied on narratives of backwardness and culturally violent practices to defend the U.S. contribution to a global fund. Using the examples of "honour killings, widow burning, and female genital mutilation," Clinton compared "traditional" practices of violence against women to violence against LGBT individuals based upon customs and religion. Using a common-sense approach to communicating the (supposed) exceptionalism of U.S. queer tolerance (only when regulated and managed), Clinton explicitly used gender-exceptional language to make sense of new foreign policy objectives. Pointing to the need to target particularly "hostile" nations, she congratulated the United States on the repeal of "Don't Ask, Don't Tell," a move to allow gay individuals to serve openly in the military, even as LGBT people remained unprotected in the Equal Opportunity policy, transgender people could not yet serve openly in the miltary, and gay marriage was still illegal in most states. Of course, even with recent changes to marriage and military access, there continues to be widespread homophobia and transphobia across the nation.

Puar (2007) claims that these types of sexual exceptionalism discourses (e.g., the United States claiming that it is a leader in LGBT rights) function in various powerful ways. Two vectors of such power are how the United States and Israel, in particular, can transcend the violence of empire and "gloss over [their] own policing of the boundaries of acceptable gender, racial and class formations" (8–9). Using the example of

both Islam and Palestine as the "Orientalist wet dream" of sexual exceptionalism, Puar argues that Israel's modernity is reaffirmed when its
occupation of Palestine is obscured by its "ascendancy" in LGBT rights
(14). When Israel comes to stand in for the most progressive and safe
space for queers in the Middle East, in opposition to Palestine in particular, the state's human rights abuses (homophobic violence toward its
own citizens as well as those it occupies) are glossed over and even justified. The stabbing of Pride Parade marchers in Jerusalem in 2015 should
overturn this misunderstanding of Israel's safety for LGBT people; yet,
because of the power of "pinkwashing," this incident was largely treated
as an isolated event (British Broadcasting Corporation 2015).

The association between LGBT rights and women's rights in the
Hillary Doctrine reveals how the United States positions itself as an
authority for condemning human rights abuses globally so that a common-sense discourse of moral superiority has become ascendant (Grewal
2005, 150). In the post-9/11 period, both genderwashing and pinkwashing are implemented, and sometimes simultaneously mobilized, in
militarized and securitized responses to the events of 9/11, with "misogynist" and "homophobic" Arab and Muslim people playing counterparts
to American progressive liberals and failed states and underdeveloped
nations being disproportionately targeted as human rights abusers.
Nowhere is this more apparent than in Clinton's response to the mass
shooting at an LGBT club called Pulse in Orlando, Florida.

On June 12, 2016, just as I was completing final revisions of this
book, Omar Marteen shot and killed fifty individuals and injured fif-
ty-three more, most of whom were queer and transgender people of
colour. In response to the massacre, Clinton, in the running for president, suggested that "radical Islam" had fuelled the "terrorist" attack.
Defending herself against Republican candidate (and now President)
Donald Trump in the urgent race for leadership, she claimed that, "if
he is somehow suggesting I don't call this for what it is, he hasn't been
listening. I have clearly said we face terrorist enemies who use Islam to
justify slaughtering people. We have to stop them and we will. We have
to defeat radical jihadist terrorism, and we will" (qtd. in Gass 2016). For
many, such declarations vilify Muslim citizens of the United States—
adding to ongoing and deepening Islamophobia in the nation—and
skirt around the issue of violence against sexual and gender minorities

in a country where anti-LGBT bills, bathroom debates, murders of trans-gender women of colour, and inconsistent and hostile treatment of same-sex couples applying for marriage licences are rampant. For me, such a response is consistent with the Hillary Doctrine: although the target (read women) has changed, the discursive manufacturing of urgency tied to American national security objectives remains fully intact.

CONCLUSION

Women's rights have become central to security discourses in U.S. foreign policy in the post-9/11 period. Global violence against women in particular is presented as an urgent security issue. Underdeveloped nations are understood to have high rates of violence against women, are assumed to be terrorist breeding grounds, and thus pose a security threat to the United States. Both the Hillary Doctrine and the proposed International Violence against Women Act reveal how concern for women's rights marks a shift in post-9/11 foreign policy objectives toward security and development. By linking security and development to moral concern for women's rights, actual American interests, including legislating imperial occupation and control in countries of interest, strategies to assert global hegemony, and continued militarization and securitization, are genderwashed in feminist languages.

By fleshing out the concepts of security and insecurity as they have been developed in post-9/11 literature on women's rights, I extended Duffield's (2010) conceptualization of the development and security nexus to understand how violence against women is situated as an *in/security* imperative in U.S. foreign relations. The intertwining of development and in/security interests has relied on a common-sense notion of women's rights as an urgent concern, illustrated by the inaugural Quadrennial Diplomacy and Development Review (2010), which emphasizes women's rights as a national security concern. The Hillary Doctrine's phrase "it's not cultural; it's criminal," repeated several times by the former secretary of state, not only framed the QDDR document but also paved a new road into the debate on cultural relativism versus universalism, which has been at an impasse, while also shoring up support for exporting criminal justice and militarized responses to violence against women. In interrogating the best practices exported by the United States, I provided a context with which to understand the proposed I-VAWA. Investments in police, military, and peacekeeping forces to prevent and respond to violence against women, as outlined in I-VAWA, are misguided. Given the U.S. military's human rights abuses abroad, and the epidemic of rape and sexual assault within the institution, I-VAWA places primary importance on American foreign interests at the expense of appropriate anti-violence strategies.

Within the development and in/security nexus, the urgent American concern for violence against women is highly manufactured. By linking security and development to a concern for women's rights, the foreign interests of the United States are genderwashed. From the Hillary Doctrine to the proposed International Violence against Women Act, gender issues are receiving far more attention at the level of foreign policy than ever before because they are linked to a post-security agenda. This agenda manufactures urgency around the issue of violence against women and allows for failed responses to it to take precedence over more suitable anti-violence initiatives. Although the promotion of women's rights globally is important, if not essential, to eradicating violence against women, I-VAWA's promotion of military, peacekeeping, and police training to respond to such violence reveals how manufacturing urgency around the issue conceals the fact that security interests are paramount and will be sought at the expense of women's well-being. Consequently, strategies to eradicate violent practices rely on their suitability to established American security interests, not on their effectiveness in eliminating violence against women globally.

The urgency to end this violence is politically constructed. Discourses of urgency allow for the securitization and militarization of responses to violence against women because they rely on already established strategies. Importantly, ending this violence *now* does not allow for the time to explore other possibilities or to engage critically with proposed laws, best practices, or discursive manoeuvres that further entrench global misogyny and ignore women's well-being.

CHAPTER 2

THE WORLD BANK CARES ABOUT VIOLENCE AGAINST WOMEN

||||||||||||||||||||||||||

*The World Bank (1993) estimates that, globally, 9 million
disability-adjusted life years (DALYs) are lost each year as
a result of rape and domestic violence. This figure is greater
than the DALYs lost due to all forms of cancer, and twice
those lost by women as a result of automobile accidents....On
the macro level, the cost of responding to domestic violence
drains budgets for the health, justice, housing and other
sectors, and drags down overall growth and productivity.*
—Alys Willman, "Valuing the Impacts
of Domestic Violence"

Violence against women is an urgent issue because it is a costly
one. According to the World Bank, female survivors of violence are
drains on the economy because they often require social services
and health care. Women are also less productive at work when
they have experienced violence because they often sustain physical
injuries or emotional harm. In its 2009 publication *The Cost of Violence*,
the World Bank (2009a) makes the case that violence of all kinds is a
pressing issue for the development industry because of the associated
costs. One chapter of the report is focused on violence against women

and names it one of the most urgent issues facing development since it blocks both economic growth and development (iii).

To communicate the urgency of the issue, the World Bank report uses a measurement to cost-out violence against women called disability-adjusted life years (or DALYs). This is a mathematical formula that, to put it most simply, measures the quality of life by comparing the productivity potentials of individuals with their experiences of disease and disability.[1] In the report, the World Bank uses this measurement to argue that disabilities, impairments, and traumas resulting from violence against women prohibit women from living up to their individual productive potential, and given that survivors of violence are a drain on the economy the development industry should take the issue seriously. With every act of violence costing economies money, the time is now to eliminate violence.

DALYs were originally designed by the World Health Organization to calculate the global "burden" of disability, impairment, and disease and the effectiveness of health-care interventions (World Bank 1993, 2009a; World Health Organization 2008). According to the World Health Organization (2008, 3), DALYs can calculate the burden of disease for the state by measuring the gap between "current health status and an ideal situation where everyone lives into old age, free of disease and disability." At the World Bank, DALYs are used to measure the costs/benefits of interventions in health and social ills.

Communicating the issue of violence against women in economic terms creates a sense of urgency around the issue for the World Bank. According to an interview that I conducted with Alys Willman, a former senior social development specialist for the Fragility, Conflict, and Violence team at the World Bank, violence against women rarely catches the attention of the organization, and those within the bank interested in issues of gender inequality have to be "opportunistic." Willman (2009) authored the chapter on violence against women entitled "Valuing the

---

1   DALYs measure the costs of disability, disease, and impairment related to a person's productive potential (World Bank 2009a). The World Bank differentiates between impairment and disability, with the former defined as a temporal injury and the latter as a chronic illness. However, the disability rights community might define impairment and disability differently and more politically. Here I use these terms as the World Bank has employed them.

Impacts of Domestic Violence: A Review by Sector" in the larger World Bank report. In it, she claims that gender advocates in the World Bank cannot generate "stand-alone" gender projects because they are not always economically driven, but they can create a sense of urgency around gender issues within other major and mainstream projects that have clear economic mandates.

This manufacturing of urgency around the issue of violence against women within a development organization is very interesting, especially when analyzing an organization such as the World Bank. It is ostensibly an apolitical organization; according to its 1944 "Articles of Agreement," the World Bank is prohibited from being political. Gender, like other human rights issues, is not apolitical, and Willman maintains that gender enthusiasts in the organization "have to go where [they] are invited to go." Since, as she suggests, "economists don't believe what they cannot measure," the urgency to eliminate violence against women must be manufactured by its quantification (personal communication, 2012). Scholar Jane Parpart confirms this strategy, stating in an interview in 2012 that, "in the development business, you have to convince people that [violence against women] is a problem that can and must be solved."

In this chapter, I consider how economic language is used to manufacture urgency around the issue of violence against women from gender advocates in the World Bank and the implications of such discourses for the well-being of women in practice. I am concerned here with how economic language is used to promote solutions to violence, such as economic empowerment programs that do little more than reproduce status quo gender work at the World Bank. Economic objectives are used by gender advocates in the organization to justify the issue of global violence against women in a way that can be "heard." Rather than conceptualize this violence as an important issue itself, the World Bank considers it important only when it is coupled with other development objectives.

By unravelling the mathematical and ethical complications of the DALYs measurement and its deployment, I establish that the World Bank requires Third World women to be "properly productive," with bodies able to undertake labour. Here I employ Robert McRuer's (2006) *Crip Theory: Cultural Signs of Queerness and Disability*, a foundational work in critical disability studies, to explain how the World Bank requires women to be "flexible" so that the organization's economic growth plans can be successful. I use the terms "overcoming," "adjusting," and "resiliency" to argue that ability (in contrast to disability) is specifically required of racialized women globally. In other words, women need to be able-bodied to live up to their individual productive potential. This means that they cannot sustain injuries from violent incidents because their bodies are needed for labour. As I see it, this is why the World Bank considers the issue of violence against women to be urgent.

To make this argument, I explore the World Bank's economic empowerment initiatives for women, which overwhelmingly cen-tre employment as a solution to gender inequality. I investigate how women are required to remain flexible in disabling conditions of pre-carious workplaces, where they are habitually employed. Violence against women is manufactured as an urgent concern economically by linking anti-violence narratives with the expectation for racialized women to "overcome" injuries and get back to work. Ultimately, I inves-tigate here how communicating the urgency of violence against women through economic language in the World Bank both narrows the defi-nition of such violence and limits possible solutions to it because more "political" solutions cannot be taken seriously by economists at the World Bank.

SPEAKING THE LANGUAGE OF INSTITUTIONS

When violence against women is measured as an economic cost, there is increased potential for the issue to gain both traction and investment from the World Bank. Given its influence on member countries, and on the development industry more generally, any approach to eradicat-ing violence against women is welcome by some gender experts. In fact, it is difficult to critique innovative approaches to ending this violence, especially by "femocrats" working under constraints such as those at the World Bank. When made visible as an anti-violence tool, economic measurements such as DALYs appear to be uncontroversial to a range of actors. As Bedford (2009, 208) argues in her critical work on gender and the World Bank, "one might as well be against puppies." Surely, ending violence globally is a priority for all feminists and anti-violence advocates. For women who have been injured or disabled by violent acts, the visibility of the issue on a global scale is crucial. For women who have missed workdays and lost income because of an impairment or disability caused by gendered violence, and for those who have made claims for services and rehabilitation because of such violence, it is clearly associated with real costs to their quality of life.

However, the World Bank's DALYs measurement instrumentalizes disability, and the issue of violence, to further the organization's economic agenda. This is a clear manufacturing of urgency around the issue, for the World Bank does not actually take seriously violence against women in its myriad forms; rather, it deploys a call to end such violence to serve the organization's other interests and commitments. My criticism of its DALYs measurement is not an all-embracing disapproval of the notion that violence against women incurs individual and economic costs. Instead, I target DALYs as a problematic formula that represents violence against women as only an individual and economic issue. I do so to illustrate how, in the development industry, anti-violence strategies are narrowed, confined, and depoliticized by coupling the issue with mainstream objectives, such as economic growth. When the issue is communicated as urgent through economic language, its complexity is lost at the expense of swift solutions already in place at the organization. By communicating the importance of violence against women as a development issue, the World Bank responds in ways critiqued by feminists as ultimately failing women. It is the manufacturing of this violence as an urgent development concern through discourses of economic growth that I am most concerned with here.

As an anti-violence advocate, I cannot consent to the World Bank's production of much of the most influential knowledge about violent practices and how to eradicate them. Although the actual investments in eradicating violence against women are underwhelming at the World Bank, the institution consistently circulates its "comparative advantage" in gender issues discursively (World Bank 2006, 2009a).[2] A member of Gender Action claimed that "for all the research that the World Bank

2   According to members of Gender Action, a watchdog organization that I interviewed in 2012, the World Bank has three current projects dealing explicitly with gender-based violence in post-earthquake Haiti, the Côte d'Ivoire, and the Democratic Republic of Congo.

has accumulated on gender, including gender based violence, the organization does very little about it in terms of its investments." At the time of our interview, the World Bank only had three projects dealing explicitly with gender-based violence; in post-earthquake Haiti, Côte d'Ivoire and the Democratic Republic of Congo. Given that the World Bank's overall project investments exceed 50 billion dollars a year, Gender Action claimed that the World Bank's actual interest in VAW in terms of monetary investments was a "drop in the bucket" (personal communication, 2012). As analysts of the organization have pointed out, the World Bank is predominantly known for being *the* "knowledge bank" above and beyond its actual banking practices, meaning that regardless of how it spends its money, the organization generates powerful knowledge about development and, as I argue in this chapter, disability and violence against women (Bergeron 2006a; Kapoor 2008). The World Bank has influence on the transnational level, and even if it does not act on its own research the knowledge that it produces has real power (Gender Action, personal communication, 2012).

In this chapter, I place the World Bank's (2009a) *The Cost of Violence* report at the centre to investigate how the organization communicates violence against women as a pressing concern to its own members and to understand better the possible outcomes of such representations on women's well-being. As I will demonstrate, the use of DALYs by the World Bank enacts two interlocking discursive moves: (1) DALYs rely on a particularly racialized and ableist conception of life-worth based upon a Third World person's productive potential in the workforce; (2) DALYs rely on an economistic framework suggesting that the only site of Third World women's empowerment is the workplace. Given the economic opportunities available to Third World women, I take the World Bank to task for how it promotes workplace empowerment opportunities as both a response to and a prevention of violence against women. I argue that through the DALYs calculation the World Bank situates such violence, and its disabling effects, within an individual and economic narrative. By focusing on empowering individual women through self-help and entrepreneurial engagements, other forms of violence—including institutional, state, and economic violence and racialized violence—are obscured to the detriment of women worldwide.

OUTLINE

In the first section of this chapter, I provide a brief outline of gender work performed at the World Bank to understand how the organization has historically approached social development issues. I provide a critical analysis of the organization's neo-liberal development models from a feminist standpoint and outline the organization's historical promotion of women's empowerment through "mainstreaming" gender into the economic-focused work of the World Bank.

In the second section, I explore how the DALYs measurement of the cost of violence against women manufactures urgency around the issue to demonstrate the complications of such violence being conceptualized as solely an economic issue. Wrestling with the representative grammars associated with the DALYs, I employ McRuer (2006, 2010) to "crip" it. In other words, I analyze it for how it treats disability as a category of analysis and privileges able-bodiedness. I take issue with how narratives of adjustment, resiliency, and overcoming function in the World Bank's neo-liberal development agenda, especially in terms of its rhetoric of urgency. I argue that measuring violence against women as a cost to the economy renders racialized women's able-bodiedness compulsory and disability as a liability to the neo-liberal state.

In the third section, I consider how the ableist nature of DALYs relies on both flexible economic relations and flexible bodies that overcome injuries. I argue that the World Bank functions as "the normate" by being a flexible institution and by disciplining Third World bodies to further privilege flexibility (Garland Thomson 1997). Ultimately, I argue that the World Bank's apparent benevolence toward people with disabilities, or bodies that do not "fit" development schemes, including survivors of violence who cannot work because of disability or impairment, secures the success of neo-liberal development schemes. I question the impacts of discourses of urgency in terms of how they play out on people's bodies and conceptualizations of their value. To this end, I highlight how, in this case, discourses of urgency present Third World women survivors of violence as needing to adjust, to be resilient, and to be flexible in the context of World Bank–enforced neo-liberal economic schemes that require their productive labour.

In the fourth section, I use the examples of micro-credit, micro-enterprise, and export processing zones (EPZs) to examine how employment programs encouraged by the World Bank are often disabling environments and can intensify women's experiences of violence to argue further the fallacy of the DALYs measurement. Introducing the concept of "racialized ableism," I outline how Third World women's "potential productivity" is embedded in racist and ableist notions of cheap and flexible labour. I use the case of the maquiladoras in Mexico, and micro-credit programming more broadly, to illustrate the intersections between economic restructuring and violence against women to suggest, ultimately, that DALYs cannot account for the complexity of this violence, nor can employment opportunities solve this issue. Instead, discourses of urgency manufactured by the DALYs measurement locate the answer to the problem of violence in a violent location.

Finally, in the fifth section, I investigate how women are made to "fit" into market schemes, including cosmetic-based "good for business" models championed by the World Bank who teach women to be both flexible in their labour and pretty at the same time. Providing a crip reading of the organization's most-championed approaches to women's empowerment, I consider racialized ableism as central to economic empowerment models for Third World women and one important consequence of discourses of urgency. Using cosmetic-based micro-entrepreneurial engagements as an example, I demonstrate the connections among how racialized bodies are understood as ideal for flexible, cheap labour, the implications of racist beauty ideals on work-based empowerment, and the flexibility required of Third World women's bodies in terms of their labour and productivity.

GENDER AND THE WORLD BANK

Before setting out the World Bank's (2009a) *The Cost of Violence* report, I will provide an overview of the organization's history of work on gender to situate my analysis within a sophisticated body of feminist literature on the World Bank.[3] Only recently has the bank deviated from a purely economic focus by integrating social development issues such as gender,

---

3   See, for example, Bedford (2009); Bergeron (2006a); Kuiper and Barker (2006); Marchand and Parpart (1995); Moser, Tornqvist, and van Bronkhorst (1999); and Saunders (2002).

sustainability, violence, conflict, and crime, as well as disability, into its work. In addition to external pressure from other development institutions, feminist activists, and academics, the World Bank's increased attention to gender is reflective of changes in the core mandate of the organization (Moser et al. 1999, 11). During the 1990s, the social costs of Structural Adjustment Programs became a public relations minefield for the World Bank, with many feminists in particular pointing to increases in poverty, poor health, and unemployment, especially among women in the adjusted Third World. For example, the "Fifty Years Is Enough" campaign established by activists in 1994, and now a transnational network of grassroots organizations and activists, openly and vehemently criticizes the World Bank's long history of "bankrolling disasters," meaning that its questionable megaprojects and neo-liberal globalization schemes have had devastating social, environmental, and economic impacts (Fox and Brown 1998, 4–5). As a response to critiques, in the 1990s a human development approach took centre stage at the World Bank, and the question of gender was popularized because of establishment of the Social Development Group within the World Bank. In opposition to solely economic sectors, this group focuses on people-centred development and poverty alleviation (Moser et al. 1999, vii).

According to feminist economists, the World Bank centred a social development agenda in the post–Washington Consensus era with a new gender approach at its core (Bedford 2009; Kuiper and Barker 2006). Former President James Wolfenson is understood to have influenced reform of the World Bank in response to heavy and harsh criticism of Structural Adjustment Programs, in which the organization played a key role. Known as the "renaissance banker," Wolfenson was determined to improve the organization's image under the watchful eyes of activist organizations such as Women's Eyes on the Bank (Bedford 2009, 2; Weaver 2010). Although some critics of the World Bank have called his approach to reform "old wine in new bottles" (Cling, Razafindrakoto, and Roubaud 2003, 111), others have documented the positive impact of his tenure on the gender agenda (Bedford 2009; Bergeron 2006a; Kuiper and Barker 2006; Weaver 2010). According to Weaver (2010, 77), Wolfenson's appearance at the UN Fourth World Conference on Women in Beijing in 1995, and the myriad reports and action plans prepared for the conference, meant that gender inequities were being given more attention than they ever had before by the World Bank. Importantly, Wolfenson made a commitment at Beijing to create a policy framework to mainstream gender in the World Bank (Barker and Kuiper 2006, 1). Although the organization had established a sector for Women in Development (WID) almost twenty years earlier, the first policy report on women was not published until 1994, the year prior to the Fourth World Conference on Women (Jahan 1995, 24–25). The World Bank's visibility at the conference marked the start of a new development era for the organization.[4] Significantly, the World Bank began to seek advice from critical outsiders and developed an External Gender Consultative Group.[5] From a gender "lunch group" in the late 1970s, to the development of a Gender and Development Unit in the newly formed Poverty Reduction and Economic Management network in 1995, it seemed that the World Bank had heard its critics (Weaver 2010, 77–78). Reforms to the organization meant that its only gender-focused group was no longer marginalized but (visibly) centred within a poverty-reduction team (Bedford 2009). Although the place of the Gender and Development Unit in the network gave it more authority, it continues to have limited ability

---

[4]   The WID framework was established in the first half of the UN Decade for Women and Development, and it argued for women's integration into development. Esther Boserup's (1970) foundational work *Woman's Role in Economic Development* marked the inauguration of the WID movement, arguing that women in Africa were bound to subsistence agriculture and informal work, while development had brought opportunities for men in formal employment. In the 1990s especially, feminist academics, policy makers, and activists reassessed WID. In opposition to it, Women and Development (WAD) emerged as a Marxist feminist critique of modernization theory, drawing heavily from dependency theory in arguing that development is an inherently unequal capitalist project that has sustained previous colonial exploitative practices (Visvanathan 1997, 19). When Gender and Development (GAD) emerged in the 1980s, proponents not only charged WID with privatizing women's empowerment but also claimed that WAD privileged class issues and women's productive capacity over gender relations. Instead, it sought to establish a framework that considered men's and women's gender issues in relation to development (Saunders 2002, 8–9).

[5]   Originally, fourteen individuals from national women's groups, non-governmental organizations, as well as academics sat on the External Gender Consultative Group at the World Bank (Weaver 2010, 77). According to the World Bank's GAD website, there are now only seven individuals who sit on the consultative group, many of whom are trained economists and come from the financial sector (World Bank 2011b).

to influence other research networks and teams at the World Bank, and it does not have power over central operations (Weaver 2010, 78).

Yet gender issues are central to the World Bank's current rhetoric, especially with regard to its economic development mandate. This is very important since the World Bank is known as a "knowledge bank." As Bedford's (2009) key work on discourses of "family" and "partnership" in the World Bank demonstrates, Wolfenson was a key figure in centring gender terminology and feminist values in the post–Washington Consensus reform of the agenda of the organization. Although its megaprojects, austerity measures, and persistent neo-liberal development models were, and remain, highly criticized by development practitioners and activists, many feminists are cautiously supportive of the World Bank's gender focus, even if it is only rhetorical (Bergeron 2006a; Kuiper and Barker 2006).

Feminist scholars point out that women's voices were central to reformed World Bank rhetoric (Bergeron 2006a; Kuiper and Barker 2006). They emphasize how Wolfenson in particular used "human dramas" to tell tales of how the organization was committed to gender equality (Bedford 2009, 7). For example, according to Kate Bedford (2009, 1) he once used the story of a young girl whom he met in Mali to pronounce the World Bank's vision of a "new and better world" that would improve the lives of women and girls. Bedford notes that the organization used carefully chosen stories from the Third World, and the "soft" faces of gender advocates, quieting its critics. When the World Bank was met with backlash in an April 2000 protest against Bretton Woods Institutions, the organization's gender staff were highly visible in the media response (Bedford 2009, 8). Feminized responses, often at the expense of actual engagement with feminist critiques of the organization and its work, are suspect. As I explored in Chapter 1, this use of women's voices, without feminist values, marks a "genderwashing" of the institution's work.

For some, the focus on gender inequities should be applauded. The World Bank has listened to its critics and has incorporated some of the most sophisticated challenges to its development agenda. In particular, it has responded to feminist criticisms of its technocratic and solely economic approach to development. The organization now emphasizes human rights, subaltern voices, empowerment, partnership, and bottom-up development in its research and knowledge-making practices. This marks a significant change in its work. Yet, given the broad range of feminist scholarship critical of the reform of the World Bank, the extent to which the organization has fully incorporated feminist values in practice remains unclear (Cornwall and Eade 2010; Miller and Razavi 1998).

In 2001, the World Bank published *Engendering Development: Through Gender Equality Rights, Resources, and Voice,* which marked a decisive shift away from solely economic approaches to an empowerment agenda. However, Bergeron (2006b) emphasizes a particularly feminist concern with the World Bank's power in establishing and circulating gender and development discourses in general. She argues that the organization as a knowledge bank legitimates particular ways of perceiving reality while excluding others (see also Kapoor 2008). Offering a critique of the reform of the World Bank, she suggests that *Engendering Development* takes a multidisciplinary approach to gender and development in that it brings together economic and social development models. Yet it does so without challenging their fundamental assumptions. As Bergeron (2006b, 127) maintains, the World Bank's integration of cultural and social models must be contextualized within the broader development community's "fascination with new theoretical innovations" in the field of economics. Regarding more recent gender agendas, Hester Eisenstein (2009, ix) even criticizes the incorporation of feminist values into the work of major institutions such as the World Bank as a blatant co-optation of "women's energies into the project of corporate globalization."

It is important that the World Bank's incorporation of gender analyses be fully acknowledged. Given the power of the organization to produce knowledge on "best practice" approaches in the development field, its gender work has both expansive reach and influence. Although the World Bank continues to promote economic growth as development, policy makers in the organization now take into consideration the social effects of interventions and work more thoughtfully to consider gender equality issues. Although three presidents have succeeded Wolfenson, gender remains on the World Bank's agenda. Now, more than ever, gender issues are integrated into the principal mandate of the institution. Whereas previous World Bank reforms made gender issues more visible, the organization now argues that women are the *key to development.* However, rather than include women as important elements of its development agenda, the World Bank now recognizes that *women are the linchpins of economic growth.* For the institution, women are not full agents in their own lives but can be moulded into full agents of development if encouraged by it.

WOMEN ARE GOOD FOR BUSINESS

Following Wolfenson, Robert B. Zoellick continued to be involved in gender agendas. Speaking about the organization's most recent Gender Action Plan (GAP) entitled Gender Equality as Smart Economics (a project that ran from 2007 to 2010), Zoellick stated that "the empowerment of women is smart economics….Studies show that investments in women yield large social and economic returns" (World Bank 2011a). In an internal interview for the World Bank (2009b), Danny Leipziger, vice-president of the Poverty Reduction and Economic Management network, claimed that in a conference in 2006 the World Bank was asked to do a better job of mainstreaming gender. Leipziger claimed that mainstreaming gender in all activities is not feasible all at once, so the institution has chosen to focus on its economic sectors, where it sees itself as having a comparative advantage. Unfortunately for women, the "buzz" around gender could quickly be replaced with more "trendy" development agendas (Smyth 2010).

For now, gender remains central to the focus of the World Bank. Quoting facts and statistics about women's likelihood to repay microcredit loans and reinvest in their families while praising their high rates of productivity, Zoellick argued that investing in women was just good economics. The most recent GAP called for the empowerment of women through intensifying and scaling up gender mainstreaming in economic sectors. The World Bank (2006) argues that this new approach will "give gender issues more traction" (1). Women's empowerment "is about *making markets work for women* (at the policy level) and *empowering women to compete in markets* (at the agency level)" (3). The GAP promotes market-based empowerment initiatives with measurable and quantifiable results (15).[6]

---

6   The World Bank (2006, 2) regards the most recent GAP as a plan of...

The World Bank (2006) claims that the focus on women's empowerment at work is rational: women's capacities overshadow current investment opportunities, and thus not investing in women would be inefficient. According to the World Bank's *World Development Report: Gender Equality and Development* (2012, 237), the jobs accompanying growth, and thus development, such as the expansion of manufacturing and services activities, are the most appropriate venues for investing in women, citing evidence that "greater gender equality enhances economic efficiency and improves other development outcomes." For the World Bank, reducing gender discrimination could increase worker productivity by 25–40 percent, depending on the state of the labour sector at hand.

Additionally, women's empowerment has more wide-reaching effects. The World Bank (2012, 238) asserts that, "in an economically integrated world, even modest improvements in the efficiency of use of resources can have significant effects, *giving countries with less discrimination and more equality a competitive edge*. Of course, not just the economy will benefit from gender equality; women themselves stand to gain from the economic plans of the World Bank. Its latest gender report argues that working women are empowered to make decisions in their households (100). Tapping into feminist theories of empowerment, it claims that agency can be understood as women taking advantage of economic opportunities to gain more power in other areas of their lives (150, 237).

In the context of ongoing criticisms of the World Bank's neo-liberal policies and the incorporation of women's empowerment into its fold, this chapter argues that calculating the cost of violence can be read as an extension of the organization's economic mandate to make space for both gender issues and disability issues. It can also be understood as a mathematical tool for communicating to an organization the urgency

---

...intensification for its gender mainstreaming framework that will allow the organization to become a global leader of women's empowerment. The GAP matches funding for projects and research that include gender concerns in the sectors of labour, land and agriculture, private sector development, and infrastructure. In the spring of 2009, the World Bank (2009b, 6) was funding 149 activities in seventy-three countries. Beyond the concern of this short-term plan are "human capital" issues such as health care and education as well as social and cultural issues that affect women's access to markets.

of violence against women, which, regardless of reforms in social development, continues to focus on economic growth as the most important development objective.

THE COST OF VIOLENCE

According to the World Bank, violence exacts a high cost for development. In *The Cost of Violence*, the World Bank (2009a) maintains that countries dealing with conflicts, or in post-conflict transitions, are only half the problem. High levels of violent crime, street violence, domestic violence, and other kinds of "common violence" have directly hampered poverty reduction efforts and barred progress (iii). According to the report, in over sixty countries over the previous ten years, violence "directly reduced economic growth" (iii). Half of the sixty countries experienced large-scale conflicts, and the other half dealt with the effects of common violence, such as domestic violence. Although some common violence is causally connected to conflict, the World Bank argues that countries with high levels of common violence are shown to be unstable over time. Significantly, this argument is reflective of the development and in/security nexus that I explored in Chapter 1. The World Bank considers the impacts of conflict and war, but its focus on violence against women in particular is found in a chapter on domestic violence.[7] Considering the physical and psychological impacts of violence, the World Bank defines domestic violence as acts that hinder women's ability to work. The report uses the term "domestic violence" to describe the most common form of violence experienced by women.

The Cost of Violence (World Bank 2009a) begins from the assumption that individual productivity is essential to economic growth and that those fully able-bodied are the most productive, whereas disabled bodies are less productive and thus less valuable. DALYs, as a measurement tool, allow the World Bank to quantify the years of possible productivity lost because of disabilities or injuries at the hands of violent perpetrators.

---

7   The World Bank (2009a, 6–12) cites military spending; destruction of capital, investment, and capital flight; effects of civil wars; and "organized violence," including internal and external conflicts and terrorism, as affecting development and growth. Violence against women is not explicitly mentioned in this section.

Here it is important to reflect on the World Bank's work on gender historically, especially the history outlined above; the organization is most concerned with the household unit. Since economic models of development habitually begin with the household unit, it is important to note the assumptions behind the measurement of violence. Using DALYs to measure domestic violence relies on the assumption of nuclear and heterosexual family units. Such assumptions ignore female-headed households, non-monogamous and same-sex units, and intergenerational family structures. As I will demonstrate throughout this chapter, this assumption means that the World Bank ignores violence experienced by women outside the household unit. Problematically, domestic violence[8] is incorrectly delinked from other forms of violence, and there is no consideration of how women globally face different struggles in their experience of violence.

According to the World Bank (2009a), violence against women is an urgent matter for development because the number of disability-adjusted life years lost because of domestic violence is larger than those lost as a result of all forms of cancer and twice those lost as a result of automobile accidents. In 1993, the World Bank estimated that 9 million DALYs were lost globally as a result of sexual and domestic violence (58). Citing individual and macrolevel expenses such as medical care, legal proceedings, as well as time and productivity lost because of injury, long-term trauma, and suffering, and the costs of caring for survivors of violence, the World Bank maintained that violence is inefficient for developing economies attempting to progress (58, 62). The association between costs to the economy and violence against women is not a new argument for the World Bank. In 2001, it recognized that men's violence against women and sexual aggression lead to negative outcomes for development. It asserted that men's patriarchal power effectively decreases women's productivity, causes absences from the workplace, and leads to an increase in homelessness. Furthermore, violence against women was seen as a cost for governments since survivors of abuse often have increased needs for judicial and police services (World Bank 2001, 77–79). Although unsaid, there is a marked contradiction

---

8   Whereas the World Bank uses the term "domestic violence," I use the term "violence against women" to remain consistent in this book.

between the needs of survivors and the priorities of contemporary neo-liberal economic policies endorsed by the World Bank—the truly urgent issue at play. Increasing the need for social services conflicts with neo-liberal policy prescriptions, which the organization endorses, that call for drastic cuts in government spending. The impacts of such cuts are not urgent issues; rather, they are allocated for later if considered at all.

World Bank employee and author Willman (2009) maintains that violence exacts a cost for individual women, families, communities, and the economy. Again, she makes this argument to both the World Bank and a public audience to generate urgency around the issue of violence against women at an organization that requires an economic focus for all its projects and policies. According to her research in *The Cost of Violence*, the disability-adjusted life years measurement is the most appropriate way to calculate the actual cost of violence for development. The DALYs method estimates the burden of diseases, accidents, and forms of violence. It is calculated "as the present value of the future years of disability-free life that are lost as a result of illness, injury, or premature death" (81). It is a complicated formula, and here I attempt to break it down into simpler terms: disease, impairment, death, disability, or effect of violence is weighed against age, demographic, and work potential to see how many productive years are lost.

The DALYs measurement was originally developed by the World Health Organization to quantify appropriate resources for health-care measures and to extend and better human lives. The measurement has come under harsh criticism by scholars of health, who have called it unethical. Since DALYs calculate the cost of disease and disability, the measurement has been criticized for being invested more in lowering the number of disability-adjusted life years than in controlling global disease. In other words, increasing the number of high-quality life years, and thus lowering the number of low-quality life years, are perceived by critics to be more important than holistic health initiatives. Additionally, DALYs are criticized as a "normative judgment" that prioritizes the health of youth while masquerading as neutral. Since DALYs consider young people as having more productive years ahead of them than older people, scarce resources are reserved for those at their peak in the market economy (Anand and Hanson 1997).

According to critical disability theorist Nirmala Erevelles (2006), the World Bank uses DALYs to measure a person's potential productivity and thus possible contribution to economic growth. Based upon her work on the DALYs measurement, Erevelles claims that the World Bank cannot award severely disabled people medical care entitlements because they are considered to be "unproductive." In fact, the institution suggests that people with disabilities are liabilities to the state. Even when public health interventions are considered cost efficient, the organization relies on neo-liberal self-help narratives in its work on disability. In the 1993 World Bank report that first introduced DALYs, the organization argued that governments should not pay for all health-care interventions measured as cost-effective because households would privately purchase cost-effective health care when informed about their choices. Such neo-liberal prescriptions rely on perfect information and a competitive marketplace in which individuals are free to choose to invest in health-care interventions. Although the World Bank does not place a monetary value on human life, buried in economic jargon, statistics, and graphs it measures quality of life and defines it in economic terms.

Although most measurements of violence only include the economic costs associated with social and medical services, the World Bank claims that DALYs are a more complete measurement. It calculates DALYs lost because of death by taking all cases of death from violence and grouping them by age, sex, and region. By subtracting the age of premature death because of violence from the life expectancy for the age and demographic group, the World Bank (2009a, 81) can measure the cost for the potential productivity of women. Importantly, the organization pays attention to disability only in terms of its costs. The loss of quality of life because of an injury or disability is calculated by taking the average period of impairment (either recovery or death) and multiplying it by a numerical weight assigned to the severity of the injury compared with death. Estimated death loss and disability loss are then combined, with an allowance added to discount the value of years lost as one ages (later years of life are valued progressively less because bodies are less productive when old) and for age weights (different values are assigned to lives lost at different ages since young bodies [peaking at twenty-five] are more productive and thus economically valuable).

DALYs are complicated, yet for gender advocates at the World Bank they are necessary to convince the institution that the issue of violence against women is urgent. The World Bank is not the first, or only, organization in the development industry or elsewhere to resort to costing violence against women to communicate its urgency. According to an expert brief for the United Nations by Tanis Day, Katherine McKenna, and Audra Bowlus (2005), every effect of violence is costly. Effects of violence against women are costly both for services and for lost income and reduced profit. Like the World Bank, the researchers for the United Nations claim that measuring the economic costs of violence helps us all to understand the issue better (14). According to the researchers, economic measurements remove debates about violence against women from the realm of social issues and "locate it in the realm of concrete fact" (14). Social issues do not manufacture urgency, since the connections between violence against women and systemic oppression require careful and nuanced untangling. Instead, economic and concrete facts are used to communicate the issue as pressing in a way that can easily be understood by those who might not be convinced otherwise.

For some, economic measurements are indeed more easily understood than complex social realities, and such evidence-based measurements can communicate the urgency of ending violence against women to economic organizations and businesses that might not otherwise pay attention to the issue. That gender researchers and policy makers at the World Bank have found a way to attract the attention of the organization marks a phenomenal success. Economic facts that make sense to the World Bank are essential to the incorporation of feminist interests into its work, and DALYs in particular reveal how gender advocates manufacture urgency around the issue.

DALYs present a complex puzzle for thinking about how the issue of violence against women is made urgent in the development industry, because, as I argued in Chapter 1, defining violence by its association with cost creates a narrow range of "appropriate" responses to the issue. As many feminists have pointed out in a thorough body of work on the World Bank, its economic and calculated development interventions are highly technocratic and often mismanaged. Framed by such a feminist dialogue, DALYs can be considered an intensified technocratic language of development, and yet it is more than just an expansion of well-known

World Bank neo-liberal development schemes. Disability-adjusted life years represent the World Bank's ableist assumptions about the *quality* of human life. If urgency is manufactured at the expense of fully conceptualized definitions of violence against women and ableist assumptions about the value of individuals, then feminists must wrestle with the organization's mathematical equations and economic models. Such a grappling is also a crip task. In other words, an analysis of how DALYs are used to quantify the cost of violence must consider how a narrow conceptualization of disability is harnessed to the project of manufacturing urgency to end violence against women.

CRIPPING THE WORLD BANK

In an address in 2004 at the first World Bank disability conference entitled Disability and Inclusive Development: Sharing, Learning, and Building Alliances, former President James Wolfenson emphasized the inclusion of people with disabilities in development by reminding the audience that "gender was...given a backward place until [the World Bank] discovered that the key to development was, in fact, women" (quoted in Dingo 2007, 93). According to Wolfenson, people with disabilities, like women, are the *keys* to development. Without their inclusion, progress will be barred. Although people with disabilities have not historically been understood as key development players, organizations such as the World Bank are ensuring (at least discursively) that they are "mainstreamed" into development. To be sure, the institution appointed an adviser for disability issues in 2004. Under the presidency of Wolfenson, disability was brought to the forefront of the World Bank's social development agenda. Such examples demonstrate the institution's foray into "disability and development."[9]

In his address, Wolfenson maintained that people with disabilities, to be included within the development industry, should also be "mainstreamed" into the work of the organization, especially in terms of bringing people with disabilities into the economic mainstream (Dingo

---

9   Following the popularization of "gender and development," I use the term "disability and development" to describe the incorporation or inclusion of disabled subjects and disability issues into the fold of hegemonic development praxis.

2007, 95). To overcome their exclusion, people with disabilities would have to "fit" development schemes.

For disability studies scholars and activists, disabilities are too often characterized as needing to be overcome. Scholars maintain that narratives of overcoming are often coupled with rehabilitative narratives that rely on stories of personal tragedy overcome by heroism (Clare 1999, 8) or technical intervention (McRuer 2006). For scholars Tanya Titchkosky and Rod Michalko (2009, 1), disabilities are popularly regarded as "stemming from function limitations or psychological losses which are assumed to arise from disability." It is assumed that disabilities occur because of a terrible misfortune and at random. It is how disability is hegemonically problematized, in the development industry and elsewhere, as individual and requiring sympathy that is at the crux of disability studies. Scholars and activists working within the "social model" of disability rather than the "medical model" (described above) do not deny the problem of disability but locate it "squarely within society" (Oliver 1996, 32). For activists and critical theorists, institutional barriers that impose restrictions on non-normatively abled bodies cause disabilities. Disability theorist Rosemarie Garland Thomson (1997, 7) writes that "the ways that bodies interact with the social engineered environment and conform to social expectation determine the varying degrees of disability or able-bodiedness." Although physical impairments are physiological facts, how assumptions are made about how one must interact with the world, and the socio-political meanings of such interactions, are culturally understood as a disability (Oliver 1996).

For McRuer (2006) able-bodiedness, like heterosexuality, is compulsory. That is, it too masquerades as normal and natural. Borrowing from Adrienne Rich's (1983) foundational essay "Compulsory Heterosexuality and Lesbian Existence" (1983), he argues that able-bodiedness is always in process, always being made and remade, and always already failing and being recouped. Using the concept of flexibility, McRuer argues that both heterosexuality and able-bodiedness have no natural origins but long histories of being manufactured (8). This masquerade of so-called natural able-bodiedness requires flexibility. That is, bodies perceived as being flexible are those that make it through crises, can manage the crises, or show potential to manage them. Highly flexible bodies are able to adapt and perform as if the crises never happened. Moreover, a flexible body does not draw too much attention to the crisis or its multiple effects. Doing so would be to perform or act out inflexibility (17). McRuer's notion of flexibility is central to my research. Significantly, I conceptualize urgency in a similar manner. That is, it can be instrumentally manufactured but must always be remade and sustained.

In a later article entitled "Disability Nationalism in Crip Times," McRuer (2010) maintains that disability studies have yet to grasp possible interventions in global political and cultural issues. Although he asserts that disability is already at work in queer projects, disability studies have much to learn from the trajectories of transnational queer theory. Expanding on the remarkable work of Puar (2007), McRuer argues that queer studies that recognize the neo-liberal management of heterosexuality and homosexuality and other queer subjectivities are the most noteworthy. Neo-liberalism has always functioned in and through cultural and identity politics. It organizes material and political life by gender, race, class, sexuality, nationality, and—I would argue—disability while obscuring how these organizing terms intersect (Duggan 2004, 14). Predominantly, neo-liberalism is understood in terms of economic policy and trade. Yet it has "cultural politics," including turning global cultures into "market cultures" (12). Personal responsibility and privatization are two key markers of the cultural politics of neo-liberalism. Questions about such politics, including normalcy and flexibility, are posed as a call for further crip scholarship on people with disabilities globally, and help to unravel the complications of using the DALYs measurement to elicit an urgent response to violence against women. In many ways, this chapter is an answer to the call for research in transnational crip studies.

EMPOWERMENT AND FLEXIBLE LABOUR

To provide a thorough crip reading of the World Bank's (2009a) *The Cost of Violence* here, I consider the impact of DALYs on the definition of violence against women and the power of the discursive circulation of disability narratives in the field of development. Equally important is my investigation of how DALYs are used by the World Bank to create urgency around the implementation of market-based solutions. To recapitulate, according to the World Bank's 2009 report, women are vulnerable to gendered violence because they lack economic autonomy.

When working, they are not only being empowered but also helping to shore up national growth and thus supporting development. When disabled or impaired because of violence, women are not empowered, and therefore they are not living up to their productive potential.

Significantly, even as the World Bank (2009a) employs the DALYs measurement to think about violence, it does so without explicitly addressing violence against women with disabilities. According to the *World Report on Disability* published by the World Health Organization and the World Bank (2011, 59), people with disabilities are at greater risk of violence than those without disabilities. This indicates that women with disabilities might be at much greater risk of violence than women without disabilities. Although it uses the term "disability-adjusted life years," the World Bank pays no attention to disability itself, suggesting that the concept is only a tool to help quantify violence against women as a development inefficiency. Given that DALYs help the World Bank to argue that violence against women is a pressing issue for development because it is a cost for women's productivity at work, the organization's conceptualization of economic engagement as empowerment requires critical analysis.

Bergeron (2006a) maintains that the emphasis on women's empowerment has often meant overcoming "traditional" roles and moving into the market economy. In fact, throughout development discourse in the 1980s, development was imagined to take place in the public sphere rather than the private sphere of the household. Often the household and women's role in it were presented as counterparts to the modern economy and even treated as obstacles to it. According to Bergeron, "The traditional sector was seen to be the cause of economic backwardness, something to be transformed through the development process....Third World women were often portrayed as the most backward in [their] society, 'ignorant, poor, uneducated, tradition-bound, domestic family oriented' (Mohanty 1991, 56), who could only be empowered by integration into the capitalist labour market" (22). In many ways, the World Bank's use of DALYs to measure violence against women pits the traditional against the modern. That is, by conceptualizing unempowerment within the so-called traditional sphere of the domestic, and empowerment within the modern public sphere, the World Bank positions women's emancipation within this long-running and tedious debate. Conceptualizing disabled and injured women as lacking the ability to work in the public sphere, the World Bank argues that their inability to become properly employed blocks their ability to become empowered. Although the organization uses DALYs to measure the cost of violence for the economy in terms of service provision for disabled and injured women, it makes it clear that women must move from the domestic sphere into the productive sphere for development and economic growth, and empowerment as an accompanying objective, to occur.

Rejection of the traditional in favour of the modern is a well-researched concept in the development field, especially in terms of women's labour. However, as both Bergeron (2006a) and Bedford (2009) assert, the domestic is not completely rejected by growth-focused economists. Rather, the heterosexual and nuclear family is often used as the symbol of a national and transnational family of cohesion, shared values, and goals as they relate to development. Bedford (2009, 9–10) argues that in this family the World Bank is surely the patriarch. Power relations and conflicts are often marginalized in this metaphor of the family (Bergeron 2006a, 23). At the World Bank, former President Wolfenson often spoke of ideological dissent as "gossip" that would break apart the World Bank family (Bedford 2009,10). Similarly, in development discourse, culture is used to point to dissent within the global family. "Black sheep" national cultures are the ones that stagnate development, not global power relations that create and sustain inequalities. For the sake of the family, the World Bank, as the patriarch, is set on a trajectory "good" for the whole unit.

Women's bodies are particularly important to this imagined transnational familial development. Historically, postcolonial nationalism used women's bodies as bearers of tradition associated with the historical and mythical nation before colonization. In resisting Western powers, Third World national elites encouraged the return to so-called traditional women's roles. Chatterjee (1993) states that the focus of postcolonial nationalism on women's traditional roles was pursued alongside modernization and development. For postcolonial governments, state-led development was seen as a way of gaining support in newly sovereign countries, while the return to tradition marked their resistance to imperial powers. In discourses of development, the struggle between modernization and tradition continues to be debated on women's bodies. Women are viewed as the bearers of both progress and tradition. To overcome tradition, viewed as retarding development, the

development industry has particularly emphasized women's empowerment in the economic sphere. Although feminists have criticized the
development industry's emphasis on economic empowerment initiatives for women, the World Bank's gender and development praxis
continues to endorse market-based empowerment, what Elisabeth M.
Prügl (2015) calls "neoliberalised feminism." Left out of such gender
and development policy schemes are essential questions about what
type of labour opportunities are most available to Third World women
in a flexible economy and how the World Bank continues to seek cheap
labour as an empowerment initiative for women even as it negatively
affects their lives. When urgency is manufactured, the issue of violence
against women is narrowed to speedy solutions, such as employment
initiatives, and feminist concerns about such solutions are left for
another time. One such question regards how disability is instrumen-
talized in the urgent process of empowering women.

DISABILITY AND NORMALCY

To understand the instrumentalization of disability in manufacturing
urgency around the issue of violence against women, here I return to
disability and crip theories to think through the concept of normalcy
and its connection to the World Bank's understanding of the value of
human lives. According to the DALYs measurement of the cost of violence, so-called normal able-bodiedness is conceptualized as the only
legitimate way of being in the world and the only version of the good life.
To be empowered, for the organization, is to be able-bodied. According
to Garland Thomson (1997, 6), disability functions as the self-evident
conceptual opposite of able-bodiedness. In this way, legal, medical,
political, and cultural narratives produce the idea of disability as the
opposite of normalcy. In disability theory, the ideal of being normal is
represented by the figure of the "normate." Arguing that people with
disabilities (abnormal) at the margins constitute the centre (normal),
Garland Thomson claims that the normate are those who, by bodily and
cultural capital (including gender, race, class, and sexual supremacy),
enter a position of authority and wield their power.

Although disability theorists generally speak about human bodies in
relation to the figure of the normate, here I use the concept of bodies

more broadly to include organizational bodies, including organizations that make up the development industry. Conceptualizing institutions, and even global systems, as bodies is not new. In fact, biological metaphors of the economy were highly popular in the eighteenth and nineteenth centuries. According to feminist economist Bergeron (2006a, 8), Adam Smith regarded the economy as a "social body," while Jean-Jacques Rousseau compared the economy to a living entity with different organs and functions. She asserts that the economy was presented as an unruly feminine subject that had to be controlled and disciplined, but this conception later gave way to more mechanical metaphors of a masculine, machine-like system. Although neo-liberal economics is often represented as a self-regulating and rational machine, understanding how global bodies or institutions masquerade as normal, natural, and neutral within this self-regulating machine is an important research trajectory. The World Bank might claim that its development interventions rely on objective information and policy making, but its neo-liberal prescriptions and powers on the international level are not normal or natural but manufactured.

The World Bank, among other large financial institutions, occupies the space and power of the normate. It might be thought of as a global normate figure that functions as a significant representation of development's impressive accumulation of power. Located in the United States—with all of its former presidents being white male American citizens, billions of dollars in annual funding, in-country offices across the globe, and a focus on economic productivity for development and growth—the World Bank functions as a normate figure. Wielding cultural and capital power attributed to the white-led, masculinist, heterosexist, and ableist organization, it is equally buttressed by the racialized and impoverished Third World individuals whom it purports to help. The World Bank sets the standard in terms of normalized and naturalized flexibility, requiring the able-bodiedness of Third World women, and in terms of neo-liberal economic relations in which insecurity, precariousness, and flexibility are paramount. The organization functions to normalize and naturalize neo-liberal flexibility in terms of its development agenda, including the promotion of obligatory trade policies, investment opportunities, and cutbacks in state spending. Thus, the World Bank not only wields cultural and capital power in its banking arrangements with less powerful clients but also is a normaliz-ing figure in the development industry.

As a knowledge bank, it is a cultural figure whose boundaries are shored up by the bodies marked as other (Kapoor 2006, 28). That is, as the centre of development policy, the World Bank marks itself as the self by marking Third World bodies as impoverished, backward, and needing help. Contextualized by a tenacious history of colonial repre-sentations of the other (McClintock 1995), and by more recent charity models in development discourse (Heron 2007; Kapoor 2006), the World Bank functions as the self or centre. As the normate, it not only positions its institutional power and economic philosophy as normal but also actively produces and maintains normalizing narratives of development praxis. At both the macrolevel and the microlevel, flexibility—overcom-ing, adjusting, and being resilient—is normalized, encouraged, and sometimes even required by the World Bank.

FLEXIBILITY AND BENEVOLENCE

In the context of development and its most hegemonic discourses, the World Bank emerges as a highly flexible body, or normate figure, benev-olent to and tolerant of those who need help adjusting and coping under the pressure of poverty. According to McRuer (2006), flexibility is double-edged. He argues that a flexible body thrown into a crisis of opposition must perform as though a destabilization has not occurred and demonstrate a "dutiful (and flexible) tolerance toward the minority groups constituted through these movements" (18). The valuation of flexibility occurs within a climate of tolerance, in which there is profit in flexibly complying with and accommodating "diversity" (18). Of course, the manufacturing of tolerance in development praxis is not new, yet it continually needs to be revealed since it produces and main-tains itself.

The World Bank situates itself as a benevolent transnational power with a "comparative advantage" in helping the less fortunate. Even as it self-constructs an identity as a global justice and even a humanitarian leader, its flexibility (read benevolence or tolerance) must be managed against the backdrop of mounting critiques of its work. As McRuer (2006) notes, normate bodies learn from oppositional movements, and the World Bank has learned from oppositional discourse: namely, environmental and gender equity critiques (Bedford 2009; Weaver 2010). In fact, the organization explicitly defines its tolerance in profitable terms, arguing most recently that women are "good for business" (World Bank 2011b, 238). In this way, its flexibility occurs as an "epiphany" on the bodies that must flexibly comply (McRuer 2006, 18).

The concept of overcoming—understood here as flexibility, resiliency, and adjustment—is important to the study of the World Bank, and especially to the impact of manufacturing urgency around the issue of violence against women, because it underscores the importance of connecting economic empowerment initiatives to the functioning of disability and ability. So, while complicated, crip theory is our best chance, in my opinion, of understanding how the World Bank creates a sense of urgency around the issue of violence against women and the impacts of such measurements on the framing of solutions: namely, labour-based empowerment.

FLEXIBLE LABOUR IN THE GLOBAL ECONOMY

David Harvey (1990, 124) claims that, following Fordism and the economic crises of the 1970s and 1980s, global economic relations have entered an era termed a "'flexible' regime of accumulation." This era is marked by flexible labour: temporary, contract, mobile, and replaceable. Other scholars have dubbed this change a "new international division of labour" made possible by the cheap labour available in the former colonies and now Third World countries (Eisenstein 2009, 25). According to feminists, the "flexible regime of accumulation" is highly gendered and racialized. As Bergeron (2006a) notes, multinational corporations taking advantage of opportunities within economies entering the global marketplace established factories and other workplaces in the Third World ultimately preferring female workers (Desai 2002, 16). The pressure to reorient national economies to manufacture for export and to house outsourced services has feminized the global labour force by increasing women's exploitation as employees of choice in manufacturing sectors and in low-paid service and informal economies. In neo-liberal terms, providing a "comparative advantage" in cheap labour offers employment and encourages economic growth. Revealing the pillars of global white supremacy, which includes the provision of cheap labour by racialized bodies (Smith 2010), the feminization of labour has relied on stereotypes of nimble-fingered, inherently docile, and hard-working Third World women to justify their suitability for repetitive and monotonous work (Bergeron 2006b, 130; Eisenstein 2009, 26; Erevelles 2006, 27; see also Fernández-Kelly 1983).

Extending well-known feminist theories of flexibility, I argue that the flexibilization of employment is both racialized and ableist, relying on conceptions of normal bodies in regard to productivity while securing cheap labour from racialized women. The feminization of employment increases the number of racialized women in the global workforce and changes the conditions of work: namely, the further flexibilization of labour. The valuation of flexibility has increased the availability of temporary, part-time, contract, mobile, replaceable, and home-based work and has specific bearings on questions of disability and ability. As my analysis below demonstrates, the feminization and flexibilization of labour require able-bodiedness in disabling environments.

This requirement of able-bodiedness is overlooked by gender advocates at the World Bank, who use the DALYs measurement to manufacture urgency around the issue of violence against women. When the organization's gender analysts claim that violence against women matters because it is costly for development, they are also arguing that women need to be working in order to be empowered and to become less of a drain on the economy. A crip reading of the World Bank's empowerment initiatives for women illustrates that the institution not only instrumentalizes disability in the DALYs measurement by using it only as a method of measuring quality of life but also requires a particular able-bodiedness of women in a flexible economy in which their labour is exploited and in which women find themselves in potentially violent and disabling circumstances.

EXPORT PROCESSING ZONES

The growth of export processing zones (EPZs) and the increase in service work for women in the Third World demonstrate the flexibilization and feminization of the workforce and exemplify the impact of conceptualizing violence against women as an urgent issue in relation to women's economic empowerment. For the World Bank, this is not a new approach to women's inequality. In fact, the DALYs measurement of the cost of violence has given old solutions new urgency.

According to Eisenstein (2009), EPZs grew in number from seventy-nine in twenty-five countries in 1975 to more than 3,000 in 116 nations in 2002. In 2002, employment in these zones was estimated to be approximately 42 million people. In many cases, the increase in EPZs was established under World Bank– and International Monetary Fund–sponsored neo-liberal conditions that forced Third World economies to access foreign direct investment with few protections. EPZs, characterized by their lack of trade barriers and unregulated working conditions, rely on a young, cheap, and fairly uneducated labour force vulnerable to exploitation. In search of cheap labour, multinational corporations have obtained extensive profits from investing in EPZs.

Problematically, EPZs are known for the suppression of labour organizing and unsafe working conditions, which often lead to disability, impairment, and even death. Eisenstein (2009) suggests that there is a high turnover in jobs in EPZs because of disabilities caused by unsafe work and the preference for young, childless women. Under the corporeal pressures of monotonous and repetitive work along the global assembly line, the average worker lasts just five years in a garment factory before injuries and other health-related issues force her to retire. Research on garment factories in Southeast Asia and Latin America have documented muscular-skeletal disorders, eyesight injuries, stress and fatigue, skin complaints, and reproductive hazards. In electronic factories in India, workers have reported digestive diseases, hair loss, back pain, and stress, among other bodily injuries (Meekosha 2011, 676).[10] In 2013, a garment factory collapsed in Bangladesh, killing at least 1,127 and injuring hundreds of others. In the garment sector in Bangladesh,

---

10   Although women surely have been exploited by labour conditions in EPZs, they have also been active resisters. As both Aihwa Ong (1987) and María Patricia Fernández-Kelly (1983) discuss, Third World women engage in work stoppages, resist long hours without breaks, and use religious or cultural celebrations to refuse work and to organize workers in EPZs. Moreover, transnational networks of solidarity have emerged to pose strong resistance to neo-liberal policies and Structural Adjustment Programs that have shaped the labour conditions of EPZs (Desai 2002, 18).

which employs mostly women, workers have a high risk of injury or death because of unsafe working conditions (Uddin 2013).

Organizations working on the ground in Bangladesh organize against violence both within and against their communities. According to the Bangladesh Center for Worker Solidarity (2013), in addition to sustaining injury and disability, women are at risk of suffering gendered violence, specifically physical and verbal abuse by their employers. This group actively connects the issue of economic violence of global restructuring to violence against women, an issue ignored by the World Bank in its focus on economic empowerment via the DALYs measurement. Export processing zones are complicated sites of economic empowerment for women. They can provide women with income, and according to the World Bank more economic autonomy within the household, but its models cannot account for violence associated with this site of labour. As the organization's use of DALYs suggests, violence against women is a cost for economic growth. Yet violent practices both within workplaces and within communities in which there has been concentrated economic restructuring are ignored by the organization. In fact, the use of DALYs to manufacture urgency around the issue of violence against women means that possibilities for organizing against economic violence, as a manifestation of violence against women, are foreclosed.

One of the most well-known EPZs is that of the Maquiladoras in Ciudad Juárez, along the American-Mexican border, which, as both activists and scholars point out, has an extreme culture of femicide. In the context of thinking about anti-violence initiatives in development, exploring such a site of the global manufacturing system is essential. Since the World Bank's (2009a) *The Cost of Violence* report considers work as a means of empowerment for women, and as a site that will ultimately make them less vulnerable to violence, one must consider the violence that women experience at work. Although the DALYs measurement places violence against women in the home, and considers that it can be overcome through work, clearly such violence is not confined to the private or traditional realm.

As Kathleen Staudt (2008) suggests, there are many lenses through which to analyze the violence in Ciudad Juárez. The Maquiladoras are often analyzed by international scholars as a site of global neo-liberal reordering. Since the Mexican government's Border Industrialization

Program was established to facilitate foreign direct investment and global free-trade regimes to be globally competitive and to develop, the city has become home to hundreds of factories employing more that 200,000 workers, over half of them women. Staudt argues that structural violence is experienced from "a global economy that has shrunk the real value of earnings in the export-processing economic development model that dominated in Juarez" (7–8). On top of inadequate shelter, food, and wages, the fact that over 370 women have been murdered since 1993 has inflicted terror on the population (x). Although the families of those missing, raped, and/or murdered in Ciudad Juárez have rallied for justice, there has been little response nationally and internationally by governments, global institutions, and the development community. Theories of serial killers and drug cartels are popular among some scholars, yet violence within the home has simultaneously become common, suggesting a broader and more systemic cause of violence within the community, in which gender conflicts have been sparked by changing patterns of labour for meagre wages and are related to securitization of the American-Mexican border (143). Staudt is clear to separate domestic violence from what is understood as femicide, but it might be more useful to conceive of these "types" of violence as interconnected.

Since DALYs calculate the burden of impairment and disease on women's productivity, femicide in Ciudad Juárez can be partially understood through this measurement of the cost of violence. Interpersonal violence has risen in areas where women are actively employed in EPZs, and DALYs would be able to quantify the productive years lost because of this violence. They might also create a sense of urgency around this pressing issue. However, DALYs are not holistic enough to account for the violence of economic restructuring, the displacement and disappearance of women, and insecurity at the border between the United States and Mexico, where EPZs are built. So, though DALYs can manufacture urgency around some practices of violence, they actively ignore others.

MICRO-CREDIT

Aside from employment in EPZs, the most flexible labour (read temporary, mobile, and replaceable), and also the most available to Third World women, is micro-credit. Habitually considered the "cure-all" for underdevelopment (Isserles 2003, 38) and women's inequality, micro-credit has become a sort of "motherhood" development initiative (Parpart, Rai, and Staudt, 2002, 52)). That is, micro-credit provides both *participatory* and *empowering* opportunities, two of the many dominant buzzwords of the gender and development lexicon (Smyth 2010). According to Prügl (1999), feminists and gender experts who promote micro-credit programming argue that providing small loans to groups, especially women, for generating micro-enterprises is a highly effective way to reach poor and marginalized women, to distribute messages of health care and education, and to support widows and wives of abusive husbands (85). Proponents also argue that micro-credit programs have increased women's self-confidence and given women a greater voice in decision making within the household. Giving poor young women credit can be a source of empowerment. However, initial micro-credit programming was laced with gendered instruction rules for women as housewives and mothers. Using the rhetoric of motherhood and womanhood, proponents of micro-credit argued that women were more likely than men to repay loans and use money responsibly to support their families. For Prügl, motherhood was transformed from being understood as economically inactive to being understood as breadwinning. Women were understood as being cautious in their use of household money. They were often cited as being more likely than men to buy food, clothing, and other necessities for their children. The combination of motherhood and income earning, home and work, arose as necessary and desirable. Home-based work emerged as a way for women to help develop the nation while also not disturbing their domestic and reproductive duties (75).

As noted by Robin G. Isserles (2003), micro-credit became increasingly popular at the height of neo-liberalized development, emerging in the development industry as a women's equality initiative highly compatible with neo-liberal austerity measures. Founded upon ideologies of individual responsibility, micro-credit appeared to be a perfectly suited "pull up your boot straps" approach to overcoming underdevelopment. As ideas of efficiency, privatization, and self-initiative combined with skepticism of state-led development initiatives directed at mainstream development thinking, micro-credit emerged as a successful market-based, entrepreneurial initiative. Additionally, the effects of neo-liberal prescriptions such as privatization, devaluing of currency, and opening of markets to foreign direct investment limited employment opportunities within the formal sector and enlarged the informal sector (41). Critics of micro-credit programming have thoroughly illustrated the impact of informal economic opportunities marked as "Band-Aid" approaches to global economic power structures and especially how they often obscure the operation of global capital and power. Since individuals are accountable for making their own labour opportunities, there is a sense that they are at fault for their poverty and must be responsible for overcoming it.

Moreover, as women's empowerment initiatives, micro-credit and small entrepreneurial engagements are often misplaced. As Aminur Rahman's (1999) research suggests, women are often pressured to join loan groups by their husbands and other male family members. Although women can gain credit and income through such programming, it remains unclear the extent to which resources are allocated equally within the home and how much decision-making power women gain. Since the World Bank's measurement of the cost associated with violence against women depends on the idea that work will empower women and make them less vulnerable to violence through economic autonomy, the distribution of resources must be thoroughly considered. However, DALYs cannot account for violence associated with work-based empowerment measures since they rely on women's productivity as the solution to violence, not a potential factor, and the key to economic growth for development.

Not only do micro-credit initiatives assume the existence of heteronormative and nuclear households, but also they are based upon, and rely on, asymmetrical power relations such as peer discipline and gender binaries to control the repayment of loans. For example, whereas men are cast as too difficult to work with, women are portrayed as submissive and compliant. Moreover, the most marginalized women are understood by donors and credit lenders to be less reliable than those owning property or those who have other family earnings, especially those of employed husbands (Rahman 1999). Aside from discursive and structural violence in micro-credit programming, violent practices in the home have also been reported by women accessing micro-credit where gender relations are disrupted by both labour and micro-credit programming obligations, such as time spent at community meetings and high debts incurred by women who cannot repay them (Rahman 1999, 73, 76).

Because the World Bank (2009a) recognizes labour and productivity as the goal and positive outcome of anti-violence and empowerment initiatives, violence is considered an urgent issue only because it is an obstacle to economic growth. When gender relations have been reorganized by women's work, and violence against women has increased, the World Bank has found innovative ways to protect their interests. Publishing research reports on men, and including men in gender project requirements on the ground, the World Bank has emphasized the transformation of "bad" men into properly heterosexual, loving husbands and fathers and equal domestic partners (Bedford 2009). As I argue elsewhere, such policy and programming efforts rely on racialized narratives of Third World men as needing to be transformed from "dangerous" to "dad" and ignore non-normative family structures in the process (Mason 2012). Instead of considering how micro-credit and small entrepreneurial programs fail women, the World Bank has attempted to make micro-reforms in interpersonal relations by centring men in its work as "partners" (Bedford 2009). Although the Beijing Declaration and Platform of Action emerging from the UN Fourth World Conference on Women in 1995 asserted the importance of counting women's reproductive labour as work, international financial institutions continue to conceptualize women as non-workers. When the World Bank considers non-productive labour, it is men's relationship to care work that is considered in need of transformation rather than the economic empowerment models that require women to work in the "productive" sphere (Bedford 2009; Mason 2012).

Of course, micro-credit programming must be analyzed in its relationship not only to violence against women but also to disability. In addition to the potential for increased interpersonal violence, workers in the informal economy face disabling environments caused by the lack of protection from unemployment, the lack of health-care benefits, and wages below the poverty level (Desai 2002, 17). Since much of the labour occurs within the home, there are no regulations on women's work conditions, including how many hours a day women work and how much time they are given for breaks. Such labour conditions reveal how disabling work environments are ignored by gender policies (Desai 2002, 19). When violence against women is defined as interpersonal violence against individuals, the World Bank wilfully ignores the varied manifestations of violence against women. Again, this is the risk of manufacturing urgency around such violence using costing mechanisms such as DALYs—definitions of, and responses to, the violence are narrowed and in this case depoliticized. Although gender advocates in the World Bank might be required to give the issue of violence against women an economic spin to ensure that it is understood as imperative to development policy and programming, thinking through its impact on women's well-being should not be left for later.

Since EPZs and micro-credit initiatives primarily target women as employees, and since the World Bank considers women's work as synonymous with their empowerment, it is important to consider the profit-seeking behaviours of multinational corporations that benefit from such neo-liberal development models. World Bank–promoted austerity measures open underdeveloped economies to the competitive global economy, and women's labour is highly intertwined with the trajectories of transnational capital and neo-liberal development. Individual women might find autonomy and power in their work and personal income, but how racialized bodies are sought for being cheap and highly flexible remains suspect. As Meredith Turshen stated, "violence against women is never seen as a consequence of neo-liberalism" (personal communication, 2012). When violence against women is conceptualized as interpersonal violence that inhibits women's productivity at work, institutional, state, and economic violence are made invisible in the process.

WOMEN'S TIME: ADJUSTMENT AND LABOUR

As feminist development experts Moser et al. (1999, 7) maintain, the assumption in the 1970s that women needed to be brought into development relied on an "elastic" conceptualization of their time in which their labour was understood as being highly flexible. The Structural Adjustment Programs of the 1980s, and other austerity measures since then, have negatively affected women's family and work lives by relying on their adjusted time, and many women successfully, if not painstakingly, have "adjusted." These programs intensified the trade-off between women's productive and reproductive expectations. In fact, Desai (2002) argues that women are now doing more non-producer work than before the rollout of the programs. Because of neo-liberal restructuring all over the world, including the West, women have become responsible for more care work on top of their precariously flexible employment. Women's health deteriorates under austerity measures because of stress, reduced food consumption, and violence often coupled with the rebalancing of gender roles in the home. Because of poor nutrition and vitamin deficiency, work-related accidents, and environmental pollution, neo-liberal restructuring adversely affects mothers and their children—especially with feminization of the workforce and privatization of health care in adjusted economies. Women are often subjected to potentially disabling conditions at work, and without government-funded health care women and their children must either pay for the high cost of private services or go unseen by medical professionals (Erevelles 2006, 28). Thus, austerity measures by themselves are violent and gendered. However, in discourses of development, violence against women is rarely conceptualized in this way. In *The Cost of Violence* (World Bank 2009a), manufacturing urgency around the issue is permitted through the DALYs measurement, and it ensures that the violence of neo-liberalism will not be considered.

Given how well many women perform flexibility by adjusting to the "double" and "triple" burden of productive, reproductive, and community work (including health care) under neo-liberal austerity measures, which have decreased if not eradicated the social safety net, it is no wonder that the World Bank views women as the key to economic growth: women are proving to be flexible.

Of course, the flexibility of women is coupled with resistance to neo-liberal models of development. Organizations such as the Self-Employed Women's Association have been instrumental in unionizing informal workers, implementing work cooperatives, and providing support networks for women in India (Desai 2002, 19; Mohanty 2003, 165). Although excluded from the World Bank's conception of empowerment, such collective organizing has been instrumental in challenging the economic vulnerability of self-employed women in India. Importantly, how the Self-Employed Women's Association collectively mobilizes against social, economic, and political disenfranchisement and exploitation is foreclosed as a possibility for transformative change, or a space for anti-violence organizing, by the World Bank. By challenging the flexibility of informal work relations, its resistance can be understood as inflexible.

To recapitulate my crip analysis of the World Bank, flexibility is defined by McRuer (2006) as a body that can survive crisis either by managing it or by showing that it has the potential to do so without ever making visible the specificities or realities of the crisis. To draw too much attention to the crisis would be to perform or act out inflexibility. To resist neo-liberal austerity, creating awareness and resisting flexible employment and the elastic conception of women's time, is to act out inflexibility or to make visible the crisis of development. Such crises, of course, are not considered urgent. Instead, they are considered ordinary and ongoing.

According to the DALYs measurement used by the World Bank, women who are impaired or disabled by various forms of violence or unsafe work environments are also inflexible bodies. When women cannot work, they are pathologized, considered unable to "fit" into current market schemas or empowerment models and thus needing to overcome their experiences of violence. In *The Cost of Violence*, the World Bank (2009a) asserts that leading a productive life is most valuable. In response to questions of violence against women, the institution maintains that lost disability-adjusted life years are not only a cost for the economy but also a cost for women's productivity. When women are unable to work or to work at their most productive potential because of disability, impairment, or illness caused by violence, the World Bank suggests that their lives are of lower quality. Of course, it is reasonable to assume that, when experiencing violence, one might be undergoing a lower quality of life. Problematically, all disabled or otherwise impaired individuals, unable to live up to their productive potential as outlined by the World Bank, are positioned in this category of low-quality life.

In the World Bank's conceptualization of disability, bodies not able to overcome their particular disability or impairment are considered to be inflexible. The organization's representation of normal corporeal functioning involves flexibility—*being resilient, adjusting*, and *overcoming* impairments, disabilities, and diseases to move closer to the ideal set by the normate figure. Disability theorists argue that social, economic, and political conditions constitute "disablement" as a deviation for the normal or ideal body (Clare 1999). According to neo-liberalism, to be disabled is to have a body unable to be properly productive in the capitalist labour economy, unable to adjust, and unable to be flexible. Disability theorists have powerfully demonstrated how the term "productivity" is not transhistorical or neutral. It is dependent on "a historical context," and "the present demands of (global) capital" require an "ease in which multinational companies can extract maximum profits from [their] workers and nation-states can extract low-wage and unpaid labour from [their] citizens" (Erevelles 2006, 30). Productivity is also a highly racialized concept in this context. Third World subjects are understood to be "cheap" labour in the global economy. Understanding how feminization of the global workforce can be attributed to (often Western) racist and patriarchal constructions of Third World women as nimble-fingered and docile, constructions that have culminated in the degradation and flexibilization of women's employment through economic restructuring, is essential to feminist challenges of the World Bank's promotion of economic empowerment models for women.

In the post–Washington Consensus era, optimally flexible bodies can move forward from the crisis of the Structural Adjustment Programs of the 1980s and 1990s and subsequent neo-liberal development schemes. According to the World Bank's newest gender report (2011b), women are exceeding expectations in labour and productivity, a key to economic development. The World Bank claims that women have successfully adjusted, making up the majority of manufacturing, retail, tourism, and communications services, but women earn less than men even though they work more (18). Because of time spent on household labour and a lack of regulations in the workplace that leaves opportunities for gender discrimination, the gap between men's and women's earning and productivity is high (20). The World Bank also attributes income and productivity gaps between men and women to women's lack of agency in the home. Arguing that domestic violence silences women and disallows decision making on household spending, the organization argues that women must be given the chance to enter the economic sector to obtain greater power at home (21). The World Bank argues that the gender gap in productivity, earning, and thus agency could be lessened if businesses realized the potential of investing in women.

BEING BOTH FLEXIBLE AND PRETTY: WOMEN ARE "GOOD FOR BUSINESS"

As I have already explored in this chapter, the World Bank promotes anti-violence interventions through economic opportunities for women. The organization argues that women would gain income, and subsequently power in their households to make decisions, and thus be less vulnerable to violence by their male partners. When unable to work because of impairment, disease, or disability caused by violence, women are unproductive and inefficient for development, according to the DALYs measurement. Violence against women is an urgent issue and must be solved because it impedes good business, economic growth, and national development. However, disability is named only as an indicator, not as a conceptual apparatus or lived reality. That disability is used to measure cost but otherwise ignored illustrates the impact of discourses of urgency on framing the issue and the narrowness of the organization's response. Disability is an issue not integrated into the analysis but left for later.

In the *World Development Report 2012: Gender Equality and Development*, the World Bank (2012, 238) makes "the business case for gender equality." Providing a case study of Belcorp in Peru and Hindustan Unilever in India, the organization attempts to demonstrate "how using innovative business models to invest in the female workforce can be good for business and bring tangible change to women's lives" (238). Using a scheme popularized by the American cosmetic company Avon, Belcorp (also a cosmetic company) pays women to sell its products informally to their personal and professional networks. According to the World Bank, women are integral to the success of Belcorp since they make up over 80 percent of its workforce as sellers of its products. The company gives its 650,000 beauty consultants opportunities to become entrepreneurs and offers other group activities to empower them. The World Bank asserts that Belcorp realized early on that "promoting women's empowerment was a sound business strategy" (238). Communicating how women are key to "good economics" depends on understanding their empowerment as being located in the public sphere.

According to the World Bank (2012), Hindustan Unilever has increased its business by discovering a "comparative advantage" in employing women, and liberalization of India's economy and opening up of markets to foreign multinational competitors such as Procter and Gamble have increased pressure on Unilever to increase profits (238). Given the valuation of flexibility in the global economy, multinational firms have sought flexible labour. Unable to reach small villages in India through formal distribution, Unilever began to invest in female micro-entrepreneurs to sell its products to their networks. Depending on 45,000 female workers, this system of informal distribution has helped the company to tap into over 3 million homes in 135,000 villages in rural areas of India. Not only has this program empowered women through increased incomes according to the bank, but also it is improving hygiene in rural India (238).

Borrowing from the business model of Avon to employ women and empower them is not surprising given that the company has been involved in both a Look Good, Feel Better breast cancer campaign and a global anti–domestic violence campaign. In Canada, for example, women are encouraged to show their solidarity with and support for women who have experienced domestic violence by wearing a special necklace designed for the initiative, with all Canadian proceeds going to anti-violence organizations and UN Women (Avon 2011). Moreover, Avon has "found the power" in Third World women and now invests in Africa, Latin America, and Asia (Dolan and Scott 2009, 207). Citing Susan Bordo's (1993) *Unbearable Weight: Feminism, Western Culture, and the Body* and Naomi Wolf's (1991) *The Beauty Myth: How Images of Beauty Are Used against Women*, Catherine Dolan and Linda Scott (2009) suggest that some feminists might question how a cosmetic beauty company could empower women since feminist theory has often perceived cosmetics as both a cause and a sign of women's oppression. Instead, I follow Priti Ramamurthy's (2003) argument that feminist research should focus on global commodity chains and explore how Third World subjects are interpellated in the activity of consumption. According to Ramamurthy, women are not duped by multinational corporations selling goods, and feminists must understand that women's production and consumption are always already situated in transnational complexity.

Whereas some critical scholars of beauty highlight thinness, makeup regimes, and biopolitical governmentality, here I take up the issue of racialized ableism as it relates to anti-violence interventions. As I have already criticized DALYs for their ableist assumptions of proper productivity here, I extend my critique to suggest that female

Third World survivors of violence are "rehabilitated," made to "fit," or "recuperated" by World Bank empowerment projects. Such initiatives are framed by an ideal of corporeal modernity based upon racist and ableist notions of normalcy. Especially important to the study of DALYs as a measurement of violence against women are the intersections of disability and empowerment in how women who survive violence are heralded as being empowered in economic and ableist terms. That is, when empowerment is sought in the economic sphere, the production and consumption of beauty products related to an idealized or normate body must be understood within the broader objectives of the World Bank and as being intimately connected to how urgency around the issue of violence against women is manufactured at the expense of their well-being.

BEAUTY, DISABILITY, AND COLONIAL CONTINUITIES

Rather than enter the debate about cosmetics as being oppressive or liberating for women, it is important to ask more complex questions about "global feminism" and the beauty industry, especially since cosmetics are currently being used to secure women's employment and corporeal modernity transnationally. As Jennifer Fluri (2009) maintains, the impact of the beauty industry must be contextualized by political and economic systems. Arguing that "the body acts as the site for the imprinting of social constructions of gender, race, sex and sexuality as well as the countering of these gendered, social norms," Fluri maintains that the definition of beauty, makeup, and even visibility of the body are harnessed to a larger project, including support for the war on terror (251). As her case study on Beauty without Borders reveals, modernity and beauty regimes interlock intricately. Extending her work, I maintain that "corporeal modernity" also relies on notions of disability and normalcy. For example, *Vogue* magazine and cosmetic company Estee Lauder, in partnership with Physiotherapy and Rehabilitation Support for Afghanistan, a non-governmental organization working on issues of disability in the country, fund Beauty without Borders. Undoubtedly, the link between racism and ableism, written on the bodies of women, must be taken into account. Beauty myths not only rely on standards of unattainable and feminized beauty for women but also are ableist. In the beauty industry, able-bodied normalcy intersects with gender, sexuality, race, and class to produce an ideal representation.

As a World Bank–attested "best practices" company, Hindustan Unilever manufactures and sells skin-whitening cream in India, among other products. According to Evelyn Nakano Glenn (2008), light skin for women is associated with (hetero)sexual desirability and operates as social capital. The production and marketing of lightening products are incorporated into the transnational flow of goods and capital. In particular, large multinational corporations have become major players in the field, spending huge sums of money on research and development of skin-whitening products, advertising them, and selling them to both mass and special markets. For example, Unilever's skin-care line Ponds provides cold creams in Europe and North America and whitening creams in Asia, the Middle East, and Latin America (296).

Although the effects of globalization have surely increased the production and consumption of skin-whitening products, the promotion of "whiter" and "lighter" skin has a much longer and tenacious history. As Anne McClintock (1995, 207) illustrates in *Imperial Leather: Race, Gender, and Sexuality in the Colonial Contest*, Victorian cleaning products were "peddled globally as a God-given sign of Britain's evolutionary superiority, and soap was invested with magical, fetish powers." Not only does McClintock connect soap, cleanliness, and whiteness to a "cult of domesticity" in Victorian women's homes, but she also suggests that soap marketing communicates ideas of social value and racial hierarchy. With colonial expansion and the extrication of palm oil, coconut oil, and cottonseed oil from West Africa, New Guinea, Ceylon, Fiji, and Malaya, soap became central to women's "proper" sanitation of the home. It was also marketed abroad as a civilizing technology, often portraying black bodies in particular as being in need of cleansing. In Pears soap advertisements, for example, black and white boys were often pictured together in a bathroom in which the black boy looked at water and soap as foreign objects and the white boy taught him how to wash himself (213). Often the racialized boy's blackness was literally scrubbed off, leaving a whitened body as the intended outcome. Hygiene was integrally associated with whiteness, lightness, and superiority by colonial regimes, and the commodity of soap became associated with imperial acts of benevolence. Representations of Africans in particular as unhygienic, dirty, and undomesticated became a social disciplining technique at home and abroad, but they also helped to violently enforce cultural and economic values that used blackness as a reflection of uncleanliness and racial inferiority and whiteness and lightness as a reflection of civility.

The World Bank's promotion of Hindustan Unilever as a "best practice" approach to women's empowerment is a "colonial continuity" (Heron 2007, 38). It is significant that, as a foremost producer of knowledge on development, the World Bank (2012, 238) emphasizes the expansion of hygiene and cosmetics to rural parts of India, supposedly where people do not take part in proper rituals of cleansing. Moreover, the lack of attention paid to Unilever's skin-whitening products and the imposition of standards of beauty, often Western-influenced, on a number of cultures with their own standards of beauty is closely connected to a colonial continuity of racialized ableism in the World Bank's work. Unilever's Fair and Lovely products are some of its most popular in India, where women are asked to be small entrepreneurs and sell products to their networks across the country. Interestingly, Unilever has launched the Fair and Lovely Foundation, whose mission is to encourage the economic empowerment of women across India. Using marketing campaigns that depict lighter-skinned women as being employed and desirable by men, the company depicts having dark skin as painful and depressing. Glenn suggests that the Fair and Lovely line is used to illustrate how "dark skin becomes a burden and *handicap* that can be *overcome* only by using the product being advertised" (2008, 298; emphasis added). Although it is problematic to collapse race onto disability, how racism and ableism fold into each other is especially interesting here.

Given how the World Bank measures the cost of gendered violence in relation to productivity, and then promotes small entrepreneurship as a best practice model of empowerment, relying on women's flexible labour, it is important to articulate how racialized ableism supports the marketability of beauty products. Conceptions of normalcy are central to practices of beauty where women with disabilities are often represented as being undesirable and asexual, needing to be "fixed" or "cured" to be desirable, and not depicted in popular beauty campaigns. Moreover, whiteness is central to international beauty campaigns, with able-bodied white women being the focus of most beauty images produced.

Although the World Bank (2012, 174) notes cultural beauty standards and social norms, such as foot binding in China, as violent practices, the organization remains silent about the violence inflicted on racialized and disabled bodies through the promotion of skin-whitening creams and other beauty products that promote a type of aesthetic normalcy. Nor does it consider the health impacts of such creams, which include ingredients such as mercury, a poison that damages the nervous system, and surely are connected to questions of global disability (Saint Louis 2010). However, such concerns about the disabling effects of products that women are asked to both buy and sell are not urgent concerns. Instead, they are reserved for later. Where the World Bank considers violence against women, social norms are understood to be cultural and local, and empowerment is seen to be economical. The World Bank pays no attention to the empowerment or disempowerment of women who manufacture beauty products in global factories, and even less attention is paid to how women are asked to be both the producers and the consumers in these economic growth schemes.

WORTHY VICTIMS: "FITTING" INTO MARKET SCHEMES

The change from representing Third World women as a minor and sometimes irritating diversion from more urgent issues to the very agents of development marks a decisive shift in the work of the World Bank. How did women become victims worthy of its time? Yasmin Jiwani (2010) argues that there is a tension between worthy victims and those who can be forgotten. Using the notion of a "doubling discourse" to describe an ambiguity in the representational frameworks of Afghan women, Jiwani argues that representations of monolithically oppressed women who lacked agency were often interchanged with depictions of women who were more involved and interactive toward the end of the decade following the events of 9/11. In a media studies analysis, Jiwani notes that Afghan women began to be represented as survivors rather than victims. Arguing that "consumer capitalism turns on the cultivation of potential Others as consumers," she suggests that Afghan women could be recuperated through the Beauty without Borders initiative since they were being taught how to be more like "us," though still a few decades behind, and becoming consumers of beauty products (68).

Like the Afghan women in Jiwani's (2010) research, the World Bank's promotion of Belcorp's and Hindustan Unilever's small enterprises for women's empowerment is a type of rehabilitative program in which women are not only asked to sell beauty products but also become the foremost consumers of those products. Their worthiness for intervention depends on their rehabilitative potential. That is, the *survival, resiliency,* and *flexibility* of women who have experienced violence are heralded in and through their incorporation into good business opportunities as the linchpin of economic development. In other words, violence against women is an urgent issue because paying attention to it is profitable.

Here I use the term "rehabilitation" to conceptualize how women are made to fit market-based strategies. Born from post–First World War medical practices, rehabilitation focused on the restoration of rank honour and "true function" of those disabled or impaired by acts of war (McRuer 2006, 111). Discourses of rehabilitation outside the confines of disability have a long history in the lives of people of colour. Offering the example of Roderick A. Ferguson's *Aberrations in Black*, McRuer asserts that systemic inequities have often been understood through the logic of rehabilitation, focusing on black family life for signs of non-normativity and pathology that must be overcome. As Barbadian feminist Eudine Barriteau maintains, the shift in development discourse from women to gender, and to men in particular, coupled with depoliticization, has resulted in a "men at risk" narrative in Jamaica that has problematically pathologized racialized men and non-(hetero)normative family structures, which include the employment of breadwinning women in "pink collar" labour (Jackson and Pearson 1998, 8).

Calculating the value of anti-violence interventions based upon an individual's productive potential is at the core of the World Bank's rehabilitative logic. In fact, "mainstreaming" disability has been framed within a rehabilitative logic at the World Bank. As Rebecca Dingo (2007) argues, the organization has often represented people with disabilities as requiring technical and technological interventions to make them better "fit" workplaces in order to take part in the development of their national economies. Women and people with disabilities are perceived by the World Bank as requiring recuperation and are worthy victims only if they can be integrated into capitalist production and consumption. Importantly, such narrow visions of anti-violence against women schemes foreclose other possibilities for such work.

Importantly, by speaking the language of the institution, internal gender advocates working to manufacture urgency around the issue do so under the constraints of the mandate of the World Bank and are therefore forced to find ways to solve violence against women through neo-liberal economic policies. Whereas violence against women has not been a major concern of the economically focused organization historically, nor has disability, the use of DALYs by gender experts in the World Bank reveals that eliminating such violence must be economically focused for the institution to take it seriously, and inappropriately it instrumentalizes the reality of global disability in the process. DALYs present violence against women as an urgent issue because it is costly and because dealing with it will be more cost effective than not dealing with it, but it does not allow for a more nuanced or deep analysis of the issue. As I have demonstrated in this chapter, violence manifests itself in workplaces and is inextricably connected to global economic restructuring processes. Thus, empowerment through work will not solve violence against women in a neo-liberal economy that relies on violence to function and often results in disabilities and impairments for female workers. Violence against women cannot be solved by manufacturing a sense of urgency around the issue using ableist measurements such as DALYs.

CRIP THEORY MATTERS TO DEVELOPMENT

My focus in this chapter on cripping development reveals not only how normalizing narratives of ability are central to the World Bank's work on preventing violence against women but also how the concept of overcoming—adjusting, being flexible, and coping—has a much broader impact on development itself and makes space for new and stimulating dialogues in the field. At the crux of such dialogue among disability studies, crip theory, and development should be a thorough engagement with the experience and representation of people with disabilities globally as well as the globalization of disabilities. As a special issue of *Wagadu: A Journal of Transnational Women's and Gender Studies* entitled *Intersecting Gender and Disability Perspectives in Rethinking Postcolonial*

Identities argued in 2007, disability studies should be pursued trans-nationally. This special issue published foundational scholarship on the possible intersections between postcolonial theory and disability but also warned of the dangers of collapsing the complexities of each field. Specifically, Mark Sherry (2007, 10) warned that the rhetorical, metaphorical, and symbolic connections between features of postcolonialism such as exile, diaspora, apartheid, and slavery and experiences of disability such as deafness, psychiatric illness, and blindness are too often made in each discipline. As Sherry states, "rather than simply bemoan disability as a symbol of the horrors of imperialism, a far more interesting approach is to unpack the power dynamics which link the two experiences, both in practice and in rhetoric" (16). Although colonialism and imperialism are intimately connected to experiences of impairment, poverty, and disease, it is not enough to use disability as a symbol of the effects of occupation and control. In response to this special issue, the *Journal of Literary and Cultural Disability Studies* published an issue in 2010 focused on "disabling" postcolonialism. Contributors expanded the analysis of postcolonialism and disability in *Wagadu* to think through how critical disability theories and decolonizing methodologies could intervene in postcolonial studies and enlarged the focus of disability studies to include regions of the world other than the West.

Like popular discourses about disability, development is also popularly conceptualized as a project of overcoming. That is, just as people with disabilities are charged with overcoming them, so too people living in poverty are charged with overcoming it. Critical development, post-development studies, and decolonizing methods have revealed how development discourses rely on an ideal of normalcy. In this case, the ideal is set by the developed Global North, or so-called First World, and the developing Global South, or so-called Third World, must overcome, be flexible, and adjust to catch up.

For many development theorists and practitioners, the development project began with President Truman's inaugural address in 1949, in which he argued that Third World poverty needed to be addressed for the sake of global security, to fight communism, and to offer the rest of the world a "fair deal" (Escobar 1995, 3; Saunders 2002, 1). For other scholars, development has a much longer history. To truncate the colonial lineage of development is to disavow its long ideological history.

The term "development" itself emerged in the English language in the eighteenth century alongside ideas of human evolution and progress, and then it broke away from biological (and heavily racialized) notions of growth into "teleological views of history, science and progress in the West" (Watts 1995, 47). The idea of development popularly known in the field today is a specifically Western concept since many non-Western languages have no equivalent term. For some critical development scholars, development is not only a Western idea but also a concept that emerged as a discourse about the mythical superiority, or normalcy, of Western society and reflects how the West imagines itself through spatialized and racialized hierarchical differences. In practice, the idea of countries being able to progress or overcome is used to justify interventions abroad, though the ability of countries to catch up, mimic, or join the developed world is greatly debated (Ferguson 2005).

Popular in foreign policy, the term "development" (re-)emerged at a time when many countries of the Third World were formally decolonizing. Following the Second World War, the United States was at the height of its power and used its influence to promote progress through practices of modernization. Various development theories have risen and fallen in popularity since the 1950s, but hegemonic models of development continue to rely on narratives of linear progress. Such models were built upon the assumption of Western cultural and economic superiority and the necessity of Western intervention to teach others how to overcome their poverty. As post-development theorists such as Arturo Escobar (1995) argue, the "problem" of Third World poverty was "discovered" through the "developmentalization" or "clientalization" through techno-representation, such as statistics, of the discursive and materially constructed Third World.

The problem of underdevelopment is often understood without historicization, politicization, and structural context by development "experts." Similar to popular advocacy related to disability, there is a large helping industry in the field of development (Heron 2007). Without collapsing the complexities between disability and development, it is interesting to note how disability and underdevelopment are similarly characterized as stemming from unfortunate events, and overcoming those events is the responsibility of those affected by them, at times with help from those better off. In the context of neo-liberalism, self-help is also imperative to charity models of both disability and development. Such connections between disability studies and development studies suggest that there is more work to be done.

CONCLUSION

The DALYs measurement organizes itself around the idea that disease, impairment, and disability must be overcome. The World Bank's (2009a) report *The Cost of Violence* suggests not only that productivity is lost as a result of violence but also that women's work is the most important aspect of their empowerment. It is not just the World Bank's quantification of violence against women that is of concern. Importantly, DALYs provide a numerical justification for the utilization of women's flexibility to obtain returns on investments in economic development as women's equality interventions. In this way, violence against women becomes something that can be measured through economic formulas, and interventions become associated solely with labour-based empowerment. Although development organizations rarely use the terms "feminist" and "feminism" (Smyth 2010, 145), gender advocates at the World Bank have harnessed feminist language of rights, voice, participation, and empowerment to roll out technocratic and economic frameworks to end violence against women while relying on discourses of adjustment and resiliency, or overcoming, to promote women's inclusion in the labour economy. With a "pull yourself up by your bootstraps" neo-liberal mentality, women are encouraged by the World Bank to survive, adjust, and cope with extreme global injustice through labour-based and entrepreneurial engagements.

I have assembled World Bank literature, various gender- and development-focused texts, and disability, crip, and feminist scholarship to demonstrate how calculating the cost of violence against women using the DALYs measurement relies on both an ableist notion of life worth, as connected to the ideal productive body, and Third World women's flexible labour relations. The World Bank communicates the cost of violence against women as a pressing concern within the structure of neo-liberal development models, which means that gender advocates within the organization have to manufacture urgency to eradicate violence against women in line with the World Bank's economic agenda. This framing has served the interests of transnational capital at the expense of women's well-being.

A brief history of the World Bank's gender and development work illustrates how the DALYs measurement is an expansion of the well-known emphasis on empowering women in the market sphere. A crip reading of the World Bank's anti-violence initiatives demonstrates the need to consider disability in the way that the organization attempts to solve the issue in addition to how it calculates its cost. Women's flexibility, resiliency, and adjustment—or their ability to overcome—are central to an ongoing expansion of neo-liberal development, in which women's empowerment is a means to an end. The World Bank's good-for-business models, for example, further articulate the interlocking of gender, race, and disability regimes through the exploration of cosmetic-based entrepreneurial initiatives that rely on women being flexible, pretty, and white.

A thorough analysis of the World Bank's use of DALYs to measure the cost of violence against women reveals that, regardless of how mathematically complex and nuanced, it cannot account for all types of violence. Moreover, justice for violent acts requires more than labour market activities for women's empowerment. Relying on narratives of flexibility, the World Bank habitually locates the issue of violence, and its disabling effects, within an individualizing narrative rather than considering how violence and disability are systemically and structurally propagated. Using DALYs to measure violence against women as a cost for women's productivity and the economy directly shapes the World Bank's technocratic approaches to ending violence against women. The institution's manufactured concern with this violence demonstrates its actual concern with the flexibility of racialized women or their ability to overcome, adjust, and remain resilient by gaining flexible employment in a neo-liberal global economy in which flexible labour is most valued. In other words, DALYs reveal that the World Bank requires racialized women to overcome gendered violence, adjust under neo-liberal restructuring, and have resilient bodies in disabling conditions. At the intersections of disability, violence, and neo-liberal development, global sexism, racism, and ableism secure one another. Thus, how the World Bank continues to seek racialized bodies for cheap and flexible labour, and as consumers of products sold by multinational corporations, as women's empowerment remains suspect.

Problematically, the World Bank's measurement of the cost of violence against women has little to add to innovative or holistic approaches to ending this violence globally. DALYs calculate the cost of the loss of women's productivity as a result of violence and measure the cost effectiveness of interventions. They do not measure the reduction in violence against women or the cost of violence for women's well-being beyond losses in productivity. The mathematical complexity of the economic measurement suggests that DALYs not only obscure the complexities of global violence against women but also secure the expertise of the World Bank at the expense of grassroots organizing against violence. Although the organization seems to focus on women's rights, it continues to focus on their responsibilities to the neo-liberal state. Thus, violence against women is an urgent concern for the World Bank insofar as women's flexible labour, time, and bodies are understood to be key to economic growth.

The urgency to eliminate violence against women is constructed by gender advocates at the World Bank using economic language. As my study of American foreign policy and the World Bank demonstrates so far in this book, discourses of urgency invoke already circulating languages, ideas, agendas, and strategies so that a concern for violence against women makes sense to the target audience. Economic and political discourses are not neutral but social and cultural constructs. Having investigated how violence against women has come to be communicated as a pressing concern for development, I now turn to how this urgency is felt. In Chapter 3, I investigate the affective politics of anti-violence campaigns to understand how emotional responses to gendered violence produce a sense of urgency around the issue.

CHAPTER 3

THE UNITED NATIONS WANTS YOU TO CARE ABOUT VIOLENCE AGAINST WOMEN

||||||||||||||||||||||||

Break the silence. When you witness violence
against women and girls, do not sit back. Act.
—Ban Ki-moon, UN Secretary-General

Violence against women has long been an urgent concern for feminist scholars and activists, yet the issue has gained the full attention of the United Nations only within the past two decades. The United Nations officially recognized violence against women as a human rights concern in 1993 with the Declaration of the Elimination of All Forms of Violence against Women, but it was not until 2006 that the organization called for a comprehensive study of such violence globally. As its first comprehensive commitment to eliminating this violence, the United Nations launched the UNiTE to End Violence against Women campaign in 2008 (UN 2012a, b). UNiTE includes a database of resources, an Internet-based knowledge-sharing centre, a group of men's leaders, and a complementary Say NO advocacy and awareness campaign. At the height of its advocacy, the UNiTE campaign aimed to enforce national laws on violence against women, implement national action plans, develop data on the prevalence of such violence, address sexual violence in conflict, and increase public awareness and social mobilization by 2015. UN Secretary-General Ban Ki-moon explicitly supported the UNiTE initiative, which suggests that the issue is being presented as imperative for the organization from the top down.

According to an interview that I conducted in 2012 with Todd Minerson, director of the White Ribbon Campaign, and participant in UNiTE's men's leaders project, UNiTE is the first initiative to both coordinate and feature global efforts to eliminate violence against women by bringing "all stakeholders into a conversation about gender-based violence." Minerson claimed that a coordinated global effort to eliminate this violence is a welcome initiative that connects with many other development concerns. He suggested that "violence is not going away and urgently needs to be addressed." At the time of my interview with him, UNiTE was building upon social media platforms and aiming to bring what is "happening on the ground" to the global level, meaning that it has to be presented in a way that is "palatable for the average person that does not understand how the UN system works."

Those who support and speak for the campaign claim that the time is *now* to end global violence against women. UNiTE has drawn the attention of well-known activists such as Archbishop Emeritus Desmond Tutu and the "father" of micro-credit enterprises, Muhammad Yunus, as well as celebrities such as Charlize Theron and Nicole Kidman. According to Theron, the messenger of peace for the United Nations, "we're *at a time* where people just want to join together and cause change. People don't want to live like this any more" (quoted in UN 2012a; emphasis added). Echoing her remarks, Ban Ki-moon (2011) stated that "more and more people are understanding that violence against women is everyone's responsibility....We need to change attitudes."

For women who have experienced gendered violence, the time to end it has always been now, yet the temporal pressure of the UNiTE campaign structures how such violence is understood as particularly pressing at this moment. Such violence does not have a crisis moment; rather, it is an ongoing reality of global misogyny, and discourses of urgency manufacture a feeling to match crisis thinking. In this chapter, I argue that urgency functions within the UNiTE campaign as what Gould (2009, 3) has termed "political feelings." UNiTE communicates the urgency of eliminating violence against women in a way that affects those who will, in turn, express emotion by taking action. Using stories of pain, trauma, and suffering, as well as narratives of empowerment and agency, this campaign aims to make one feel and then act quickly on that feeling in ways deemed appropriate by the United Nations. Resembling other awareness campaigns, the initiative works to affect, and be affected by, its audience. By collecting stories of respondents who say no to violence against women, the campaign can claim global reach, and its success is marked by the political feelings that it instills in its audience. The campaigns are focused on both awareness and social action and function as a "one-stop shop" for people who know little about the nuances and reality of global violence (Minerson, personal communication, 2012).

The UNiTE campaign and the Say NO initiative can be analyzed through a critical lens that will reveal the representational politics of the campaign. As the United Nations deploys images, text, and video to communicate the scope of the issue and suitable responses to it, a discursive analysis of the campaign is important. Although the representation of violence against women has been explored in sophisticated critical feminist literature, affect has yet to be studied in the context of the development industry. To fill in this gap, I centre political feelings in my analysis of the UNiTE and Say NO campaigns. I explore common and expected feelings related to a global anti-violence awareness and advocacy campaign, including feelings of being overwhelmed, desperate, and feeling pity for victims, and I account for less predictable ones, including feelings of hope and empowerment, in addition to accounting for how some political feelings might be disallowed by the discourses of urgency manufactured by the campaigns.

OUTLINE

In this chapter, I expand Gould's (2009) groundbreaking work on the affective nature of ACT UP's HIV/AIDS activism. I ask, How are political feelings generated, cultivated, and contained by the UNiTE to End Violence against Women campaign? How do political feelings shape awareness campaigns and global advocacy efforts as well as the bodies on which emotions "stick" (Ahmed 2004a)? By centring the UNiTE and Say NO campaigns, I feel my way through the affective economy of the initiatives, specifically paying attention to how calls for urgent action orient participants toward particular political feelings. I maintain that affect is not spontaneously generated but functions in line with systems of oppression, and I subsequently adopt Ahmed's (2004a) notion of affect and her cultural theory of emotions. Indebted to her concept of affective economies, my analysis of political feelings in the UNiTE and Say NO campaigns is aimed at understanding how emotions circulate among bodies, gain affective value in their repetition, and stick to bodies.

Although a sophisticated and thorough body of feminist literature has been published on the representation of violence against women in the Third World, I point to the lack of attention to affect. As a complement to the important work of postcolonial, transnational, Third World, and critical race feminist scholarship, I maintain the importance of considering how affective responses are evoked by representations of such violence in the development industry.

As a site of anti-violence work, the United Nations provides a complicated archive for exploration. Concerned with the political feelings that are permissible and those that are foreclosed in the UNiTE campaign, I outline a brief history of anti-violence work at the organization to situate UNiTE within an analysis of the forms of activism that have flourished or faltered at the organization. Feminists have been mobilizing officially at the United Nations around the issue of violence against women since the UN Decade for Women (1975–85). However, such mobilizations are far from straightforward. The outcomes of the UN Conferences on Women provide a context for understanding how the United Nations currently approaches the issue of this violence.

Turning to the UNiTE to End Violence against Women campaign, my analysis focuses on "The Situation" overview (UN 2012b) and "UNiTE Worldwide" (UN 2012c) interactive map on the campaign's website. Expanding Amin Alhassan's (2009) notion of "telescopic philanthropy," I explore what it might mean to *feel* telescopically. Employing the idea of "telescopic feeling," I analyze the political feelings that are both possible and foreclosed by representational frames: namely, individual and benevolent responses to an issue "over there" and how emotions associated with violence against women stick to bodies linked to the spaces targeted for intervention (Ahmed 2004a). In particular, I argue that telescopic feeling prevents participants from making broader and more complex connections between the West and the "rest" by limiting the scope of possible feelings.

I also follow the circulation of affect in UNiTE's Say NO campaign (UN 2012d). Focused on how participants can "take action" now to end violence against women, I consider the affective possibilities of saying no and making donations for change. Since these are the two most visible forms of action available to participants on the UNiTE website, I explore how their emotions are evoked through their orientations to other bodies. Aligned with those who want to help, I maintain that the urgency of the Say NO campaign generates a body of "do-good" donors in contrast to a body in need of aid. The urgency of such click-campaigns creates not only a space for individuals to have feelings of sympathy for victims but also a sense of belonging and empowerment by taking action against violence: the "aboutness" of the campaign is centred on the agency of the participant (Ahmed 2004a, 21). By evoking a sense of urgency through the emotionality of Say NO, these texts position the United Nations and the UNiTE participants as agents of change. As I illustrate, narratives of individual pain and suffering in particular obscure the complexities of violence against women and promote monetary donations as a solution to the issue. The urgency of this campaign forecloses possibilities for other political feelings, including those that might lead to collective action against global systems of oppression that secure women's vulnerability to violence. As Enloe (2004) reminds us, issues regulated for now too often leave feminist questions and concerns for later. A radical feminist critique of development itself, the UN system, and global violence against women would align participants toward negative political feelings that might actually prohibit participants from donating to the UNiTE and adjoining Say NO campaigns, and thus they are less urgent questions and relegated to later.

THE UN APPROACH TO VIOLENCE AGAINST WOMEN

The Declaration on the Elimination of Violence against Women (UN 1993) is the most comprehensive human rights text regarding the issue to date, and it marks a remarkable feat by feminist and anti-violence advocates to have the issue recognized at the international level. In the original Convention on the Elimination of All Forms of Discrimination against Women adopted by the General Assembly (UN 1979), there was not one reference to violence against women. However, following the UN

Decade for Women (1975–85) and the Fourth UN World Conference on Women in Beijing (1995), the issue of this violence moved to centre stage in the United Nations. Since the UNiTE campaign arose from the Office of the Secretary-General, it suggests that violence against women is now at the centre of UN policy making. To understand how violence against women has urgently emerged at the United Nations with introduction of the UNiTE and Say NO campaigns, we need a historical context for mobilizations around this issue by international feminist activists.

MEXICO

In 1975, the First UN World Conference for Women was held in Mexico City. Reflecting Cold War politics, countries belonging to the United Nations sat divided in three blocs: the Western nations, the Southern countries belonging to the Group of Seventy-Seven (most formerly colonized), and the Eastern nations (communist and other socialist countries). Whereas the Western bloc pushed for development, the Eastern group argued for peace, and the Southern bloc demanded a new international economic order (Joachim 2007, 73–74). Central to the discussion of women's equality was the framing of how to make changes in the lives of women. Equality through redistribution and progress through development were the two major competing frames within which inequality was understood (Joachim 2007, 77). Although violence against women was brought up as a major concern, especially for Third World women, the integration of women into development schemes was one of the most controversial subjects of the conference. The "Report of the World Conference of the International Women's Year" (UN 1976, 5) claimed not only that the problem of underdevelopment was a result of "unsuitable internal structures," including the lack of female integration into development, but also that the problem of underdevelopment rested in the "profoundly unjust world economic system," including structures of development. Importantly, the Group of Seventy-Seven argued that women's inequality should be understood as being inextricably linked to unequal global economic and political conditions stemming from colonialism and imperialism (Joachim 207, 81–82). Although women differed in terms of preferred solutions to their inequality, the report claimed that they came together under the banner of global sisterhood,

recognizing that their differences were overshadowed by their experiences of sexism and that their awareness of patriarchy made them
"natural allies in the struggle against any form of oppression, such as is
practiced under colonialism, neo-colonialism, Zionism, racial discrimination, and apartheid, thereby constituting an enormous revolutionary
potential for economic and social change in the world today" (UN 1976,
3). The official report not only claimed that women should fight together
against colonialism and neo-colonialism but also called on international cooperation to end "foreign occupation, Zionism, apartheid, and
racial discrimination in all its forms as well as the recognition of the
dignity of peoples and their right to self determination" (UN 1976, 13).
Significantly, much of this history of UN conferences has been obscured
or forgotten, especially since executive summaries and action plans
from the conferences have not included such revolutionary discourse.

In Mexico City, violence against women was officially framed as physical and emotional abuse, often perpetrated by men. Although the Group
of Seventy-Seven argued for the integration of structural and economic
concerns into conversations on the issue, the objectives of the UN Decade
for Women set at the conference in Mexico followed structures of development rather than redistribution by calling for extended education in
the Third World, the modernization of agriculture, and women's involvement in development as solutions to some of the issues. According to
the Group of Seventy-Seven, development and technical intervention
would offer considerable possibilities for improving the well-being of all
people, but *it was a new international economic order that would radically
reshape women's lives*. According to the report's appendix, participants
from Albania asserted that "many parts of the Plan [of Action] did not
adequately reflect the concerns of all the women of the world" and maintained that "the struggle for women's emancipation had to be waged first
and foremost against colonialism, racism, and apartheid" (UN 1976, 44).

COPENHAGEN

During the second UN World Conference on Women in Copenhagen
(1980), women met to review the targets of the first half of the Decade
for Women and commit to a plan of action for the second half. The
Copenhagen conference was arguably the most heated meeting in the

UN Decade for Women. Development again took centre stage at the conference as the solution to women's inequality, while Third World women
continued to argue in favour of a new international economic order and
maintained that international peace depended on the elimination of
imperialism, colonialism, neo-colonialism, apartheid, Zionism, and foreign occupation (UN 1980). At Copenhagen, the language of colonialism,
imperialism, and Zionism, and recognition of the plight of Palestinian
women in particular, were blocked by the Northern countries, including
Germany, the United Kingdom, and the United States, which asked that
these issues be dealt with in more "appropriate forums" (Joachim 2007,
85). Problematically, such opposition by Western powers to contextual-
izing women's issues within global power structures of domination and
exploitation meant that violence against women, among other issues,
was left ahistoricized and disconnected from the global political economy. For example, violence against women was included in the report by
citing participants' calls for policy measures and research on the extent
of the issue. Domestic violence in particular, took centre stage with the
establishment of shelters and treatment options in member countries
as an urgent recommendation (UN 1980).[1]

NAIROBI

The Third UN World Conference on Women occurred in Nairobi (UN 1985)
and was aimed at reviewing the accomplishments of the UN Decade for
Women. To avoid another politicized conference, U.S. delegate Maureen
Reagan (daughter of President Ronald Reagan) argued for a change in the
decision-making rules through an amendment regarding "general agreement." Margaret Kenyatta, daughter of the former president of Kenya
and leader of the Nairobi conference, wanted a successful conference so
as not to damage Kenya's international reputation, and she became an
unexpected ally for Reagan. When the United States threatened to walk
out of the conference if the term "Zionism" was used in the "Forward
Looking Strategies for the Advancement of Women," Kenyatta offered

---

1   As Narayan (1997) demonstrates, this call for more shelters for survivors
    of abuse across the world is a strategy based upon assumptions of similar
    experiences of violence by women transnationally, and it disregards local and
    national economies, structural resources, cultures, and the needs of women.

to substitute a more palatable phrase regarding the discrimination that women face globally (Joachim 2007, 94–95). According to the official report on the Nairobi conference, the United States not only disagreed with the language of colonialism, imperialism, apartheid, and racism but also rejected the claim that Third World poverty stemmed from inequitable economic relations and foreign occupations (UN 1985, 17). The United States also voted against the inclusion of references to the failings of official development assistance, accumulating debt, and trade protectionism that negatively affected the economies of developing nations. Moreover, the United States rejected any mention of apartheid and calls for sanctions against and liberation for South Africa and Palestine. With regard to Palestine, the United States voted against a paragraph that condemned the oppressive practices of the Israeli state, especially its treatment of women, stating that it contained "tendentious and unnecessary elements into the Forward Looking Strategies document which have only a nominal connection with the unique concerns of women" (UN 1985).

Depoliticization of the conference proceedings also occurred through an overreliance on statistical data on women's issues. Before the Nairobi conference, convenors conducted the World Survey on the Role of Women in Development and shared the results with participants. Themes of water, sanitation, education, industrialization, and trade were spoken about as technical issues in the Third World that required Western assistance. Although there were methodological problems with survey distribution, collection, and lack of aggregated statistics on women, the data successfully tilted the meeting away from questions of power and redistribution and toward women's issues as they related to economic development (Joachim 2007, 95–96; Pietilä and Vickers 1996, 10). Of course, not all women experienced the conference in this way. According to an interview that I conducted in 2012 with Eva Rathgeber, a Canadian development consultant, Nairobi was an exciting conference and there was a diversity of women all moving in the same direction. However, in 1985, "most feminists did not have a good understanding of violence against women. We were just starting to recognize this as an issue."

At the conference, ending violence against women was a top priority on the official agenda, and more than 100 workshops at the adjoining NGO forum were devoted to this issue. Joachim (2007, 116) argues that, though this was a major achievement for feminists, it meant that activists began to lose control over how the issue was defined by "experts" in the field. Following the conference, the UN Branches for the Advancement of Women and for Crime Prevention and Criminal Justice and the Centre for Social Development and Humanitarian Affairs called an "expert meeting on domestic violence" in 1986. NGOs and other women's organizations, with a few exceptions, were not participants but observers of "experts" such as criminologists, social scientists, and lawyers from the First World. The primary aim of the meeting was to share information about violence against women since little was known about the previously invisible and "private" issue. Experts argued that, without information about the numbers of women affected by violence, governments and international bodies were unlikely to take the issue seriously. Problematically, but not unlike other feminist organizing at the time, the experiences of North American women (primarily white) came to stand in for all women's experiences of violence. At the first UN meeting of leading experts, violence against women was most popularly understood as an act perpetrated by mentally ill men or as a result of alcohol abuse, stress, and provocation—when it occurred in the West. By contrast, violence against women in the Third World was attributed to cultural "backwardness" (Joachim 2007, 118).[2] Furthermore, Western nations continued to promote development as a cure-all for societal ills in the Third World, including violence against women. Although experts were successful in making the issue important at the United Nations, its narrow framing was problematic. As transnational and Third World feminists, including Mohanty (2003) and Narayan (1997), and anti-violence advocates, including INCITE! (2006) and Smith (2005), argue, and as I explored in Chapter 1, the hyper-visibility of racialized people as "backward" and the criminalization of violence against women lead to both misrepresentation of the issue and imposition of failed approaches to solving it.

---

2   Although this is true of the conceptualizations of violence against women at the Nairobi conference and subsequent meeting of experts, such representations of the issue continue to be prevalent, if not overwhelming, in current explanations. That is, how the issue has been framed historically continues to resonate in current definitions. For example, North America continues to rely on the criminalization of men (especially men of colour) to combat the issue, which suggests that there is little connection between the prison-industrial complex and how mainstream anti-violence organizations mobilize against violence against women (INCITE! 2006; Smith 2005).

BEIJING

In 1995, the Beijing Declaration outlined the centrality of preventing and eliminating violence against women and girls. In the report, violence against women is considered an obstacle to achieving equality, development, and peace. Where conflict and peace are mentioned, the terms "racism," "apartheid," and "neo-colonialism" are noticeably absent. Moreover, while violations of the human rights of women are accounted for, "murder, torture, systematic rape, forced pregnancy, and forced abortion" are disconnected from unequal global power relations, and the names of occupying forces are undocumented (UN 1995, 9). Although sustainable development is heralded, the call for a new international economic order is not mentioned in the official report. It is unclear that Third World women ceased to call for a change to uneven global economic systems in this space. However, because the Beijing Declaration relies so heavily on depoliticized discourses of empowerment and human rights, it is arguably the least politically charged text to emerge from the UN World Conferences on Women.

According to Maxine Molyneux and Shahra Razavi (2006, iv), the "'Beijing conference' was a landmark in policy terms, setting a global policy framework to advance gender equality." Both the Plus 5 and the Plus 10 conferences that followed the Beijing conference affirmed policies but did not set radically alternative agendas. Thus, the Beijing Declaration set and maintains the stage for international mobilizations for women's equality. Significantly, its legacy in terms of anti-violence agitation is that it set the issue of violence against women within the context of development and human rights and separate from radical calls from Southern voices to restructure the global political economy. The collective and powerful voices of the Group of Seventy-Seven who called for an overhaul of existing structural relations were thus silenced in this space. According to Desai (2005, 323), the mantra "women's rights are human rights," spoken by Hillary Clinton, became "paradigmatic" in Beijing. Arguing that human rights complement rather than conflict with neo-liberalism, Desai asserts that the emergence of the "rights discourse" at Beijing as both a hegemonic language structure and an influential ideology "coincided with the domination of the neo-liberal discourse" at the United Nations (323). That is, as women's

rights were articulated as human rights, critiques of neo-liberalism—
the overwhelming global economy construct—fell to the wayside. This
change in discourse has had important implications for agendas on
women's issues. According to Molyneux and Razavi (2002), most governments have fulfilled their trade treaties and obligations to the World
Bank, for example, rather than their human rights agreements since
Beijing. Noting that most Third World women participated in adjoining but separate forums, rather than the official Beijing forum, Desai
(2005) argues that the United Nations is a site for agenda setting but
hardly a space for transnational feminist solidarity building. Claiming
that Western participants in particular see the United Nations as a
space to "aid" Third World women, Desai maintains that the organization might no longer be the appropriate space for Third World women's
political activism (323), especially those agitating against violence at the
intersections of women's equality, neo-colonialism, occupation, imperialism, and neo-liberalism. Yet it remains the key site for top-down
agenda setting, given that feminist mobilizations against violence continue to occur there.

FROM BEIJING TO UNITE

Given the tenacious history of women's activism at the United Nations,
what does it mean for anti-violence work there now? If Third World
women have little access to and power in the organization, then how
are "their" problems being addressed? Although the United Nations
has drawn considerable academic and activist criticism of its membership, internal power relations, and structure of the Security Council,
it remains a central site for claims to international gender equality.[3]
According to Amartya Sen (2006, xvii),

---

3   The United Nations was born in the aftermath of the Second World War,
     and its original mission of peace building soon became secondary to that
     of development as countries in Africa and Asia became independent.
     Reflected in the structure of the Security Council, including the veto power
     for the victors of the Second World War and its ideology and language of
     development, the United Nations mirrors neo-colonial rule and uneven
     global power structures even as it promotes itself as a political leader of
     global equality.

even though the United Nations is often separated out these days for particular chastisement for being ineffective (or worse), the UN and the intellectual and political movements associated with it have contributed greatly to making our world a bit less nasty and more livable. And even though women had to fight to be heard and influence the making and working of this grand institution, the constructive impact of women's ideas and leadership can be seen in nearly every field in which the UN has made significant contributions.

Regardless of criticism of the institution, the United Nations has a global state-based membership, policy and monetary power, a foundation for a sizable audience, and broad and sophisticated media and social media outreach. Reaching millions by disseminating information via the Internet, national strategies, and the policy adoptions of member states, as well as funding local advocacy and grassroots organizing, there might be no better place for an anti-violence initiative to be housed. Even as the United Nations as a site for women's activism remains precarious, especially for Third World women who have historically struggled to gain meaningful access to and power in the institution, it remains a crucial site for agenda setting for the development industry and trans-national feminist mobilization. Thus, it continues to be a complex and important site to inquire about women's issues, gender equality, and representations of Third World "problems."

UNITE TO END VIOLENCE AGAINST WOMEN

According to the UNiTE campaign (UN 2012a), violence against women is a universally unjustifiable crime but exists in all parts of the world. UNiTE maintains that persistent discrimination against women lies at the root of the issue and that violence against women is unconfined to any culture, region, or country. Importantly, the campaign attends to the intersections of ethnicity, caste, class, migrant or refugee status, age, religion, sexual orientation, marital status, disability, and HIV status with women's experiences of violence.[4] Unexpectedly, the campaign

---

4   Unsurprisingly, race is not considered an important factor in UNiTE's...

material includes a discussion of violence against Indigenous women and police violence against those in custody, a global issue habitually obscured or ignored by mainstream anti-violence organizing and the development industry. As pointed out by Prügl (2015, 620), unexpectedly the "neoliberalisation of feminism yields a diverse range of outcomes, contradictions and sometimes even openings for 'progressive' agendas." And though UNiTE considers the systemic and structural roots of violence an example of such a progressive agenda, the campaign problematically maintains that the *primary* manifestation of violence against women is men's violence against their intimate partners. It does so by defining "The Situation" of global violence against women (UN 2012b).

Highlighting cultural practices such as dowry murder, honour killing, and female genital mutilation/cutting, the campaign overwhelmingly represented violent practices as exoticized practices of "backward" Third World cultures. The focus on these cultural narratives does particular discursive work for the awareness campaign. Emphasizing the most "extreme" forms of violence against women, as opposed to more ordinary and ongoing practices, UNiTE's overview functions as a "colonialist stance" (Narayan 1997, 59). That is, though UNiTE aims to bring all practices of violence into one global awareness campaign, it does so by presenting other women's experiences as the most extreme.

Although it is clear in the campaign's overview that violence against women is global, the Global South is highlighted and becomes the intended focus for the audience. Using an interactive map entitled "UNiTE Worldwide," the global geography of violence against women, and the UN's work, is highlighted in colour. As Canada and the United States, for example, literally fade into the background on the map, Southern countries become hyper-visible through colour as the targets of intervention. Obscured from the view of UNiTE participants

---

...intersectional analysis of violence against women globally. Critical race scholars have developed "intersectional theory," including Kimberle Crenshaw (1991), who coined the term, which makes the campaign's inattention to race a massive oversight. According to Uma Kothari (2006, 2), discourses of development rarely include the term "race," and development actively considers race "relatively unimportant in shaping inequalities, injustice and poverty." Instead, other categories of social differentiation—such as ethnicity, religion, and culture—are perceived to have the greatest significance.

are Northern countries, not highlighted and thus unmarked as being gender inequitable. As Mohanty (2003, 243) maintains, the division between the "Western/Third World"—or "North/South," "local/global," or "developed/underdeveloped"—presents the world through divisions between oppositional and unconnected spaces that disallow points of connection and distance between women across numerous dimensions. In particular, the experiences of Indigenous women vulnerable to poverty and violence through the impacts of colonization of the so-called developed world are actively obscured by such representations.

In addition to the ongoing problem of focusing on issues of violence against women that historically have been made hyper-visible by Western feminists and development experts, the aim of the global campaign lacks the intersectionality or transnationality that it claims. Extreme cases require urgent responses, since they are considered the most pressing, whereas ordinary or ongoing violence against women, and undoing the web of intersections among state-sponsored, structural, and interpersonal violence, are earmarked for later.

Focusing on the Global South (via colour highlighting), the "UNiTE Worldwide" map highlights particular cases and spaces of violence even as it attempts to create awareness of the issue as global.[5] The map functions as a neutral representation among other awareness-raising materials, yet cartographic projects must be problematized. According to Neil Smith and Cindi Katz (1993), the purpose of mapping is to produce a scaled representation of a space such that the representation is considered accurate for a particular purpose, but mapping is a particular political project too often deployed as a technical and objective practice: "Mapping involves exploration, selection, definition, generalization, and translation of data, it assumes a range of social cum representational power, and as the military histories of geography and cartography suggest, the power to map can be closely entwined with the power of conquest and social control" (69). Importantly, maps do not only define an area of inquiry but can also give new forms to sets of problems. Functioning as "absolute spaces," spaces that read as high or

---

5   Here I use Global South and Global North instead of the discursive constructs of the Third World and the West to mark how the practice of geographic mapping is essential to the affective economy of the UNiTE campaign.

extreme violence against women because of their colouring (in contrast to spaces not highlighted by colouring) are mapped onto recognized locational coordinates divided by imposed nation-state boundaries and borderlands by the UNiTE campaign. The scaled representation of violence against women in the form of a map produces a specific form of the problem and creates a spatialized dimension to what can be known and *felt* about the issue.

Thinking about how the UNiTE map highlights the geography of violence against women is essential to understanding how the map as a representation circulates within discourses of the campaign. As a scaled representation, the map is limited to countries of concern to the United Nations and targets of its investments and interventions. This highlighting of some spaces over others creates a sense of urgency in dealing with extreme cases of violence or where violence is understood to be a pressing rather than benign or non-threatening issue. Moreover, the interactive nature of the map gives participants a sense of control over the knowledge produced about violence and UNiTE's anti-violence initiatives that "pop up" at the click of a mouse on the colourful spaces. Mastery of knowledge is offered to a participant in terms of the visible simplicity of a colour-coded map, but it is also felt as flesh knowledge. That is, the map offers affective possibilities by evoking bodily intensities coded as emotions of control, understanding, excitement, and ease. Such affective and emotional reactions to the map are not neutral but orient participants toward "political feelings" in the most basic sense of the term. This map not only generates the participant's feelings of control but also communicates to viewers that the United Nations is the primary agent of change, for its anti-violence initiatives pop up in the spaces of extreme and thus urgent violence. Thus, participants are invited to feel comfortable with and even proud of the United Nations for taking control of, and trying to fix, an urgent global problem.

AFFECT AND FEELING

Whereas affect refers to states of being rather than the expression or interpretation of emotions, the political and economic circulation of affect is central to the field and to my understanding of this UNiTE map (Hemmings 2005, 551). Affect refers to bodily sensations, and emotion can be understood as what is *captured and coded* as feelings and responses. According to Brian Massumi's introduction to Deleuze and Guattari's (2000) *A Thousand Plateaus*, affect is not an emotion or feeling. Feelings are personal and emotions are social, whereas affect is a preconscious experience of intensity. Those interested in affect seek to describe or interpret intensities without making meanings of bodily capacities. Emotions or feelings, then, can be understood as "embodied meaning-making" in which affective responses are understood in comparison with past experiences, and emotions are projections of those feelings as communicative strategies with others (Wetherell 2012, 3). Affective circulation, and its impressions, can be understood by tracing how bodily capacities self-reflect, react, and loop back. As Silvan Tomkins (1963) asserts, the contagious nature of a yawn or smile demonstrates how affect is transferred between bodies. That is, a smile is transferred to others, doubles back, and increases its original intensity and resonance. A smile is understood as happiness because of meaning-making practices around our affective capacities.

Although theorists of affect disagree on the definitions of and distinctions among affect, emotion, and feeling, here I use the term "affect" to denote a preconscious and prediscursive bodily sensation such as the heart pounding, the body becoming sweaty, or the gut being wrenched. Subsequently, I use the terms "emotion" and "feeling" to describe the codification of affect or the attachment of sensation to discourses, ideas, narratives, and meaning-making practices. I understand feelings to be constructed through past experiences, and thus they are personal, but I also understand feelings as political. Consequently, I also deviate from Massumi's (2000) suggestion that only emotions are social.

Although I am particularly interested in affect theory for how it reveals the social and cultural construction of urgency in anti-violence campaigns, I also understand both emotions and feelings to be social in terms of how we understand them through discursive structures embedded in personal experiences. I conceptualize both feelings and emotions to be the conscious making of meaning of bodily sensations informed by dominant signification, so that being "gut wrenched" is understood as a feeling of sadness, devastation, or guilt and projected through emotionality. Using Gould's (2009) conceptualization, I also think about feelings as being *politically* generated and circulated.

Although theorists of affect have specifically attended to how it fastens to objects randomly, Clare Hemmings (2005, 559) argues that the most important theory of affect emerging in the field attends to social frameworks of inequality. While not holding identities in place on a fixed map of subjectivity, affect theory must consider how affective attachments "serve to satisfy drives or social norms." Citing Frantz Fanon's (2008) and Audre Lorde's (1984) descriptions of affective responses to their blackness, Hemmings maintains that affective attachments can be *unsurprising*. Fanon (2008, 11–12) writes:

> "Look, a Negro!" It was an external stimulus that flicked over me as I passed by. I made a tight smile.
>
> "Look, a Negro!" It was true. It amused me.
>
> "Look, a Negro!" The circle was drawing a bit tighter. I made no secret of my amusement.
>
> "Mama, see the Negro! I'm frightened! Frightened! Frightened!" Now they were beginning to be afraid of me. I made up my mind to laugh myself to tears, but laughter had become impossible.

And Lorde (1984, 147–48) writes:

> The AA subway train to Harlem. I clutch my mother's sleeve, her arms full of shopping bags, christmas-heavy. The wet smell of winter clothes, the train's lurching. My mother spots an almost seat, pushes my little snowsuited body down. On one side of me a man reading a paper. On the other, a woman in a fur hat staring at me. Her mouth twitches as she stares and then her gaze drops down, pulling mine with it. Her leather-gloved hand plucks at the line where my new blue snowpants and her sleek fur coat meet. She jerks her coat closer to her. I look. I do not see whatever terrible thing she is seeing on the seat between us....And suddenly I realize there is nothing crawling up the seat between us; it is me she doesn't want to touch....Something's going on here I don't understand, but I will never forget it. Her eyes. The flared nostrils. The hate.

Using the term "racial affect" to describe how affective attachments are driven by social oppression, Hemmings (2005) argues that affect theory must be couched in social meaning. Rather than understand affect as the intensities and sensations of random attachments, it should be understood as bodily intensities that circulate in and through history and context and as accumulations of sensations and vibrations that impress themselves on subjects and slide among and between different collective bodies. Affect generates certain emotions and political feelings in line with social inequalities and dominations. That is, affect, or bodily vibrations and intensities, are captured and coded through discourses and material realities of exclusion, hierarchies of difference, and they politically orient bodies toward feelings of hate and love, desire and repulsion, and, for the purposes of this chapter, apathy and sympathy.

Hemmings (2005) maintains that Ahmed's *The Cultural Politics of Emotion* (2004a) is one of the most important interventions in the field. Centring the "cultural politics" of emotion in her work, Ahmed tracks how emotions circulate among bodies and why and how they stick to certain bodies. Arguing that emotions are central to thoughts themselves, even as they have been marginalized in academic scholarship in favour of rational and objective approaches to theorizing, Ahmed has successfully established a theory of affective economies (4). Although she is interested in affect, her focus on emotions in particular is foundational to my understanding of the political economy of affect. Ahmed argues that emotions register the proximity of others and that objects can take on affective value, especially in their circulation. She maintains that emotions impress themselves on individual and collective bodies in the spaces between bodies and signs. Claiming that emotions are neither solely private nor inwardly oriented, Ahmed asserts that emotions are social in that they shape the boundaries and surfaces of bodies. For example, using a lengthy citation from a white supremacist website, Ahmed (2004b) claims that hate and love, as circulating emotions between bodies and signs, impress themselves on collective bodies, in this case the nation. According to her, the subject ("the white nationalist, the average white man, the white housewife, the white working man, the white citizen, and the white Christian Farmer") is presented as being endangered by others in terms of security, wealth, and jobs (117). Through hate, there is a passionate attachment to those worthy of love—those read as white: "Hate is economic; it circulates between signifiers in relationships of difference and displacement" (119). For Ahmed, emotions work as a form of capital. That is, affect does not reside as intensity within a sign or body but circulates accumulating affective value in its exchange. As communicative displays of affect, emotions are *productive* in meaning-making processes. Borrowing from Marx's concept of "commodity fetishism," Ahmed maintains that emotions gain value in their exchange and circulation over time, and like commodities under capitalism economies of affect ensure that the history of their production (labour and labour time) is obscured.

AFFECT AND VIOLENCE AGAINST WOMEN

Why study the affective politics of anti-violence initiatives? The study of affect reveals how and why we move and are moved. Thus, studying affect and campaigns to end violence against women allows us to ask how representations of such violence in campaigns are e/affective in how they make meaning emotionally and generate political feelings (Gould 2009). Expanding on the "affective turn" in the social sciences to include a study of discourses on development, I use affect theory and studies on emotion to analyze how discursive manoeuvres such as stories of violence, images, and texts can express empowerment and pain, for example, and how crucial the emotionality of texts, such as "The Situation" map, is to how we understand the issue of violence against women. As emotions move between bodies and signs, emotionality surrounding the elimination of this violence circulates in an affective economy. Importantly, such economies produce some political and emotional possibilities but refuse others. That is, as emotions circulate, participants of campaigns such as UNiTE and Say NO are oriented toward particular political feelings, emotions, and actions. Such campaigns also foreclose other possibilities for feeling because affective attachments are *driven by and reflect social inequality and oppression*. In this chapter, I maintain that, as the United Nations targets global violence against women as an urgent concern, the orientation of participants toward certain political feelings affects the outcome of global efforts to end this violence.

Expressions of women's experiences of violence are inherently affective. Stories of survivors' experiences have long shaped the history of the feminist anti-violence movement. As an issue that pushed the demarcation of public and private boundaries, the sharing of experience was essential to the establishment of publicly recognized "facts" and statistics and helped in international recognition of the issue and its eradication by making it feel "real" (Joachim 2007). Stories of women's experiences have helped to move people emotionally toward taking action. Stories told to development workers and academics, including anthropologists, circulate widely in the development industry for a variety of purposes. Using the phrase "to bring the self into the other," Spivak (2004, 556) is critical of how Third World women's stories are manipulated to serve the interests of Western philosophy, including human rights and development theory. Moreover, her work has been highly critical of the obscuring of women's voices and agency in Western academic texts (see Spivak 1988). In the essay "Under Western Eyes Revisited," Mohanty (2003) critically analyzes the representations of development discourse and argues that women's experiences are too often misrepresented as being homogeneous and simplified, without context and within the boundaries of Western saviour discourses. Mirroring this claim, Narayan (1997, 101) argues that stories of violence against women in the Third World in particular are turned into "quick-facts" of easily digestible categories of language such as "dowry murders" when they cross borders. In establishing the urgency with which Third World women's oppression must be eradicated, the complexity of the issue, along with Third World women's agency in their own empowerment, is routinely ignored or obscured.

In critical work on representations, feminist and critical race scholarship has long pointed to the material consequences of inappropriate representations, including interventions organized and deployed in the name of women's rights around the world. Given the sophisticated literature on representations of violence against women in the Third World, affect theory can be understood as complementary to thinking about discursive renderings of violence against women within discourses of development. In particular, affect theory opens up the possibility of inquiries that do not rely on the dichotomy of good/bad representations of others but ask, instead, What are the affective politics of representations? That is, by investigating the cultural work of representations, affect theory allows us to ask what are the social, political, and economic relations of affect in discourses of development in which narratives of violence against women are invoked.

Given that the UNiTE campaign has emerged within the development industry as the most extensive global strategy to eliminate violence against women, the affective politics of this campaign are particularly complex. In particular, the history of the United Nations as the location for women's organizing against violence provides a fascinating site for a study of the affective politics of a global anti-violence campaign.

AFFECT AND REPRESENTATION

Critically engaging with debates coming out of the poststructural turn in cultural theory and feminist studies, theorists of affect reject the notion that "critical thinking" must always be about pointing out what is already known about identities and locating them on a stable map in which they are conceptualized as being fixed in place. As Puar (2007) maintains, the "affective turn" invites scholars to think about the body and identity in non-essentialist ways. That is, affect theory opens up possibilities to bring the body back into dialogue without mapping static identities onto bodies or making universal claims to experience based upon how identity is read off the body. Significantly, some theorists of affect argue for bringing the body into scholarship by claiming that critical thinking is reduced too often to deconstructivist methods of revealing how discursive representations are racist, (hetero)sexist, ableist, or classist. Those critical of poststructural thinking often encourage those interested in the discursive to bring back in what is invoked as "the material": the body (Hemmings 2005). In feminist theory in particular, scholars have argued that poststructuralism overemphasizes power relations to the extent that there is no hope for the emancipation of marginalized subjects. Regrettably, the importance of poststructural projects that question both representational politics and the "cultural work they do" is overly dismissed at times by critics (Treichler 1999). In feminist, queer, and crip scholarship, important questions continue to be asked about representation and identity through a variety of theories and projects (see McRuer 2012). Furthermore, as critical race and postcolonial theorists have aptly demonstrated, representational and identity politics have "material" realities in terms of their implications for activism, policy, and solidarity work (see Mohanty 2003). I agree with Puar (2007, 212), who suggests that affect theory can be used as a *complement to rather than a replacement of* poststructural theory and representational analyses. My turn to affect theory in this chapter should not be read as a dismissal of discourse analysis. In fact, the first two chapters of this book primarily explore representational questions. However, my analysis of anti-violence campaigns requires an affective turn here because the texts that I analyze require more than representational analyses. Emotions saturate representations. My analysis of the emotionality of a text is concerned with how "emotion incites, shapes, and is generated by practices of meaning-making"; since this chapter focuses on campaigns, such analyses "invite scholarly attention to the affective dimensions of sense-making" (Gould 2009, 13).

AFFECTIVE REPRESENTATIONS "OVER THERE"

In the study of international development communication, Alhassan (2009) uses the term "telescopic philanthropy" to explain the discursive and performative functions of saviour discourses. In particular, he is concerned with how the Third World is made visible from afar. Citing *Bleak House* by Dickens, Alhassan describes how the character Mrs. Jellyby neglects both her house and her children but is obsessed with projects designed to save Africans in the Congo, ignoring problems "here" and focusing on poverty "there." Alhassan understands telescopic philanthropy to denote how discourses of development magnify, highlight, and focus on the Third World as a site for saving. Although his interest is in representation and philanthropy, my concern is with the affective capacity of telescopic philanthropy essential to understanding the affect of the UNiTE worldwide map of violence against women.

According to the *Oxford English Dictionary* (2013a), the word *telescopic* is defined as "relating to or made with a telescope." Here it is the relational aspect of telescopic philanthropy that is the most significant. As Ahmed (2004a) maintains, affect is relational. Sliding between bodies and signs and impressing itself on the surfaces of bodies, affect is not contained within an object but moves between objects. In Alhassan's (2009) conception of telescopic philanthropy, signs such as hunger and poverty that can be *seen* by (white) Western saviours by means of a telescope function to represent backwardness or lack of progress and invite charitable responses. *Feeling through a telescope*, then, is an affective project between distant bodies and those signs, and the telescope intensifies affective responses as it magnifies the lines of sight. If, as Alhassan suggests, poverty is a sign of backwardness as seen from afar, with its magnification through a telescope, feeling telescopically can be described as the affective relations between the bodies that see and those that are seen and the signs that not only signify but also generate affect, emotion, and even political feeling.

Circulating as an object that can create and shape political feelings, their direction, how they move, and to whom they stick, the "UNiTE Worldwide" map, for example, does affective work for the campaign. By augmenting participants' focus on particular countries as the most urgent and problematic, the map not only frames the representation of global violence against women telescopically but also narrows the possibilities of feeling through such representation. Telescopic feeling, then, refers to the political feelings possible in being affected and affecting from afar via a telescopic view. Limiting the scope of view, and thus the scope of feeling, telescopic feeling relies on the associations among singular or small signs and a historical archive of identification of these signs, as well as on what is obscured by the process of magnification: namely, production of the line of sight. That is, the possibilities for affective response are shaped by what can be seen and thus felt by participants as well as what goes unseen in or is obscured by the frame of focus.

In the UNiTE campaign, the scope of the initiative is narrow. Within a limited frame that highlights Southern countries as areas of pressing concern, a campaign participant is asked, or even obliged, to have affective attachments to particular countries and to demonstrate concern about specific practices of violence against women deemed most critical by the United Nations. As Hemmings (2005) suggests, affective attachments are not made at random but driven by social inequalities and discursive structures. The UNiTE campaign makes it clear that the scope of awareness and advocacy initiatives is restricted to places historically marked as "over there." Although some participants of the UNiTE campaign might reside in the places marked as urgent and problematic, the campaign relies on an orientalist conception of the "West and the rest" by demarcating the boundaries between the developed and undeveloped world, the civilized and uncivilized world, the modern and backward world. By highlighting urgent and problematic sites, the UNiTE map encourages participants to "zoom in" on the emphasized continents positioned as "afar" and disconnected from the West. Disallowing connections between violence in the West and violence in the Third World, and obscuring violence committed, encouraged, or tacitly accepted by the West, the map positions the Global South as the site of exigent intervention and the West as the intervener, regardless of the participant's place of interaction with the campaign or experience of gendered violence.

Global violence against women is an issue that can make one feel overwhelmed and confused by the various manifestations transnationally, by the levels of violence and how they intersect with other forms of oppression, as well as by the colonial legacy and imperial present within which violent practices are embedded. However, by narrowing the frame of focus, the telescopic representation of violence against women prohibits the possibility of being immobilized by a sense of confusion in the UNiTE campaign. Instead, the transnational phenomenon of this violence is made knowable, manageable, and fixable. Feeling telescopically, then, relies on the production of otherness or "over thereness" in regard to this violence to move people to act *now*. Since the issue is framed as taking place over there, participants can feel as if they are in control, that the issue is manageable, that they have the power to fix it because they know about the subject. This is an example of the affective nature of discourses of urgency. It is not that some violence against women is explicitly presented as more pressing but that an audience of such campaigns is meant to feel the urgency. Moreover, the audience can trust that the United Nations, as an expert, is already on its way to solving this urgent problem by way of the map's oversimplification of its "on the ground" work.

The UNiTE campaign has been launched in Latin America, the Caribbean, Africa, and the Asia-Pacific. Through mobilizing participants' passion to eliminate violence against women globally, these have emerged as the sites most in need of global anti-violence activism. Historically problematized as "backward" and poor (Escobar 1995), the continents that the UNiTE campaign has chosen to target are associated with an enormous archive of knowledge produced by colonizers and development experts and, I suggest, an archive of feelings (see Kapoor 2008; Loomba 1998; McClintock 1995; and Said 1978). Although feelings do not appear in the object of the UNiTE map, they are generative in the way that affect moves between the object of the map and violence against women as a sign often understood in the development community as a symptom of backwardness and a cause of underdevelopment (Carrillo 1992). Feelings of sorrow, sympathy, outrage, grief, and passion to take urgent action interlock with stereotypical and racist assumptions, saviour discourses, and political feelings of charity and benevolence made available to participants through how countries are represented as the prime targets of intervention.

Moreover, the UNiTE map functions not only as an abstraction but also as a representation of absolute space that works to fix bodies in affective relationships with UNiTE participants. The emphasis on the Global South, in both spatial terms and through the discursive practices of the campaign, positions Third World bodies in a particular place within an affective economy. The mapping of violence against women as UNiTE has done allows some bodies to be read as perpetrators of violent practices and thus targets of our disdain or sympathy. Importantly, some bodies are not represented on the map as perpetrators or victims, and thus they are not explicitly intended to be targets of affective or urgent responses, though these bodies certainly gain importance in the circulation of affect. That is, the historical accumulation of affect, expressed through emotions such as sympathy and pity, shapes not only the continents highlighted on the UNiTE map but also the continents unmarked on it. Those countries that fade into the background of the map are effectively represented as gender equitable and disconnected from the violence of Southern countries. Importantly, they are not presented as the targets of political feelings intended to move people instantly to take action (in prescribed ways) against gendered violence.

For example, as outlined in "The Situation" overview, UNiTE describes "Female Genital Mutilation/Cutting (FGM/C)" as a major concern for Africa (UN 2012b). Because the campaign highlights the continent as a space open for urgent anti-violence intervention, participants are encouraged to associate "traditional" or "extreme" practices of violence with the mapping of absolute space in which they are said to occur. As postcolonial, Third World, and critical race feminists have articulated in a thorough body of work on the representation of Third World women, oppressive practices such as violence are presented as similar, unchanging over time, culturally based, and manageable by saving women from the "dangerous brown men" who dominate them (see, e.g., Bhattacharyya 2008; Mohanty 2003; Narayan 1997; and Spivak 1988). Highlighting Africa, and focusing on FGM/C in particular, can couple UNiTE participants' feelings of pity and sympathy for victims of such acts with outrage toward, disdain for, or fear of perpetrators of such acts.

Because the UNiTE map positions the Third World as the site of urgent intervention, racialized Third World men become the objects of emotions such as scorn or fear. According to Puar (2007, 187), affect slides between bodies that look alike or "seem [a]like." Borrowing from Ahmed's (2004a) theorization of Fanon's (2008) account of racial affect, Puar (2007) understands fear to gain value in an affective economy in that it circulates between signifiers and bodies. Since emotions do not reside in bodies but move between them, subjects are bound together by affect, creating "pools of suspicious bodies" (184). Emotions such as fear and hate slide between bodies but get stuck on bodies historically associated with fear and hate. Here affect is made meaningful by associating bodily intensities with emotional expressions, histories, and systems of power. In this anti-violence campaign, racialized men from the Global South are highlighted as perpetrators of gendered violence by the construction of women from the Global South as its foremost victims. Although not all Southern men perpetrate violence against women, fear and hate, as non-residential emotions, can be materialized on any body that "could be" a perpetrator. Distinct from the visibly discerned "looks like," the concept "seems like" gestures toward the realm of affect (187). Others are made fearsome through misrecognition. Importantly, those understood as "us" are not similarly feared or hated. In the UNiTE campaign, the colour-coded map functions to evoke non-residential emotions that slide between imagined bodies that seem like one another. As contagious bodies to be feared, an entire populace with a similar profile can be targeted for intervention through misrecognition. As UNiTE makes clear through its men's leaders project, Southern men require leadership to end practices of violence against women (UN 2012e). Importantly, such feelings are already known in that fear of racialized men's violence is not a new concept but floats as a popular understanding.[6]

Such representations not only collapse complex and changing practices of violence onto entire continents with many nations, and many cultures and religions, histories of colonization and imperialism, types of nationalism and governance, but also invite particular political feelings. That is, the UniTE map communicates to participants of the campaign which sites of intervention are the most urgent, and it shapes the countries and practices of violence against women about which participants should feel passionate. As a space in which extreme forms of violence against women are understood to be practised, political feelings of fear and pity are affective responses that become possible through telescopic feeling. By highlighting only targeted countries, UNiTE forecloses the possibility of participants' feeling accountable to neo-colonization and global economic regimes, which have influenced or sustained such practices of violence, including economic violence, and how Westerners understand the issue. Instead, participants are encouraged to feel sympathy for victims in the moment, without ever making connections between the Global North and South, developed and underdeveloped, or Western World and Third World and the complex manifestations of violence against women within and between nations. Such connections are feminist concerns earmarked for the patriarchal time zone of later.

Although the UNiTE map itself does not contain affect, it appears within the larger UNiTE campaign as an affective sign. Mapping the Global South resonates with intensity within the campaign because of its hegemonic circulation within discourses and practices of development. As Ahmed (2004b, 120) maintains, affect circulates within an economy of accumulation in which value is gained over time: "The more [emotions] circulate, the more affective they become." Obscuring the historical legacy of the creation and mapping of the Third World, the emotions generated and inextricably tied to colonization—such as intrigue, fear, sympathy, and altruism—and embedded in current

---

6   See Bhattacharyya (2008) on the popularization of representations of
     dangerous racialized men, especially in the post-9/11 period.

development discourses and practices circulate with significant value in the UNiTE campaign. Moreover, given the historical archive of feelings associated with violence against women and the Third World, especially in regard to misogynist men and patriarchal cultures, the already accumulating disdain for racialized men as perpetrators of violence, and the sympathy for racialized women as the victims of this violence (when savable by white men and women), circulate with affective value. Imagined as absolute spaces, continents such as Africa emerge on the UNiTE map and in the campaign as objective forms of an urgent but manageable set of problems and invite participants not only to become aware of violent practices in the continent but also to take action immediately by making donations.

AFFECTIVE POSSIBILITIES: SAY(ING) NO AND DONATING FOR CHANGE

According to UNiTE, the campaign aims to "galvanize action across the UN system to prevent and punish violence against women" (UN 2012f). To incite action, UNiTE provides a variety of opportunities for participants at various levels, including government, civil society, and individual levels. A major component of the UNiTE mandate is to involve men and boys in the elimination of violence against women and girls. Following a decade of pursuing a "men and development" agenda among development institutions, UNiTE maintains the importance of including men and boys in the often feminized work of "doing gender" in development. For UNiTE (2012e), men are raised to accept and perpetuate sexist behaviour. However, many men feel uncomfortable with men's violence against women and seek emotional support from other men to intervene. The Say NO campaign provides role models for men to stimulate passion for the elimination of violence against women (UN 2012d).

Say NO is not just for men. According to the UNiTE website, Say NO is a "global platform for advocacy and action by individuals, governments, civil society and UN partners which initiates, supports and demonstrates local and national advocacy efforts towards ending violence against women and girls" (UN 2012d). For Secretary-General Ban Ki-moon, breaking the silence and speaking out are the keys to eliminating violence against women (UN 2012a). Launched by UN Women in 2009, the Say NO campaign uses an interactive website as well as social media to encourage participation from "people from all walks of life, online and on the ground" (UN 2012d). According to UNiTE, saying no to violence against women is vital. Citing narratives of such violence made popular by development discourse, campaign material claims that violent practices not only harm families and communities but also stunt development and undermine economic growth. Mirroring the UNiTE campaign, the Say NO website suggests that everyone has a role to play in ending the global pandemic of this violence and that "the time to act together is NOW" (UN 2012d). Saying no, in this case, is an immediate need, represented as being directly connected to elimination of this violence. Aiming to both highlight and trigger actions taken against violence against women, the Say NO initiative tries to generate support through donations to the UN Trust Fund to End Violence against Women.

To take action by saying no and donating money, participants must feel the urgency with which the global pandemic of violence against women must be eliminated now. To affect participants to effect change, the Say NO campaign material does emotional work. For example, when a participant chooses to "take action" on the website, he or she is told "we know you *want* to make a difference" (UN 2012d; emphasis added). Here the word *want* orients participants toward action, and associated emotions such as desire, ambition, and aspiration stick to the bodies of those who long to help. This "want" can provide the conditions for a collective desire and thus a collective identity for those who yearn to help. In contrast, others might be read as those who have no desire to make a difference. As an emotional text, the Say NO website invites participants to feel empowered as agents of change and to feel sorry for those who cannot help themselves. Figures of speech can generate affect, and the emotionality of text functions through both how texts move and how emotions are named in them. In placing importance on mapping the circulation of words as emotionally generative, Ahmed (2004a) argues that feelings shape different kinds of actions and orientations, such as taking action to end violence against women.

As a participant, there are many ways to take action in the Say NO campaign. Importantly, grassroots organizations have joined UNiTE, and specifically the Say NO campaign, to effect change on the ground. Organizations such as the Rainbow Women's Network have used Say NO as a platform to support lesbian, gay, bisexual, transgender, and intersex women, female ex-prisoners, and sex workers in Fiji who face violence and discrimination based upon sexual orientation or stigma related to sex work (UN Women 2012). This important work should not be downplayed. In fact, it does exactly what Ferguson (2009) and Prügl (2015) suggest—that top-down neo-liberal development work can actually crack open unexpected possibilities for feminist and transformational work. The UNiTE platform might help, in fact, to fund and support sophisticated and radical strategies to end violence against women in communities around the world. However, such optimism must be balanced with an understanding of the system at work here. According to an interview that I conducted with Todd Minerson in 2012, the sheer size and bureaucracy of the UN structure can stifle the passion and commitment of individuals to do great work. Given the complex nature of the United Nations and the issue of global violence against women, the UNiTE and Say No campaigns are simplified representations of a problem that requires a nuanced approach. According to an interview with Jane Parpart in 2012, "nuances are difficult for organizations to deal with." Although people within organizations know the complexities, they also know how to present an issue to the public.

The problem of simplicity in practice is demonstrated by how the United Nations creates an extremely accessible action for participants online, even if the outcomes of funding are multifaceted and generative. In the West, participants are asked to sign up through a petition and to donate to the UN Trust Fund. Significantly, both actions can be taken online and require little or no collective action in person. In fact, the campaign discourages collective feelings of agitation, anger, and outrage, or uneasiness with the United Nations as the most appropriate organization to fund grassroots organizations, even if they are doing incredible work. Although grassroots mobilization is encouraged for participants in countries marked with high levels of violence, as the most visible form of partaking in the initiative, Western participants are only asked to become sympathetic enough to sign up with the campaign and donate money to the United Nations. Urgency is manufactured here through the interface of the online donation system. One does not need to think about the consequences of funding structures later but can simply say no and donate now. When violence against women is constructed as urgent, it both provides an instant sense of relief for "doing something" about the issue and prompts "feel good" emotions that come with saying no and donating.

In her foundational work on social movements, Gould (2009) argues that the questions of how and why people take political action can be answered by understanding the affective realm. Similarly, analyzing the affective politics of the Say NO campaign reveals how participants are encouraged to take action against violence against women. Gould claims that the term "movement" gestures toward the realm of affect. Providing a case study of ACT UP, a direct action AIDS organization in the United States, she reveals how affect, being moved, and making movements involve bodily intensities, emotions, feelings, and passions. Analyzing how political feelings are generated, sustained, and altered in political actions, Gould is concerned with how individual feelings become collective or collectivized in social movements. Pointing to the importance of understanding how feelings shape political actions, her case study of ACT UP illustrates affective possibilities and how they are shaped by activist strategies. For example, Gould questions the limitation of possibilities for grieving the deaths in queer communities at the height of the HIV/AIDS pandemic in the United States. As members of these communities died, participants of the direct action group were called on to feel anger and outrage toward discriminatory health-care and government policies rather than sorrow and sadness. As Gould notes, by taking direct action through protests, performances, and rallies, ACT UP participants had their political feelings shaped, and sometimes foreclosed, by the movement's trajectory or "political horizon" (3).

Similarly, UNiTE's use of the phrase "take action" signals affect. Borrowing Gould's (2009) notion of political feelings, the Say NO campaign and the UN Trust Fund rely on the circulation of emotional words and the representation of objects as signs of feelings. The political feelings permissible and prohibited are constructed by the affective structure of the campaign.

SIGNING ON, SAYING NO

As part of the twofold UNiTE to End Violence against Women awareness and advocacy campaign, the Say NO initiative is a social mobilization platform on which participants are encouraged to add their names to the roster of those who have said no to violence against women. According to the website (UN 2012d), "Say NO records what individuals, organizations and governments worldwide are doing to end violence against women. Whether you volunteer at a shelter, donate, reach out to students or advocate for better policies—every action counts." Say NO claims that anywhere from "15 to 76 percent of women may be abused in their lifetime." Given this potentially large percentage, Say NO maintains that the time is *now* to end the violence. Spreading a feeling of urgency, the initiative requests that participants let UNiTE "count [them] in to make a difference." According to the website, over 5,597,648 actions had been taken as of May 2013. Gesturing toward the affective realm, a political horizon is generated in and through the initiative's emphasis on the *desire* to join, to feel a sense of belonging by being counted in, and to feel empowered to end the violence *now*. Participants are told that their voices matter, and by signing on to the Say NO campaign their voices will be added to the 5 million that have already communicated to governments around the world that ending violence against women is an urgent priority. Adding one's name to "this powerful call to take action" is expressed through political feelings.

Although an emotional response to violence against women globally is invoked in other parts of the campaign, the Say NO petition centres on a participant's experience of empowerment by joining the campaign. The language of empowerment operates through signs in the campaign, simultaneously conveying and concealing histories of power and attaching power affectively to some bodies while bypassing others. Since the Say NO campaign focuses on the emotions of participants, those interpellated as the "you" who should "want" to be counted in are the most important to the initiative. Assuming that you should want to join the campaign via signing the petition, you are allowed to enter into a relationship with those who experience violence as an individual who feels a desire to help, who seeks to be empowered by joining "this powerful campaign" (UN 2012d). Since the UNiTE campaign outlines the Third World as the site of intervention (UN 2012c), signing up with the campaign functions as an entrance into a relationship with the other. It is this form of contact with both the objects and the objectives of the campaign that solidifies the political feelings that a participant can express in it.

The focus on joining and belonging situates power within the hands of those who choose to say no and sign the petition. Thus, those rewarded for joining the campaign, rather than those who have survived violence, are allowed to feel empowered by the initiative. The "aboutness" of the campaign is those who join. In *The Cultural Politics of Emotion*, Ahmed (2004a, 21) uses an instructional letter inviting donations to end the pain caused by landmines to describe her use of the term "aboutness." Suggesting that development and humanitarian campaigns can ensure that participants are aligned with the other through differentiation, rather than through shared experiences or interests by means of solidarity, Ahmed claims that "our" feelings remain the most important. The imperative to feel something for the other is not about feelings of pain experienced by victims of landmines, for example, but about our feelings "*about* their suffering, an 'aboutness' that ensure[s] that they remain the object of 'our feeling'" (21). Thus, the affective politics of pain are as much or more about our feelings than the other's pain. For Sherene Razack (2007), this aboutness can be described as "stealing the pain of others." She argues that charitable sympathy produces a process of consumption that is the antithesis of collective outrage for the rights of others. I will return to the ideas of political feeling and charitable consumption later in this chapter.

Comparable to the case of the anti-landmine campaign letter, I maintain that the aboutness of the Say NO petition centres on our empowerment and our desire to help, to belong, to want to join the global collective of people saying no to violence. The aboutness of the campaign is not the violence that women around the world are vulnerable to, but instead the promise of empowerment in the act of saying no. Overcoming violence against women as a global epidemic, promised by the Say NO campaign, is a means by which the participant is empowered and can feel an immediate sense of belonging to a collective body of those temporally affected by the campaign.

Empowerment and belonging are sticky attachments within this affective economy. As Ahmed (2004a) maintains, the stickiness of affect, and the act of emotions getting stuck on bodies, including collective bodies, function through signs and objects, and their historical associations often work through concealment. Ahmed claims that the stickiness of an object should be understood not as an object itself being sticky but as the accumulation of affect from that which the object touches. Signs become sticky through repetition, the welcomeness of the sign, and the labour behind its repetition is concealed in the Say NO campaign. That is, if a word is habitually circulated within a set of discourses, then its "use" becomes intrinsic, and the history of its circulation is concealed. The language of joining, belonging, and being empowered is sticky because of the affective value as emotional words that circulate routinely in development campaigns. Specifically, using the language of empowerment in campaigns aiming to end poverty, suffering, and violence in the Third World is affectively sticky because the signs and objects of the Third World are regularly circulated within discourses of development.

"Empowerment" is considered a "motherhood" term in development discourses (Parpart, Rai, and Staudt 2002). In gender and development circles, empowerment is an all-embracing, and often depoliticized, discursive manoeuvre used to support a variety of practices and projects aimed at generating gender equity throughout the Third World. Empowerment is an expression that emerged from liberal feminist agitation against representations and practices that assume Third World women's passiveness, but often appearing without historical context and circulating affective value. Although the language of empowerment is often stuck to Third World women's bodies, specifically bodies historically represented as powerless, in this case participants of the Say NO campaign are promised empowerment now. That is not to say that the UNiTE campaign at large is not interested in Third World women's empowerment as a means to overcome violence against women; yet the Say NO initiative's aboutness centres on participants who say no online.

To borrow Gould's (2009) term, the "political horizon" of the Say NO campaign is shaped by language that describes the emotionality of "taking action" (UN 2012d). Importantly, the affective value of the language of empowerment, desire, and belonging in the campaign disallows anger, sadness, outrage, or grief about violent practices in their various manifestations and instead focuses on the emotional benefits that can be attained by saying no to violence. Additionally, the participant is positioned as a Westerner by way of situating her or him as a benevolent helper of others. Because the participant asked to say no to violence is differentiated from others who experience violence and require the aid of those with the power to say no and effect change, the feeling of belonging is not shared. The affective strategies of the campaign include how it generates a collective body of empowered individuals who belong through their desire to help others. In opposition are the bodies on which this affective strategy to empower is impressed through telescopic feelings. That is, a collective body of others over there who need urgent help is generated in contrast to those here and empowered to belong now.

Others enter an affective relationship with those who desire to belong and be empowered through representations of their pain. In particular, the elimination of Third World women's experiences of pain and suffering is presented as causally linked to the support and empowerment of those who sign the Say NO petition or make a donation to the UN Trust Fund.

AFFECTING PAIN: THE UN TRUST FUND

Say NO participants are also encouraged to donate to the UN Trust Fund to End Violence against Women. By asking "won't you help?" the campaign claims that "every contribution is vital. Every dollar tells women and girls who experience violence that they are not forgotten" (UN 2012d). According to UN Women (2014), the UN Trust Fund "is a testimony to the global consciousness that violence against women and girls is neither inevitable nor acceptable." As a grant-making mechanism, the UN Trust Fund supports various organizations working to address violence against women and girls. Taking action by donating to the fund orients UNiTE participants in a similar way as the Say NO petition. Generating a collective body of those who desire to help *now*, participants enter an affective relationship with those represented as being in need of urgent help. As anti-violence initiatives, the UNiTE and Say NO campaigns rely on the communication of Third World women's experiences of pain, suffering, and trauma. Using stories of their experiences of violence, the Say NO initiative aims affectively to move participants to take action by donating to the UN Trust Fund.

Physical pain and suffering as outcomes of violent practices are often described as bodily sensations. However, according to Ahmed (2004a, 15), pain that does damage to the skin's surface also opens bodies up to others. Pain circulates in the public domain, not as a discursive concept, but as an "intensification." That is, how one experiences pain not only corresponds to damage to the body and psyche but also involves meaning-making practices. Knowing pain as bodily sensation can occur only through association with other "feeling states" (23). Differentiating pain from other feelings, expressing the sensation of pain, and recognizing pain in others is what Ahmed terms "intensification." Using skin as an example, Ahmed claims that it is a shell for the body that acts as a container, but it is also where others can "impress" upon us, to use Ahmed's term, and thus pain can change the surfaces of bodies. In other words, that which separates bodies also connects them to others. Ahmed writes that "pain is hence bound up in how we inhabit the world, how we live in relationship to the surfaces, bodies, and objects that make up our dwelling places" (27). Understanding pain as a bodily sensation, but also an experience that places bodies in affective relationships with others, she asks not "what is pain?" but "what *does* pain do?" (27).

Here I ask, What does pain *do* in the context of a global anti-violence campaign? How do pain, suffering, and trauma affect women who experience violence? How do these experiences of violence and narratives of pain circulate in an affective and urgent economy? As a campaign that aims to move participants to make donations, the Say NO initiative relies on connections or attachments to be made to the survivors of violence highlighted by UniTE through storytelling. Individual women are asked to tell their stories of pain and how they have overcome pain. To be touched or moved in a certain way by this telescopic encounter with others requires an immediate affective response to pain. In the context of development, affective economies of pain are political. The expression of pain through emotion or emotional words and images gains value in their circulation and repetition in an economy that relies on donations. The alignment of participants toward donorship, rather than solidarity, is a significant outcome of this campaign, one that I will return to later in this chapter. As narratives of pain open up bodies to an alignment with others who feel empathy or sympathy, single stories of suffering also conceal historical context and complex questions of the political, economic, and social aspects of violence against women insofar as a simple monetary donation is understood as a real solution to the urgency of eliminating this violence globally.

Ahmed (2004a, 20) asks "how does pain enter politics?" Centring landmines in her discussion of the affect evoked in public discourses of pain, she studies a letter from Christian Aid to previous donors describing the pain caused by landmines. Arguing that a discursive manoeuvre of causality posits landmines as the cause of pain, and not the political and military relations in which landmines are manufactured and operationalized, relies as much on affective politics of empowerment as on the affective circulation of trauma. That is, Ahmed argues that the Christian Aid letter in question uses landmines to signify pain while also ensuring that notions of support and empowerment are linked to donations. Similar to the anti-landmine initiative, the Say NO campaign uses a variety of practices of violence against women to signify pain while ensuring that support is linked to the UN Trust Fund and empowerment to those who choose to donate. Pain as a bodily sensation related to violence is expressed through women's emotions and the use of emotional words. Political feelings, or that which participants are supposed to feel by the structure of the campaign, are attached to the stories told. Which stories are told and which are untold in the Say NO campaign reflect how participants are asked to generate attachments to Third World women. Unsurprisingly, stories of violence against women, often exoticized and culturalized in Western academic scholarship and development campaign materials, take centre stage in the campaign. Mirroring UNiTE's situational overview (UN 2012b), the Say NO campaign uses "extreme" practices of violence against women to affect its participants to act now.

In an article entitled "Cambodia: Reclaiming Life after Acid Attacks" (UN 2011a), UNiTE presents the story of Chhean, who stood up to her sister's husband in 2008 when he sold his two-year-old daughter to a trafficking ring to purchase a motorbike. When Chhean threatened her brother-in-law with a lawsuit, he threw acid on her. It burned her face, eyes, shoulder, and left hand. Chhean, a widow and sole provider for her four children, is represented as an empowered woman who aimed to save her sister's family from a violent man and experienced violence because she took action on her own. Her pain is represented through the impressions on her body left by the acid as well as her sombre facial expression as she sits in front of a sewing machine.

Through the action of sewing, Chhean is represented as being empowered. Assumed to be able to find employment, even though she is physically scarred from the violent attack, she can be understood to have overcome her pain through the support of the UN Trust Fund to End Violence against Women. Through her emotional expression presented in this image, as well as the emotional work of her story of pain and empowerment, her narrative is aimed at moving participants to donate. In particular, her story is directly connected to the work of Acid Survivors Trust International, an organization sponsored by the UN Trust Fund. According to the story, Chhean and her sister are now active in their community working with survivors of acid attacks. UNiTE claims that, "despite the scars, Chhean and Ponleu continue to build their confidence as survivors and help those around them" (UN 2011a). Not only are they represented as disabled heroes who have overcome their physical impairments (Clare 1999; McRuer 2006), but their story functions to evoke affective responses from participants.

UNiTE maintains that acid attacks are common and widespread in Cambodia and that most women "find themselves in the dark for adequate legal, medical and psychological support" (UN 2011a). With no information provided about the availability of acid as a tool to commit violence against women, as there is for guns in the United States, for example, participants are brought into this story of extreme pain and suffering through how the UN Trust Fund is positioned as the linchpin to end violence against women in Cambodia. By placing participants in opposition to others who experience violence, and aligning them with those who desire to say no, campaign materials evoke feelings of empowerment through how participants are asked to become involved with the United Nations. Although Cambodian women and local organizations are represented as agents in the elimination of violence against women, it is clear to participants that their donations will allow the United Nations to support these women and organizations to become empowered to do so. Being part of this story as the primary agent of an anti-violence initiative shapes how participants are located in the worlds created by the campaign.

In this story, participants belong to one world by their proximity to a collective body of empowered donors and make donations telescopically to another world shaped affectively through pain and suffering. Agency is in the hands of donors through the work of the United Nations, presented as a trusted source of a speedy trickle-down approach to gender equality in the development community. What is concealed through this UNiTE story is the historical debate about the United Nations as a site for women's organizing and activism as well as the NGOization of grassroots mobilization that requires structured funding regimes that limit the work of the organization on the ground (Alvarez 1999; Desai 2002; Poster and Salime 2002). The political horizon of feelings allowed is structured by stories of pain and overcoming that evoke feelings of positivity, benevolence, and pride that come with taking action via donating. In the Say NO campaign, donors' quick actions provide the necessary resources to eliminate violence, an urgent concern. Such "do good" feelings available to participants conceal both the complex history and the present process of development from these distant places of pain and suffering.

Significantly, such stories of pain do emotional work at the expense of both nuanced representations of the issue and active mobilizations against violence against women in Bangladesh. As Elora Halim Chowdhury (2011, xvi) claims, the work of organizations such as Naripokkho, which have created the "conceptual and organizational groundwork for placing acid attacks on women and girls into the global landscape" and provide services for acid survivors, is buried in the discourse of UN benevolence and self-congratulatory remarks about its work. She argues that, more than obscuring the work of these organizations, the United Nations, among other actors, actually co-opts their work, and this has resulted in a rewriting of the history that has led to public recognition of acid burning. I agree with Chowdhury that the focus on the United Nations and participants' donations obscures organizing on the ground. The orientation toward donations, rather than solidarity with groups such as Naripokkho, appropriates the historical legacy of women's mobilizations against acid attacks in Bangladesh, mobilizations that have always been urgently needed, and forecloses the possibilities of tracing this history, which would lead to very different anti-violence strategies at the transnational level.

Testimonies of pain do political work in discursive and affective realms when they are placed alongside each other. In their circulation and repetition, similar stories of pain and empowerment gain affective value. Each story arouses feelings of pity and sympathy. Such political feelings about cases of violence against women are manageable if one just says no. They can be easily overcome if one just donates. The Say

NO campaign uses many stories of violence to encourage donations. Another story comes from a woman named Laura in an article entitled "Guatemala: Young Mayan Women Shape the Future" (UN 2011b). Laura is a twenty-four-year-old Indigenous woman who lost her mother at an early age and had to leave school to take care of her eight siblings. Her father regularly used alcohol to cope, and Laura was "his regular victim." She is now an anti-violence advocate through a project implemented by Population Council Guatemala, a grantee of the UN Trust Fund to End Violence against Women. According to the website, "[Laura] wasn't always this confident. But after over a decade of beatings, she made a decision to finally stand up for herself and create a different life, one of strength and dignity." Leaving behind a lifetime of pain, she applied for an internship in gender empowerment programming, and "it was the first time in her memory that she felt valued." Citing civil war as the reason that Indigenous communities are at risk of multiple forms of violence, Say NO states that 45 percent of Guatemalan women have suffered violence in their lifetimes. Laura's story stands in for all Indigenous women in Guatemala. Although civil war and imperialism provide a context for the manifestation of violence against women in Indigenous communities, the Spanish colonization of Guatemala, which included imposition of Christianity and appropriation of land, is not part of the story. Potential donors are told that women and girls were never visible as leaders within Indigenous communities in Guatemala until the United Nations intervened and provided the resources to empower them. Since Guatemalans are presented as making war against their own people, and oppressing women and girls, Laura's story unfolds as a narrative of pain and suffering that can be rapidly overcome with donations to the UN Trust Fund. Like Chhean, Laura is presented as being empowered—but *only* by her work provided by the United Nations. Again the primary agent of change is the donor who responds to the urgent call for help. Laura's physical pain caused by her experience of violence conjures up an emotional reaction from the potential donor. Such emotions are calmed and collected through the individual action of saying no and donating money, which effectively simplifies the complexity of violence against women in Guatemala and globally.

Significantly, stories like Laura's in the campaign actively obscure Indigenous struggles transnationally. Although the United Nations points to Indigenous women's vulnerability to violence in the United States and Canada, it does not use stories of Indigenous women living in contexts of white settler colonialism. Stories of genocide, intergenerational abuse brought on by violence at residential schools, police brutality, missing and murdered women, and apathy among governments would not garner currency in the affective economy of the Say NO campaign. In fact, the anger of Indigenous women and men working with organizations such as Families of Sisters in Spirit (2013) in Canada, and their calls for solidarity, would radically reshape a global anti-violence campaign. However, such feminist concerns are left for later.

In the Say NO campaign, pain does political work. The representation of pain functions to align donors with those who experience pain. Although donors cannot feel the pain of others, they can be moved by the stories of survivors. Although it might be possible to present pain as a bodily sensation that survivors of violence experience differently across the globe, and thus share interest in eliminating violence against women in its various manifestations, the political feelings allowed in the Say NO initiative foreclose possibilities for solidarity (Mohanty 2003). Some bodies are situated as donors, whereas others are situated as needing donations. As Ahmed (2004a, 22) maintains in regard to an anti-landmine campaign, the participant is elevated to a position of power over others as "the one who is 'behind' the possibility of overcoming pain." Additionally, mitigating another's pain in this way can reinforce systemic inequalities connected to the pain experienced by women. This includes the unequal political and economic relationship between the West and Third World secured by the structure of the United Nations and its processes of global governance. As Ahmed writes,

> the West gives to others insofar as it is forgotten what the West has already taken in its very *capacity* to give in the first place....Feelings of pain and suffering, which are in part effects of socio-economic relations of violence and poverty, are assumed to be alleviated by the very generosity that is enabled by such socio-economic relations. So the West takes, then gives, *and in the moment of giving repeats as well as conceals the taking.* (22)

As Desai (2005) maintains, the United Nations remains a site for aiding Third World women but not a place for transnational feminist solidarity. Following the historical patterns of women's organizing since the UN Decade for Women, violence against women is not only narrowly understood in the UNiTE campaign in terms of men's violence against women but also disconnected from colonialism, imperialism, occupation, and war. Similar to the Beijing Platform for Action, anti-violence and gender equality strategies are diluted in terms of politics even as they are made at the epicentre of global economic and political power.

The aboutness of the UNiTE initiative remains focused on the feelings of the donor even while the focus on pain centres the experiences of Third World women. The call for action through emotional responses to stories of pain is about the donor's political feelings and the support that the United Nations can offer through voluntary contributions. Thus, the Say NO campaign communicates not only that the United Nations is the obvious institution to do the work of eliminating violence against women but also that the time to do so is now. The urgency with which participants are asked to say no and to donate positions the donor as an object of hope. The other might be the one to overcome violence, but the UNiTE participant is the one empowered by taking action urgently. By ensuring that participants immediately feel pity, empathy, and charity through emotional short stories and quick facts about violence, the campaign directs them to say no and donate to the United Nations because they now "understand" the issue. This kind of "expert" information leads them to believe that they can act quickly to respond to an urgent problem by saying no and donating money online. Alternative opportunities to support survivors of violence, such as building solidarity among survivors across borders, are foreclosed by the orientation of participants toward political feelings that can be urgently generated. Importantly, those who want to help are positioned as having agency and power. Stories of the empowerment of Third World women are about empowering Western donors to act by affectively stimulating emotional responses. By aligning participants with the United Nations as agents of change who answer the urgent call to end violence against women, the issue is not associated with collective sadness, anger, or outrage that could lead to different anti-violence strategies and different outcomes. Instead, affective value is gained as an expression of individual empowerment and hope by how it is associated with the individual donor's decision to take action.

Importantly, political feelings such as collective outrage and affective possibilities of working together in community and solidarity with women who have experienced violence are disallowed by how participants are oriented toward individual acts of donating to the United Nations online. Thus, affective attachments invited by the UNiTE and Say NO campaigns are not random but aligned with social inequalities and oppressions, which include the overarching notion of top-down development, global NGO funding structures, and processes of exclusion and hierarchies of difference marked by the current era of neo-liberal global economic restructuring that differentiate women by gender, race, class, sexuality, and ability. Campaigns such as UNiTE and Say NO do not function on their own. Rather, they reflect larger systems of charitable strategies that employ affective strategies to orient participants toward certain political feelings and away from others.

For example, in research that compares outcomes of the work done by a fat-positive feminist activist group with the Dove Real Beauty campaign, Josée Johnston and Judith Taylor (2008, 961) argue that, though Dove has a wide reach and is thus relatively effective, it relies on "feminist consumerism [that] tends to obscure and minimize both structural and institutionalized gender inequalities that are difficult to resolve and that might cause negative emotional associations with brands." In contrast, grassroots fat activism does not ask women to buy self-esteem through cosmetic products, but joins fat people in a community that refuses both sizeism and consumerist beauty ideologies. Johnson and Taylor make it clear how affective and political possibilities for change are shaped by the structure of a campaign. Orienting women to purchase their way out of poor self-esteem, the Real Beauty campaign simplifies the implications of beauty ideology and consumerism for the creation and maintenance of gender norms, racism, and ableism, even as it attempts to suggest that women should accept themselves inside and out. Importantly, the political possibility of radically critiquing beauty ideologies can affect sales of Dove products.

Similar to the Real Beauty campaign, the emotional investment of participants in campaigns such as UNiTE and Say NO rely on the commodification of support. Complicating or radically critiquing violence against women as a manifestation of gender inequality, histories of colonialism, globalization-cum-imperialism, and economic restructuring could negatively affect the political purchase of participants in the UN system. It could also open up other affective possibilities, such as accountability and anger, which would lead to new possibilities for strategizing against violence globally. Donating to the cause would not be sufficient. Emotional investments in UNiTE and Say NO rely on participants to feel empowered and in control to donate. Complicating violence against women through radical critique would not only alter the structure of the campaign and its materials but also offer participants alterative avenues to generate different political feelings. Charitable sympathy is a process of consumption. As Razack (2007) argues, consuming or "stealing" the pain of others is the antithesis of collective outrage, and such practices of empathetic purchasing cannot affectively align participants toward accountability or solidarity. Such an approach would be slower, but its outcome might actually address the real urgency of eliminating violence against women that the UNiTE campaign simply cannot.

AFFECT MATTERS TO DEVELOPMENT

Before concluding this chapter, I want to outline briefly how affect theory can be beneficial to critical, post-development, and feminist studies beyond the study of global anti-violence campaigns. Development studies are ripe for the affective turn that has occurred in cultural, feminist, and queer studies. For critical and post-development scholars, questions of the representation of development are central to the field. Critical analyses of discourses of development are important contributions, especially given the vast number of representations of Third World people and problems in scholarship, policy literature, and campaign materials produced and circulated by the development industry. Scholars such as Crush (1995), Escobar (1995), Kapoor (2008), and Mohanty (2003) demonstrate the need for understanding the power of development discourses. Here my concern with affect does not replace my interest in discursive representations but complements my focus on the discursive realm. In particular, a focus on affect adds a layer of complexity to the study of development discourses.

Scholars critical of the Enlightenment tradition within development studies have demonstrated how counter-discourses are complicit
in what they seek to reject. Indebted to Jacques Derrida's concept of
"logocentrism," Kate Manzo (1991) demonstrates that even the most
radical critiques of development have a "disposition to impose hierarchy between places and subjects, a nostalgia for origins, and a vantage
point independent of interpretation" (Watts 1995, 51). The inability of
development theories to critique wholly the "development-as-progress"
narrative is known in the field as the "development impasse" (Munck
1999, 197). In the 1990s, post-development theory became popular as it
attempted to move beyond the impasse by offering new scholarship on
development as discourse. Escobar's (1995) poststructural, specifically
Foucauldian, approach to development discourse marked the cultural
turn of development theory and effectively opened the door for poststructural and postcolonial feminisms to enter the debates on development
"beyond the impasse" (Crush 1995, 57). However, as a methodological
tactic, discursive analyses in the development field are similarly limited.
Often confined by questions of good and bad representations of development subjects, rights, and transgressive (anti-development) or liberatory
(better development) imaginings, affective theory might reveal the political, economic, and social circulations of emotions in and engagements
with development. In other words, such a turn in the field would centre
the *affectiveness* of development rather than its *effectiveness*. Specifically,
for scholars like me concerned with the power of development "experts"
to produce knowledge of, and solutions to, poverty, hunger, disease, and
especially violence against women, affect provides a crucial accompani-
ment to postcolonial and poststructural research.

In fact, post-development, critical development, and postcolonial
theorists theorize affect without naming it as a disciplinary field of
study. Focusing on the desire of development workers to help, Heron
(2007) demonstrates that the motivations of (mostly white) women, in
particular, to travel to the Third World in search of development projects
are built upon emotion. Although Heron is not concerned with affective economies within the development industry, her work reveals that
affect and emotion come into play in development. Citing attachments
to feelings of obligation, urgency, and even entitlement in her research
with development workers, she reveals that the desire for development

rests in individuals' affective attachments to others. Borrowing from Anne McClintock (1995) and Ann Stoler (1995), Heron suggests that the desire to help was built into a bourgeois identity that emerged in Europe in the 1800s especially, during which colonial regimes explored and conquered foreign territories. She argues that bourgeois identity was enveloped by "a certain sensibility" that included sympathy, desire for recognition of benevolence, and acts of charity toward those considered less fortunate and less advanced. Part of this bourgeois subjectivity was the affirmation of class relations, which not only justified and maintained exploitative labour relations locally and globally but also rationalized spatialized social relations based upon racial difference (28–30). Naming this bourgeois subjectivity a "colonial continuity" (33), Heron investigates the notions of charity and benevolence in white middle-class development workers' subjectivity in the mid-1990s. Although unconcerned with affect per se, her research demonstrates how development affectively orients the development worker toward those worthy of help and happiness and, through attachments to feelings of compassion and empathy, how the collective body of the development industry is shaped by the circulation of emotions.

Although unconcerned with development, Ahmed (2010) provides an analysis of the long history of affective relations and colonial contact. She argues that colonial expansion was motivated and justified not just by feelings related to pity and charity. She cites an article in the *Monthly Review* (1813) by John Bruce, involved in the East India Trading Company, claiming that "the *happiness* of the human race would thus be prodigiously augmented" by settler colonialism in India (29; emphasis added). The duty to be philanthropic was narrated through the expansion of happiness to the colonies. Trying to justify colonialism and control, colonizers imagined themselves to be spreading happiness to those who lacked it because of "chaos" and poverty. As Razack's (2004) critical analysis of modern peacekeeping reveals, gratefulness of the "natives" is a required emotion in return.

The infamous 1980 Live Aid concert in support of ending famine in Ethiopia demonstrates the interplay of affect and emotion in the development industry. Organized by Bob Geldof and supported by musicians such as Paul McCartney, Mick Jagger, David Bowie, Queen, and Led Zeppelin, the event was televised from both London and Philadelphia.

Throughout the concert, images of the famine appeared on large screens, and viewers were encouraged to donate money (Geldof 2012). According to Rotimi Sankore (2005), graphic images of ailing racialized children are no more than "development pornography" that uses "shocking" images to elicit affective responses.[7] Although Sankore's language is problematic, his allusion to affective economies is interesting. For Sankore, no picture could ever explain the tenacious history of "slavery, colonialism, mass murder, repression, looting, corruption, trade imbalances, and outrageous interests on dubious loans" in the Third World. Yet such images circulate with affective currency in the development industry.

Images from development campaigns are cultural texts that circulate with affective value. Signalled by the emaciated black body with eyes either pestered by flies or on the verge of tears, the development subject is produced through a political economy of representations and emotions. That is, "clientalization" or "developmentalization" of Third World subjects, to use Escobar's (1995) terms, is generated in and through affect. Affective attachments in development rely on the circulation of feelings made visible by the bodies on which they stick. Using interchangeable Third World bodies, such frames of representation used in charity campaigns such as Live Aid are too often used in the development industry. As poststructural, postcolonial, and anti-racist scholarship reveals, such representations are problematic (Mohanty

---

7   Sankore's (2005) conception of development pornography relies on the stigmatization and demonization of porn and does not provide a nuanced analysis of the complexity of the industry and those who work in it. Causally relating the filming of sex to exploitation, the notion of development porn takes aim at both the industry of development and the industry of pornography. Although I reject the anti-porn, anti–sex work framework that this term emerges from, I find it useful to point to voyeurism in development campaigns and the framing of representations of the Third World. I do not agree that one needs more shocking images to be affected or stimulated by watching porn, nor does producing shocking porn necessitate exploitation of those involved in it. However, I do agree that there is a sense of audience fatigue regarding affective responses to poverty in charity models, and thus Sankore's work remains useful insofar as it points to how development campaigns produce images and texts to provoke affective responses to shocking representations of decontextualized images, for example, of poor, diseased, sad, and starving children.

2003; Narayan 1997; Treichler 1999). More than racist representations, images of Third World bodies circulate to signal "our" collective sadness for others' suffering.

As Ahmed (2004a) argues, emotions circulate between bodies and signs and impress themselves on the surfaces of bodies. Emotions gain value in their circulation and both adhere to historical associations of feelings and representations and obscure the history of their production. As such, representations of others' pain, trauma, hunger, and experiences of violence circulate in affective economies that value benevolence rather than accountability. That is, feelings of sympathy and returned gratitude are evoked through representations of others. Circulating widely in development communication materials, such representations evoke affective responses that bind together compassionate subjects while simultaneously othering objects of pity and ultimately ignoring historical contexts and causes of pain, trauma, and suffering.

Emotions do different things to different subjects because they involve various orientations toward or away from objects (Ahmed 2004a). Cultural productions, such as those emerging out of Live Aid, reveal how emotions get stuck on certain bodies. Ahmed argues that "getting stuck" is dependent on "past histories of association that often 'work' through concealment" (13). As such, development subjects are made subjects by our pity, and their collective and unfortunate problems (read through images of pain, suffering, and trauma) are dependent on the concealment of histories of colonialism, uneven capitalism, neo-liberal globalization, and imperial projects. Unable to be explained through single stories and images, development campaign materials that rely on images of Third World individuals' pain and trauma allow pity to stick to Third World bodies, creating a collective body of poor and needy individuals while simultaneously and effectively demarcating the boundaries between us and them. Racial difference is read from their bodies as well as "endowed upon their bodies" (Puar 2007, 169). That is, images of poor and hungry Ethiopians in the context of famine, for example, are read as different and thus always already different from us. As difference slides across bodies that resemble Ethiopians under famine, difference is endowed on the entire continent, if not on the entire Third World.

Images of women who have experienced violence, or are vulnerable to violence, are used in development campaigns to manufacture a sense of urgency and to frame a way of responding to it. Third World women's bodies are read as always already different through their racialization, and this difference slides between bodies that "look like" or "seem like" vulnerable subjects (Puar 2007, 187). In the same way, pity is stuck on bodies that require intervention, and benevolence and superiority are stuck on the bodies of those willing to act. Moreover, the bodies of perpetrators are stuck with feelings of fear or hate. In development studies, racialized affects of representations must be attended to more broadly if we are truly to understand the impacts of development discourses and their circulation.

CONCLUSION

Emotions circulated within an affective economy in the UNiTE to End Violence against Women and adjoining Say NO campaigns. Outlining the scholarship on affect, and centring work on the cultural politics of emotion (Ahmed 2004a) in particular, I demonstrated the affective nature of development and of anti-violence initiatives within the development industry. I suggested that political feelings (Gould 2009) are shaped by development discourses and representational practices. Within the UNiTE campaign, the emotionality of images and texts encourages participants to be moved to take action. Borrowing from Ahmed's (2004b) conception of "affective economies," in which affect gains value in its circulation and exchange, my analysis of political feelings in the UNiTE and Say NO campaigns reveals how emotions circulate between bodies, how they gain affective value in their repetition, and how they stick to certain bodies. Expanding on Alhassan's (2009) notion of "telescopic philanthropy," I employed the term "telescopic feeling" to demonstrate the limits of affective possibilities in participants' understanding of violence against women in relation to "The Situation" overview (UN 2012b) and "UNiTE Worldwide" map (UN 2012c). I maintained that a sense of "over thereness" or "otherness" generates feelings of mastery and managerial confidence while simultaneously foreclosing the possibility of feelings of accountability and solidarity that might invite participants to make connections between the Global South and the Global North. Focusing on the Say NO campaign, I investigated how participants are asked to "take action" through a narrow representational frame. Using

the Say NO petition and requests for donations to the UN Trust Fund
to End Violence against Women, I argued that participants' feelings
of empowerment and belonging overshadow the reality of victims'
experiences of violence and conceal important histories that make
taking action through petitions and donations possible as a solution.
Generating a sense of urgency through narrowly focused, accessible,
and relatively easy steps to "eliminate violence against women now," the
UNiTE and Say NO campaigns function as practical and inspirational
campaigns to gain awareness of the issue and produce advocacy around
it. However, through telescopic feeling and individual action taking, the
"aboutness" (Ahmed 2004a) of the campaigns remains focused on participants' feelings of empowerment and control, not on the agency of
survivors. Such urgent strategies to end violence against women now
not only obscure important histories and complexities of this violence,
including the complexities of feminists working within the UN system
historically, as reflected in conference proceedings from the UN Decade
for Women, but also direct participants toward benevolent and individual actions rather than collective or solidarity-based strategies. The
latter could reveal the complexities of this violence as urgent and generate different sets of solutions to ending these practices globally.

CONCLUSION

||||||||||||||||||||||

Violence against women is an urgent and transnational problem. Women around the world experience violence connected to various social, cultural, political, and economic practices. Although the issue is pressing, in the development industry there is an "epidemic of signification" that manufactures urgency around the issue (Treichler 1999). My analysis of the discursive development apparatus focused on the construction of violence against women as a problem for the development industry to solve *now*. In conceptualizing the call to end this violence now as an urgent mode of representation, this book deconstructed the development industry's concern with the issue. Thinking about the project of making urgent, or exploring the manufacturing of urgency, allowed me to see, and then describe, the workings of producing violence against women as a "problem" for development.

The sheer number of justifications given by the development industry for why violence against women is an urgent issue constructs it as a problem for the industry to solve. As this book has unpacked and thus revealed, laborious discursive manoeuvres have led to the issue to be understood as an urgent problem for the development industry. According to the narratives mapped in this book, development and progress are stagnated by this violence. It is also a problem for development because it is a global security issue, causally connected to global violence in places with extreme poverty and gender inequality understood as breeding grounds for terrorism. Finally, violence against women can be solved by saying no and donating to the United Nations, which subsequently funds development organizations that deal with the issue.

For development experts, violence against women matters vis-à-vis other development issues. Although violence experienced by women should matter in itself, experts in the development industry have paired the urgency of ending violence against women with the urgency of other development concerns: security, economic growth, and feel-good aid. By representing such violence as urgent in combination with other objectives, rather than attending to its actual urgency, development experts and institutions successfully collapse the complexities of the issue transnationally in favour of swift and narrow solutions. The sense of urgency to combat this violence globally both represents the issue as universally solvable with similar tactics and forecloses more radical strategies, including possible solutions that might exist outside the limits of the development industry.

Three ways in which violence against women has been problematized alongside other development interests are post-9/11 national security concerns, neo-liberal economic growth, and cultural production of benevolent aid. My sites of study here—American foreign policy, the World Bank, and the United Nations—were different in terms of their institutional affiliations, development objectives, ideologies, and anti-violence strategies. These institutions and actors offer different analyses of, and solutions to, violence against women but remain committed to it as a pressing concern for development. In fact, how they differ led me to use multiple methods and three distinctive theoretical models to analyze them. Using both discursive analyses of documents and interviews with development experts, I decolonized representations of violence against women using theories of development and security, critical disability, crip studies, and affect theory. Woven into a framework of transnational feminism, this book mapped the power of development discourses at seemingly "scattered" hegemonic locations to establish that there are interconnected regimes of knowledge about violence against women in the development industry that secure both its expertise on the issue and its power to manufacture urgency around it (Foucault 1980; Grewal and Kaplan 1994). Deconstructing the project of making urgent, or analyzing representations of violence against women in development discourses, reveals a concern for the issue in the development industry as embedded in global systems of domination, including sexism, racism, classism, ableism, heterosexism, imperialism, and neo-colonialism.

RETURNING TO URGENCY

By investigating how American foreign policy makers, the World Bank, and the United Nations communicate the importance of ending violence against women, I revealed how the issue is connected to what I consider some of the most important "flavours of the day" for the development industry: national security, neo-liberal economic growth, and feel-good aid. I suggested that the urgency of eliminating this violence is established through its connection to other development objectives. Rather than an end in itself, fighting violence against women matters to development experts because it is understood as being interlinked with other goals—some of which directly contradict anti-violence strategies, as I demonstrated here.

As urgency theorist Kotter (2008) maintains, a sense of urgency must be created. That is, urgency is a manufactured feeling about, or a perception of, an issue. In my research, I found that development experts borrow from the languages, concepts, and strategies developed by feminists in their anti-violence campaigns, policies, and legislations to communicate the urgency of the issue. Pairing feminist and gender equality language with other development objectives opened up the possibility of communicating the urgency of eliminating violence against women *now* but often leaving other feminist questions and concerns for later (Enloe 2004).

Of course, it is not only violence against women that is communicated as an urgent development concern. In fact, inquiring into sites of urgency, or where one sees a sense of urgency being created discursively or affectively, might reveal more about the functioning of the development industry than the issues themselves. In other words, searching for urgency, or analyzing it as a discursive and affective manoeuvre, reveals the inner or hidden workings of *making* a certain issue a top priority in the industry. For example, the focus on women's rights in development, including gender mainstreaming strategies, has placed women's issues at the forefront of knowledge production in academic scholarship and within development organizations. Although women's rights were rarely given a place at the table in development circles in the 1980s, one would be hard pressed to find an organization within the development industry that does not deal with gender issues (at least on paper) today. Of course, this move has not been matched by financial investment. Whether sprinkled into funding proposals or taken seriously by development organizations, gender issues are constructed as urgent problems for the industry. But to what end?

I offer the idea here of manufacturing urgency to ask scholars and practitioners to think about how policy, legislative, research, and advocacy concerns in the development industry are produced and circulated. Although I connect this idea to violence against women in particular, manufacturing urgency can be used in other sites of inquiry. Given the emphasis on crisis, disaster, and emergency in mainstream post-9/11 political discourses, the idea of manufacturing urgency allows one to ask the following questions: What follows a moment of emergency? How do discourses of urgency allow such moments to endure? That is, how can these discourses maintain affective drives toward reactionary and emergency politics? Which decisions must be made now? Which can wait until later? Critically analyzing the politics of urgency allows one to think about the functioning of modes of urgency and how they are culturally, socially, politically, and economically produced.

One example, far removed from the development industry, is the manufacturing of urgency to eliminate obesity in North America. In academic literature, fat studies offer particularly sophisticated analyses of discourses of urgency. Although authors such as Charlotte Biltekoff (2007) do not position their work in relation to discourses or affective relations of urgency, studies of the "obesity epidemic" trace the cultural production of urgency around the issue. Similar to Treichler's (1999) concern with the epidemic of signification around HIV/AIDS, Biltekoff investigates the "cultural work" performed by anti-obesity campaigns, taking into account how the reformed Body Mass Index scale in the United States effectively moved previously "normal" body weights of individuals to the levels of "overweight" and "obese." Fat studies scholars reveal how the urgency to "fight fat" is manufactured. In this case, studies of the epidemic of signification of obesity reveal that control and discipline of bodies and behaviours (especially those of poor people and people of colour in the United States) build a sense of urgency around the issue while effacing structural, environmental, biological, economic, and political processes that lead to the problematizing of fatness and a national health crisis and even a national security crisis (Biltekoff 2007). Those are issues to be dealt with later.

As I was completing this book, the feminist watchdog group Gender Action alerted me to a new World Bank scandal involving violence against women. In 2016, news media began to report on the cancellation of a World Bank road construction project worth $265 million in western Uganda amid allegations of sexual violence against school-aged girls and harassment of female workers (Daily Mail 2016; Mwesigwa 2016). In a statement on the Uganda Transport Sector Development Project, President Jim Young Kim declared that "an early review of the World Bank–financed project found inadequacies in Bank supervision and lack of follow-through after serious issues were identified" (World Bank 2015). The lack of safeguarding of women's rights is not new to Gender Action. This organization has worked diligently to pressure the World Bank to take violence against women seriously and to act with urgency on the issue. Its own research with Friends of the Earth International (2011) demonstrates that development projects—including pipelines financed by the World Bank in western Africa, Eurasia, and central Asia—have made women's lives worse, not better. Although a gender safeguard policy is under review, currently the World Bank does not have one, which means that women are left unprotected while the institution continues to finance mega-infrastructure projects. What is *new* at the World Bank is a task force on gender-based violence. In the midst of the Ugandan "scandal," the World Bank responded urgently (Talley 2016). According to Elana Berger from another watchdog group, the Bank Information Center, "everyone at all levels at the bank denied that there was a problem [with the Ugandan project]." As she mentioned to the *Wall Street Journal*, "it was only after months of her group's pestering bank staff in Uganda and the head office in Washington [that] the bank's project officials...start[ed] taking the allegations seriously" (Talley 2016). Like many institutions and organizations—from the Canadian government (dealing with the publicity of systemic violence against Indigenous women) to universities (responding to sexual assault scandals on their campuses)—reactionary measures and emergency politics arise when issues left for later become public and must be dealt with *now*.

Another example of the manufacturing of urgency in the development industry is the recent focus on LGBT rights. In 2015, the United States announced a special envoy for LGBT rights following a State of the Union address in which President Obama claimed that talking about these rights globally would "make us all safer." In 2013, the United Nations launched a Free and Equal campaign focused on the human rights of LGBT people globally. Even the most "apolitical" of organizations, the World Bank, is now thinking about the costs of homophobia (Lee Badgett 2014). This does not mean, of course, that queer discrimination is suddenly and unexpectedly an urgent issue for the development industry, nor does it mean that this key moment in U.S. foreign policy, a historical UN campaign, and a change in the World Bank's focus should obscure radical and global mobilizations around sexuality, gender identity, and human rights. According to Rahul Rao (2014, 200), "the Homosexual Question" is the new marker of modernity, in which campaigns, images, and news media depictions of LGBT rights and sexual minority activism circulate to mark "a temporal phase of wider acceptance of LGBT rights and conjur[e] up visions of progress." The development industry has slowly begun to recognize LGBT rights, and as the issue of global homophobia and transphobia is taken up by the development industry it becomes a development problem.[1]

Although it is unclear that there is significant funding devoted to this new "flavour of the day," the issue is being communicated as pressing. Surely, President Obama's use of post-9/11 rhetoric about national security being connected to LGBT rights suggests that the issue is being communicated as urgent and borrows from feminist language. Yet, at the time of the appointment of a State Department special envoy for LGBT rights globally, twenty transgender women, mostly women of colour, had been killed with impunity in the United States (Kellaway and Sunnivie 2015). Although LGBT rights are being constructed as an urgent issue "abroad" for U.S. foreign policy, global human rights at home—and even national security, racist transmisogyny, and failing criminal justice systems—are the kinds of feminist and queer issues to be dealt with at another time, if at all. The end of the Obama administration and the election of Donald Trump, and his appointments of an overwhelmingly anti-LGBT cabinet, will likely manufacture another

1   Although development experts are actively beginning to think about LGBT rights, development is not being queered. That is, queering development or thinking about queer justice is not a focus of development institutions at this time.

kind of urgency in foreign policy, and academics concerned with "gay imperialism," or at least the global promotion of LGBT rights by the United States, might turn their gaze back to the domestic realm. The impacts of Trump's presidency on the development industry have yet to be seen.

Similar to eliminating violence against women, eliminating discrimination and violence against queer people transnationally is not a simple task. In fact, any aim to "mainstream" issues related to identity and oppression—including racism, classism, sexism, homophobia, transphobia, and ableism—into development, and in an urgent manner, necessitates a thorough analysis of swift solutions and emergent strategies. Certainly, LGBT rights are currently more controversial than violence against women in the West. This is not to suggest that rape culture, misogyny, or patriarchy does not exist in the West; instead, regardless of the staggering numbers of women and gender and sexual minorities who experience violence daily in the Western world, national machineries generally defend anti–violence as a concept. The feel-good or moral obligation to "save" LGBT individuals might not be as universally seductive as violence against women. Yet, as internal and external pressures and activist mobilizations continue around the issue, the development industry's foreign aid practices, foreign policy relations, and funding procedures might be influenced to claim that both homophobia and transphobia are also development problems that need to be addressed *now*.

BEYOND THE DEVELOPMENT INDUSTRY

Manufacturing Urgency has focused on the issue of violence against women as it is taken up by the development industry. Focusing on critiques of representations, especially with regard to discourses of urgency, this book has analyzed official documents, policies, reports, media coverage, and campaigns of three of the largest and most powerful development actors. I chose this focus on the development industry because my intention was to map development discourses in the vein of critical theorists, including Escobar (1995), Kapoor (2006), and Mohanty (1991, 2003). The problem with focusing on hegemonic discourses of development is that it risks reifying power by concluding that the industry is all powerful in shaping representations of and responses to violence against women. This, of course, is not the case. I maintain that the development industry remains powerful in shaping official responses to so-called urgent matters and has the funding to back them up (but rarely does); however, grassroots, community, and grounded activists are the ones who respond to the urgency to end violence against women.

Neither this book nor this conclusion is meant to provide an analysis, or even a thorough overview, of global movements to end this violence. However, throughout my research I have found incredibly inspiring ways in which feminist movements name violence against women as an urgent concern without losing feminist analyses of the issue, which, as Enloe (2004) and Jacobson (2013) inform us, are too often left to the patriarchal zone of later. These examples, which I briefly detail below, are not movements, organizations, or ideas manufactured by the development industry. They do not represent the imaginings of the gatekeepers, agenda setters, or funders of the industry. Instead, these movements and organizations are led by survivors and community activists who understand, through experience, that violence against women is always already inextricably connected to imperialism, capitalism, and war.

Thursdays in Black (2015) is one example of a grassroots global campaign that requests individuals to wear black on Thursdays as "a symbol of strength and courage" and to stand in "solidarity with victims and survivors of violence...calling for a world without rape and violence." This campaign has been around since the 1970s, and it has roots in the movement Mothers of the Disappeared in Argentina. That movement challenged the roots of violence silently by coming together and wearing black scarves in honour of family members and friends who had disappeared or been raped or abused. Importantly, it specifically targeted the loss of loved ones under military dictatorships and received critical attention for its essentialist views on women and motherhood (Elshtain and Tobias 1990). However, the simplicity of being silent and wearing black has led to the campaign being adopted in the "rape-death camps" of Bosnia, apartheid South Africa, and occupied Palestine and focuses on systemic structural conditions of violence against women, including war, imperialism, and occupation.

Even groups who focus on the levels of the local and the interpersonal demonstrate the real urgency of violence against women outside the parameters of the development industry. In India, a group of women are standing up to abusers through bystander intervention. Inspired by a woman named Sampat Pal Devi—who interrupted the domestic violence of a community member and even responded physically to stop the abuser and was herself violated—these women wear pink saris to signify womanhood and strength and work to eliminate violence against women. They specialize in self-defence training and techniques of intervention. As a way to support survivors, the women provide wedding services, including tailoring bridal wear, catering, making flower arrangements, and applying henna. Given their emphasis on domestic violence, they target men and women at marriage ceremonies for education and awareness (Gulabi Gang 2014).

One example of a global project to end violence against women that might be better known, albeit controversial, is SlutWalk. While I was writing this book, I was also working on a book chapter about SlutWalk as a transnational anti-violence movement (Watson and Mason 2015). The SlutWalk movement began in 2011 as a collective response to the victim-blaming of survivors of violence by a member of the police in Toronto. In our research, we found that SlutWalks have taken place in Canada, the United States, the United Kingdom, Australia, India, Brazil, Singapore, Israel, South Korea, Poland, and beyond. I mention SlutWalk here because it is a movement that engages in the urgency of violence against women by organizers who responded quickly to an incident of violence but did not narrow their response to focusing on interpersonal violence, claiming to empower women, or requesting pledges toward an organization—the three tactics that I have described in this book's case studies. Instead, SlutWalk in Toronto organically translated into a transnational movement without funding, governance, or expertise because of the overwhelming evidence that women around the world were being blamed, albeit differently, for violence perpetrated against them. What is clear from our research on the transnationality of SlutWalk is that women, in their own localities, are the experts in eliminating violence against them.

As a transnational feminist scholar, I wrote about SlutWalk because I wanted to map how SlutWalk around the world has taken on different names and local focuses to demonstrate the lack of efficiency of standardized approaches to global violence against women. In Singapore, SlutWalk was organized around a discomfort with reclamation of the term "slut." The organizers there asked protesters to dress in any way that they felt comfortable. In London, a faction within the SlutWalk march called Hijabs, Hoodies, and Hotpants emerged as a rejection of reclamation of the term "slut." In India in 2011, organizers used the term *besharmi morcha*, or "shameless protest," to speak to the Indian context (Kapur 2012). For critics, this protest followed on the heels of a much more relevant local protest called Pink Chaddis, in which women sent pink panties to a right-wing Hindu organization that blamed the victim of a recent sexual assault for her presence in public. For Ratna Kapur (2012), that SlutWalk was unhelpful to local feminist concerns, such as laws that do not protect women from rape, because of its focus on modesty and shame.[2] Although I maintain that the term "slut" does particular exclusionary work—and that it has not be successful in every location, especially when it has been taken on in a more standardized approach—the movement has been transformed by communities (especially through critiques), and that is inspiring.

My work on SlutWalk was a good reminder of how "trickle-up social justice" movements are more successful, especially for women's experiences of empowerment, through building and contributing to social movements for change (Spade 2011). Fighting for acceptance and visibility of an issue such as violence against women in the very institutions that discriminate against women, sponsor state-sanctioned violence against them, create conditions of precarity for them, promote and enact imperial wars and occupations that harness discourses of their rights while ignoring their well-being is a process of bolstering the power of these organizations to continue to marginalize the most marginal.

Manufacturing Urgency has described how development expertise is connected to perpetuation of violence rather than working only to eliminate it. My theoretical contribution here is to reveal the traps of buying

---

2   Kapur (2012) maintains that SlutWalk ignores the postcolonial context of India, especially the figure of the "good woman" in the struggles for independence. Kapur argues that the intersections of local patriarchies, nationalisms, and histories of colonization meant that women were represented as needing their honour and chastity protected in coverage of SlutWalk.

in to the development industry's problematization of the issue *as a development issue* and to encourage other imaginings of activism and advocacy against global violence against women that do not buy into militarization, criminalization, imperialism, neo-liberalism, or charity/philanthropy models that obscure the agency of the very communities that development organizations purport to support. Put bluntly, there are not alternative development strategies, only alternatives to this form of development.

LIMITATIONS AND POSSIBILITIES

Although this book has not sought to reveal all the ways in which gender inequality is tied to the development industry, it began from the understanding that feminism, feminist values, and gender sensitivity are both integrally and often disjunctively linked to the violence of global restructuring, which includes development and human rights interventions. I agree with Marianne Marchand and Anne Runyan (2011, 21): "[Global] restructuring is an open-ended process that creates myriad (re)interpretations and contradictions and counter-discourses and practices as activists and scholars continuously expose the politics of globalization-cum-imperialism and propose alternatives to it." Significantly, neo-liberal globalization, or what Marchand and Runyan have decisively retermed "global restructuring," is malleable to critique. That is, the pervasiveness of neo-liberalism has required global managers, such as the World Bank, to listen to external and internal critiques and include previously marginalized voices in their work. The urgent focus on gender in development and human rights obscures the working of "globalization-cum-imperialism," including the militarization and securitization of post 9/11 femininities and masculinities (16). Some feminist scholars have understood transitions to gender-sensitive policy and programming within development institutions as a remarkable success, but these transitions also mark the genderwashing of neo-liberal global restructuring.

Feminist activists, gender equality promoters, and development practitioners sensitive to gender issues and human rights work within the confines of global restructuring and are thus complicit in its processes, even as they seek to unfasten the structures of domination that effect the operations of sexism, racism, classism, and ableism in the realms of ideologies, subjectivities, and bodies and on the level of social relations. It cannot be denied, however, that the urgency created around women's rights and gender issues opens up multiple avenues for feminist activism and advocacy within the development industry, however complex. The limitations of my research here are that it focuses on policy, legislation, and campaign discourse and therefore not explicitly on the work of feminist activists and gender experts who diligently create a sense of urgency around women's issues to be heard by their organizations or communities. Instead, I have focused on how the development industry communicates the urgency of issues such as violence against women. I cannot ignore the impact of feminist activism that demands organizations such as the World Bank pay attention to women's rights. Feminist activism is behind the framing of violence against women as an issue worthy of the attention of development experts. According to interviews that I conducted with development and gender experts, there are major discontinuities between the commitment of individuals working within institutions to end violence against women and what is said about it at the global level by development organizations. As Turshen pointed out in 2012, "not everything published is part of the real 'on the ground' work." Therefore, studying the manufacturing of urgency from the perspective of feminist activists, femocrats, and advocates who work diligently to pressure development organizations and foreign policy experts to take violence against women seriously remains an important task. What feminist advocates and femocrats can accomplish within a manufactured sense of urgency around gender issues should be further studied. Research in this area might ask the following questions: What does access to the development mainstream entail? What will access to the mainstream bring, for whom, and at whose expense? Can the development industry be redeemed through the mainstreaming of feminist values, including the focus on violence against women, especially when urgency is manufactured?

Although I have not focused here on on-the-ground mobilizations of manufactured urgencies in the development industry, I have spoken to policy concerns about adopting flavour-of-the-day strategies. In my own anti-violence advocacy work, I have experienced how funding structures, election politics, language trends, and buzzwords can deeply shape feminist advocacy within organizations. In speaking to develop-ment practitioners for this book, especially the gender advocate whom I spoke to at the World Bank, it became clear to me what was to be lost and gained in using the economic language required by the organiza-tion. I maintain that counting, measuring, and costing violence against women manufactures urgency around an issue that is urgent entirely by itself, but I understand that measuring in the age of austerity and global neo-liberalism is both a survival strategy and a radical strategy. Yet I remain concerned with calls to address complex issues through number-crunching formulas. This book contributes, then, to ongo-ing discussions in feminist anti-violence communities about the im/ possibilities of working within the constraints of state-funded and pri-vate institutions. Although I wish to attest and document the inventive strategies employed by gender advocates working in the development industry, this book is also a cautionary account of how large and pow-erful organizations listen to social movements and feminist critiques, criticisms, and trends and then co-opt ideas and values for their own uses. This is not to say that feminist values and activisms are innocent until co-opted but to illustrate feminist complicity in the functioning of the development industry.

I stand behind my criticisms of how U.S. foreign policy makers, the World Bank, and the United Nations define violence against women and strategize to solve this global issue, but I understand that my research is limited by the fact that I have not studied the impacts of policies, laws, and campaigns on the ground. For example, I am aware that the outcomes of the UNiTE to End Violence against Women and Say NO campaigns might be increased funding for anti-violence organizations that might desperately need these funds to function and do progres-sive and important work. Alvarez's (2009) and Poster and Salime's (2004) research findings on funding challenges for NGOs in the devel-opment industry are two sophisticated examples of feminist research that link on-the-ground activism to funding practices and development discourses. In this book, I have focused specifically on development discourses because it is unclear how recent UN campaigns, U.S. legis-lation, and World Bank research reports at the centre of my research have impacted on-the-ground work of women's organizations in the short term. Yet my discourse analyses of documents and interviews with femocrats reveal that speaking language that has political currency in the development industry—including evoking economic jargon, using discourses on nationalism and anti-terrorism, or employing a charity frame—has consequences for how solutions to violence against women are imagined. As I have demonstrated in this book, economic solutions secure women's responsibilities to state development above and beyond human rights concerns, securitized discourses can lead to militarized responses to violence against women that can advance the insecurity of women, and feel-good strategies do little more than individualize both the problem of and the solution to violence against women at the expense of collective and radical actions to eliminate structures of oppression that make women vulnerable to violence transnationally.

By focusing on development discourses, especially on the development industry's appropriation of feminist language without feminist politics, I have revealed the neo-liberal, imperial, and neo-colonial development outcomes of manufacturing urgency around the issue of global violence against women. I have also demonstrated how these objectives are obscured by a seemingly moral, innocent, and rational call to end this violence. The need for top-down models of "doing development" is secured by development actors who make urgent global violence against women and take the lead as experts in solving a so-called development problem. That is, it is in their interest to lead the charge on this issue because revealing its complexities as a systemic global issue that interlocks with systems of gendered, racialized, classed, ableist, and heterosexist/homophobic power and other relations of rule would question development itself as a moral project. Additionally, the need for development to solve the issue of violence against women might be overshadowed by alternative struggles against this violence that simultaneously take aim at processes of global economic restructuring. Manufacturing violence against women as an urgent concern obscures those complexities and forecloses those possibilities.

REFERENCES

||||||||||||||||||||||||||

Abu-Lughod, Lila. 2002. "Do Muslim Women Really Need Saving? Anthropological Reflections on Cultural Relativism and Its Others." *American Anthropologist* 104, 3: 783–90.

Agamben, Giorgio. 1998. *State of Exception*. Translated by Kevin Attell. Chicago: University of Chicago Press.

Ahmed, Sara. 2004a. *The Cultural Politics of Emotion*. New York: Routledge.

———. 2004b. "Affective Economies." *Social Text* 22, 2: 117–37.

———. 2010. *The Promise of Happiness*. Durham, NC: Duke University Press.

Alexander, Jacqui. 2005. *Pedagogies of Crossing: Meditations on Feminism, Sexual Politics, Memory, and the Sacred*. Durham, NC: Duke University Press.

Alexander, Jacqui, and Chandra Talpade Mohanty. 2010. "Cartographies of Knowledge and Power: Transnational Feminism and Radical Praxis." In *Critical Transnational Feminist Praxis*, edited by Richa Nagar and Amanda Lock Swarr, 23–45. Albany, NY: SUNY Press.

Alhassan, Amin. 2009. "Telescopic Philanthropy, Emancipation, and Development Communication Theory." *Nordicom Review* 30: 117–28.

Alison, Miranda H. 2007. "Wartime Sexual Violence: Women's Human Rights and Questions of Masculinity." *Review of International Studies* 33, 1: 75–90.

Alvarez, Sonia E. 1999. "Advocating Feminism: The Latin American Feminist NGO 'Boom.'" *International Feminist Journal of Politics* 1, 2: 181–209.

———. 2009. "Beyond NGO-ization? Reflections from Latin America." *Development* 52, 2: 175–84.

Amnesty International. 2010. "The International Violence against Women Act (I-VAWA) (S.2982, HR.4594)." Issue Brief No. 2. http://www.amnestyusa.org/sites/default/files/pdfs/ivawa_ib2.pdf.

Anand, Sudhir, and Kara Hanson. 1997. "Disability-Adjusted Life Years: A Critical Review." *Journal of Health Economics* 16: 685–702.

Aroon, Preeti. 2010. "International Violence against Women Act Approved by Senate Foreign Relations Committee." *Foreign Policy Magazine*, December 15. http://hillary.foreignpolicy.com/posts/2010/12/15/international_violence_against_women_act_approved_by_senate_foreign_relations_committee.

Avon. 2011. *Speak Out against Domestic Violence*. http://www.ca.avon.com/PRSuite/domestic.page.

Bangladesh Center for Worker Solidarity. 2013. *Bangladesh*. http://www.solidaritycenter.org/content.asp?contentid=448.

Bedford, Kate. 2009. *Developing Partnerships: Gender, Sexuality, and the Reformed World Bank*. Minneapolis: University of Minnesota Press.

Bendery, Jennifer. 2012. "Violence against Women Act Shouldn't Cover Same-Sex Couples, GOP Congresswoman Says." *Huffington Post*, May 14. http://www.huffingtonpost.com/2012/05/14/violence-against-women-act-same-sex-couples_n_1516281.html.

Bergeron, Suzanne. 2006a. *Fragments of Development: Nation, Gender, and the Space of Modernity*. Michigan: University of Michigan Press.

———. 2006b. "Colonizing Knowledge: Economics and Interdisciplinarity in Engendering Development." In *Feminist Economics and the World Bank: History, Theory, and Policy*, edited by Edith Kuiper and Drucilla Barker, 127–41. New York: Routledge.

Berlant, Lauren. 2007. "Slow Death (Sovereignty, Obesity, Lateral Agency)." *Critical Inquiry* 33, 4: 754–80.

Bhabha, Homi. 1984. "Of Mimicry and Man: The Ambivalence of Colonial Discourse." *Discipleship: A Special Issue on Psychoanalysis* 28: 125–33.

Bhattacharyya, Gargi. 2008. *Dangerous Brown Men: Exploiting Sex, Violence, and Feminism in the "War on Terror."* New York: Zed Books.

Biltekoff, Charlotte. 2007. "The Terror Within: Obesity in Post 9/11 U.S. Life." *American Studies* 48, 3: 29–48.

Blakeley, Ruth. 2006. "Still Training to Torture? U.S. Training of Military Forces from Latin America." *Third World Quarterly* 27, 8: 1439–61.

Bordo, Susan. 1993. *Unbearable Weight: Feminism, Western Culture, and the Body*. Berkeley: University of California Press.

Boserup, Esther. 1970. *Woman's Role in Economic Development*. New York: St. Martin's Press.

British Broadcasting Corporation. 2009. "U.S. Military Sex Attack Reports Up." March 18. http://news.bbc.co.uk/2/hi/7950439.stm.

Brooks, Rachelle. 1997. "Feminists Negotiate the Legislative Branch: The Violence against Women Act." In *Feminists Negotiate the State: The Politics of Domestic Violence*, edited by Cynthia R. Daniels, 65–82. Lanham, MD: University Press of America.

———. 2015. "Jerusalem Gay Pride: Six Stabbed 'by Ultra-Orthodox Jew.'" July 30. http://www.bbc.com/news/world-middle-east-33726634.

Bruce, John. 1813. "Bruce's Report on the East India Negotiation." *Monthly Review*: 20–37.

Burns, Robert. 2013. "Soldier in Sexual Assault Office Accused of Abuse." Yahoo News, May 14. http://news.yahoo.com/soldier-sexual-assault-office-accused-abuse-000206696.html.

Canadian Broadcasting Corporation. 2013. "Sexual Assault Threatens Trust in Military, Obama Says." May 24. http://www.cbc.ca/news/world/story/2013/05/24/us-obama-military-sexual-assault.html.

Canadian Women's Foundation. 2015. "The Facts about Violence against Women." http://www.canadianwomen.org/facts-about-violence.

Carrillo, Roxanna. 1992. *Battered Dreams: Violence against Women as an Obstacle to Development*. Publication No. WE 011. New York: United Nations Development Fund for Women.

Chatterjee, Partha. 1993. *Nationalist Thought and the Colonial World: A Derivative Discourse*. Minneapolis: University of Minnesota Press.

Chemaly, Soraya. 2011. "Violence against Women Is a Global Pandemic." *Huffington Post*, January 31. http://www.huffingtonpost.com/soraya-chemaly/violence-against-women-is_1_b_1121001.html.

Chowdhury, Elora Halim. 2011. *Transnationalism Reversed: Women Organizing against Gendered Violence in Bangladesh*. Albany, NY: SUNY Press.

Clare, Eli. 1999. *Exile and Pride: Disability, Queerness, and Liberation*. New York: South End Press.

Cling, Jean-Pierre, Mireille Razafindrakoto, and François Roubaud. 2003. "New Poverty Reduction Strategies: Old Wine in New Bottles?" In *Annual World Bank Conference on Development Economics Europe toward Pro-Poor Policies: Aid, Institutions, and Globalization*, edited by Bertile Tungodeen, Nicholas Stern, and Ivar Kolstad, 111–13. Washington, DC: World Bank; Oxford: Oxford University Press.

Clinton, Hillary. 2009. "UN Women: Peace and Security." United Nations Security Council. http://www.unmultimedia.org/tv/unifeed/d/13601.html.

———. 2010. "It's Time to Get Tough on Violence against Women." *Guardian*, December 10. http://www.guardian.co.uk/commentisfree/2011/dec/10/violence-women-hillary-clinton.

———. 2011. "Recognition of International Human Rights Day." U.S. Department of State. http://www.state.gov/secretary/rm/2011/12/178368.htm.

———. 2012. "International Day of Zero Tolerance to Female Genital Mutilation/Cutting." http://translations.state.gov/st/english/texttrans/2012/02/20120206183857su0.7688344 html#axzz4DpLV0R4g.

Cohn, Carol. 1987. "Sex and Death in the World of Rational Defense Intellectuals." *Signs: Journal of Women in Culture and Society* 12, 4: 687–718.

Connell, Raewyn, and James W. Messerschmidt. 2005. "Hegemonic Masculinity: Rethinking the Concept." *Gender and Society* 19, 6: 829–59.

Cornwall, Andrea, and Deborah Eade. 2010. *Deconstructing Development Discourse: Buzzwords and Fuzzwords.* Oxford: Oxfam Press.

Crenshaw, Kimberle. 1991. "Mapping the Margins: Intersectionality, Identity Politics, and Violence against Women of Color." *Stanford Law Review* 43, 6: 1241–99.

Crush, Jonathan. 1995. *Power of Development.* New York: Routledge.

Daily Mail. 2015. "World Bank Pulls Funding for Uganda Transport Project." *Daily Mail*, December 21. http://www.dailymail.co.uk/wires/afp/article-3369511/World-Bank-pulls-funding-Uganda-transport-project.html.

Davidson, Kavitha A. 2013. "Hillary Clinton: Countries Visited by the Most-Traveled Secretary of State in History." *Huffington Post*, June 9. http://www.huffingtonpost.com/2013/02/02/hillary-clinton-countries-travels_n_2602541.html.

Davis, Angela. 2003. *Are Prisons Obsolete?* New York: Seven Stories Press.

———. 2005. *Abolition Democracy: Beyond Empire, Prisons, and Torture.* New York: Seven Stories Press.

Day, Tanis, Katherine McKenna, and Audra Bowlus. 2005. *The Economic Costs of Violence against Women: An Evaluation of the Literature.* Expert Brief, United Nations. http://www.un.org/womenwatch/daw/vaw/expert%20brief%20costs.pdf.

Deleuze, Gilles, and Félix Guattari. 2004. *A Thousand Plateaus: Capitalism and Schizophrenia.* London: Continuum Books.

Desai, Manisha. 2002. "Transnational Solidarity: Women's Agency, Structural Adjustment, and Globalization." In *Women's Activism and Globalization: Linking Local Struggles and Transnational Politics*, edited by Nancy Naples and Manisha Desai, 14–31. New York: Routledge.

———. 2005. "Transnationalism: The Face of Feminist Politics Post-Beijing." *International Social Science Journal* 57 (184): 319–30.

Dick, Kirby, and Amy Ziering, dirs. 2012. *The Invisible War.* Chain Camera Pictures.

Dingo, Rebecca. 2007. "Making the 'Unfit, Fit': The Rhetoric of Mainstreaming in the World Bank's Commitment to Gender Equality and

Disability Rights." *Wagadu: A Journal of Transnational Women and Gender Studies* 4: 93–107.

———. 2012. *Networking Arguments: Rhetoric, Transnational Feminism, and Public Policy Writing*. Pittsburgh: University of Pittsburgh Press.

Dolan, Catherine, and Linda Scott. 2009. "Lipstick Evangelism: Avon Trading Circles and Gender Empowerment in South Africa." *Gender and Development* 17, 2: 203–18.

Du Bois, W. E. B. 1903. *The Souls of Black Folk*. Chicago: A. C. McClurg Press.

Duffield, Mark. 2007. *Development, Security, and Unending War: Governing the World of Peoples*. Cambridge, UK: Polity Press.

———. 2010. "The Liberal Way of Development and the Development-Security Impasse: Exploring the Global Life-Chance Divide." *Security Dialogue* 41, 1: 53–76.

Duggan, Lisa. 2004. *The Twilight of Equality: Neoliberalism, Cultural Politics, and the Attack on Democracy*. Boston: Beacon Press.

Eisenstein, Hester. 2009. *Feminism Seduced: How Global Elites Use Women's Labor and Ideas to Exploit the World*. London: Paradigm Publishers.

Eisenstein, Zillah. 2004. *Against Empire: Feminisms, Racism, and the West*. New York: Zed Books.

Elliot, Larry. 2016. "Austerity Policies Do More Harm than Good, IMF Study Concludes." *Guardian*, May 27. https://www.theguardian.com/business/2016/may/27/austerity-policies-do-more-harm-than-good-imf-study-concludes.

Elshtain, Jean Bethke, and Sheila Tobias. 1990. *Women, Militarism, and War: Essays in History, Politics, and Social Theory*. New York: Rowman and Littlefield.

Enloe, Cynthia. 1988. *Does Khaki Become You? The Militarisation of Women's Lives*. London: Pandora Press.

———. 1989. *Bananas, Beaches, and Bases: Making Feminist Sense of International Politics*. London: Pandora Press.

———. 2004. *The Curious Feminist: Searching for Women in a New Age of Empire*. Berkeley: University of California Press.

———. 2007. *Globalization and Militarism: Feminists Make the Link*. New York: Rowman and Littlefield.

Erevelles, Nirmala. 2006. "Disability in the New World Order." In *Color of Violence: The INCITE! Anthology*, edited by INCITE! Women of Color against Violence, 25–31. Cambridge, MA: South End Press.

Erwin, Patricia E. 2006. "Exporting U.S. Domestic Violence Reforms: An Analysis of Human Rights Frameworks and U.S. 'Best Practices.'" *Feminist Criminology* 1, 3: 188–206.

Escobar, Arturo. 1995. *Encountering Development: The Making and Unmaking of the Third World*. Princeton, NJ: Princeton University Press.

Families of Sisters in Spirit. 2013. http://familiesofsistersinspirit.tumblr.com.

Fanon, Frantz. 2008. *Black Skins, White Masks*. Translated by R. Philcox. New York: Grove Press.

Ferguson, James. 2005. "Decomposing Modernity: History and Hierarchy after Development." In *Postcolonial Studies and Beyond*, edited by Ania Loomba, Suvir Kaul, Matti Bunzl, Antoinette Burton, and Jed Esty, 166–81. Durham, NC: Duke University Press.

———. 2009. "The Uses of Neoliberalism." *Antipode* 41, S1: 166–84.

Fernández-Kelly, María Patricia. 1983. *For We Are Sold, I and My People: Women and Industry in Mexico's Frontier*. Albany, NY: SUNY Press.

Fluri, Jennifer. 2009. "The Beautiful 'Other': A Critical Examination of 'Western' Representations of Afghan Feminine Corporeal Modernity." *Gender, Place, and Culture* 16, 3: 241–57.

Foucault, Michel. 1980. *Power/Knowledge: Selected Interviews and Other Writings, 1972–1977*. New York: Pantheon.

———. 2003. *"Society Must Be Defended": Lectures at the Collège de France, 1975–1976*. New York: Picador.

Fox, Jonathan, and David Brown. 1998. *The Struggle for Accountability: The World Bank, NGOs, and Grassroots Movements*. Cambridge, MA: MIT Press.

Garland Thomson, Rosemarie. 1997. *Extraordinary Bodies: Figuring Physical Disability in American Culture and Literature*. New York: Columbia University Press.

Gass, Nick. 2016. "Clinton Breaks from Obama, Calls Orlando Attack 'Radical Islamism.'" *Politico*, June 13. http://www.politico.com/story/2016/06/hillary-clinton-radical-islam-224255#ixzz4BZcbK5FA.

Geldof, Bob. 2012. *Live Aid*. http://www.bobgeldof.com/#.

Gender Action and Friends of the Earth International. 2011. "Broken Promises and the World Bank's Gender Equality and Development Report." http://www.genderaction.org/publications/11/chad-cam-wagp-pipelines.html.

Gerring, John. 2004. "What Is a Case Study and What Is It Good For?" *American Political Science Review* 98, 2: 341–52.

Glenn, Evelyn Nakano. 2008. "Yearning for Lightness: Transnational Circuits in the Marketing and Consumption of Skin Lighteners." *Gender and Society* 22, 3: 281–302.

Gould, Deborah B. 2009. *Moving Politics: Emotion and ACT UP's Fight against AIDS*. Chicago: University of Chicago Press.

Grewal, Inderpal. 2005. *Transnational America: Feminisms, Diasporas, Neoliberalisms*. Durham, NC: Duke University Press.

Grewal, Inderpal, and Caren Kaplan. 1994. *Scattered Hegemonies: Postmodernity and Transnational Feminist Practices*. Minneapolis: University of Minnesota Press.

Gulabi Gang. 2014. "Gulabi Gang Official." http://www.gulabigang.in.

Hage, Ghassan J. 2000. *White Nation: Fantasies of White Supremacy in a Multicultural Society*. New York: Routledge.

Hall, Stuart. 1990. "The Whites of Their Eyes: Racist Ideologies and the Media." In *The Media Reader*, edited by Manual Alvarado and John O. Thompson, 9–23. London: British Film Institute.

Harman, Jane. 2008. "Finally, Some Progress in Combating Rape and Assault in the Military." *Huffington Post*, October 11. http://www.huffingtonpost.com/rep-jane-harman/finally-some-progress-in_b_125504.html.

Harrison, Graham. 2001. "Administering Market Friendly Growth? Liberal Populism and the World Bank's Involvement in Administrative Reform in Sub-Saharan Africa." *Review of International Political Economy* 8, 3: 528–47.

Harvey, David. 1990. *The Condition of Postmodernity: An Enquiry into the Origins of Cultural Change*. Cambridge, UK: Blackwell.

Hemmings, Clare. 2005. "Invoking Affect: Cultural Theory and the Ontological Turn." *Cultural Studies* 19, 5: 548–67.

Herman, Edward S., and Noam Chomsky. 2002. *Manufacturing Consent: The Political Economy of the Mass Media*. 1988; reprinted, New York: Pantheon Books.

Heron, Barbara. 2007. *Desire for Development: Whiteness, Gender, and the Helping Imperative*. Waterloo: Wilfrid Laurier University Press.

Hettne, Björn. 2010. "Development and Security: Origins and Future." *Security Dialogue* 41, 1: 31–52.

Hill, Stephen M., Randall R. Beger, and John M. Zanetti. 2007. "Plugging the Security Gap or Springing a Leak: Questioning the Growth of Paramilitary Policing in U.S. Domestic and Foreign Policy." *Democracy and Security* 3, 3: 301–21.

Hill Collins, Patricia. 1998. "The Tie that Binds: Race, Gender, and U.S. Violence." *Ethnic and Racial Studies* 21, 5: 917–38.

hooks, bell. 2000. *Feminism Is for Everybody: Passionate Politics*. London: Pluto Press.

Hudson, Valerie M., and Patricia Leidl. 2015. *The Hillary Doctrine: Sex and American Foreign Policy*. New York: Columbia University Press.

Huntington, Samuel P. 1993. *The Clash of Civilizations and the Remaking of World Order*. New York: Touchstone.

Iannotti, Lauren. 2011. "*Glamour* Goes on the Road with Hillary." *Glamour Magazine*, August 2. http://www.glamour.com/inspired/sex-love-life/2011/08/glamour-goes-on-the-road-with-hillary.

INCITE! Women of Color against Violence. 2006. *The Color of Violence: The INCITE! Anthology*. Cambridge, MA: South End Press.

International Violence against Women Act of 2010. 2010. H.R. 4594, 111th Congress, 2nd Session.

Ironstone-Catterall, Penelope. 2011. "Pan(dem)ic Now! Palliative Commodities, Anticipatory Anxiety, and the Flu." Feminist Café, University of Ottawa.

Isserles, Robin G. 2003. "Microcredit: The Rhetoric of Empowerment, the Reality of 'Development as Usual.'" *Women's Studies Quarterly* 31, 3–4: 38–57.

Jackson, Cecile, and Ruth Pearson. 1998. *Feminist Visions of Development: Gender Analysis and Policy*. New York: Routledge.

Jacobson, Ruth. 2013. "Women 'after' Wars." In W*omen and Wars: Contested Histories, Uncertain Futures*, edited by Carol Cohn, 215–41. Cambridge, UK: Polity Press.

Jahan, Rounaq. 1995. *The Elusive Agenda: Mainstreaming Women in Development*. New York: Zed Books.

Jiwani, Yasmin. 2006. *Discourses of Denial: Mediations of Race, Gender, and Violence*. Vancouver: UBC Press.

———. 2010. "Doubling Discourses and the Veiled Other: Mediations of Race and Gender in Canadian Media." In *States of Race: Critical Race Feminism for the 21st Century*, edited by Sherene Razack, Malinda Smith, and Sunera Thobani, 59–86. Toronto: Between the Lines.

Joachim, Jutta M. 2007. *Agenda Setting, the UN, and NGOs: Gender Violence and Reproductive Rights*. Washington, DC: Georgetown University Press.

Johnston, Josée, and Judith Taylor. 2008. "Feminist Consumerism and Fat Activists: A Comparative Study of Grassroots Activism and the Dove Real Beauty Campaign." *Signs* 33, 4: 941–66.

Kapoor, Ilan. 2006. *The Postcolonial Politics of Development*. London: Routledge.

Kapur, Ratna. 2012. "Pink Chaddis and SlutWalk Couture: The Postcolonial Politics of Feminism Lite." *Feminist Legal Studies* 20, 1: 1–20.

Katz, Cindi. 2001. "On the Grounds of Globalization: A Topography for Feminist Political Engagement." *Signs* 26, 4: 1213–34.

Kellaway, Mitch, and Brydum Sunnivie. 2015. "The 21 Trans Women Killed in 2015." *Advocate*, July 27. http://www.advocate.com/transgender/2015/07/27/these-are-trans-women-killed-so-far-us-2015.

Kothari, Uma. 2006. "Critiquing 'Race' and Racism in Development Discourse and Practice." *Progress in Development Studies* 6: 1–7.

Kotter, John P. 2008. *A Sense of Urgency*. Cambridge, MA: Harvard Business Press.

Kuiper, Edith, and Drucilla Barker. 2006. *Feminist Economics and the World Bank: History, Theory, and Policy*. New York: Routledge.

Lee, Matthew. 2010. "Clinton Promotes Human Rights in Papua New Guinea." *Washington Post*, November 3. http://www.washingtonpost.com/wp-dyn/content/article/2010/11/03/AR2010110301070.html.

Lee Badgett, M. V. 2014. "The Economic Costs of Homophobia and the Exclusion of LGBT People: A Case Study of India." World Bank. http://www.worldbank.org/content/dam/Worldbank/document/SAR/economic-costs-homophobia-lgbt-exlusion-india.pdf.

Lind, Amy. 2009. "Governing Intimacy, Struggling for Sexual Rights: Challenging Hetero-normativity in the Global Development Industry." *Development* 52, 1: 34–42.

Lippmann, Walter. 1922. *Public Opinion*. New York: Harcourt, Brace, and Company.

Loomba, Ania. 1998. *Colonialism/Postcolonialism: The New Critical Idiom*. New York: Routledge.

Lorde, Audre. 1984. *Sister Outsider: Essays and Speeches by Audre Lorde*. Trumansburg, NY: Crossing Press.

Macklin, Audrey. 2002. "Looking at Law through the Lens of Culture: A Provocative Case." In *Crimes of Colour: Racialization and the Criminal Justice System in Canada*, edited by Wendy Chan and Kiran Mirchandani, 87–100. Toronto: University of Toronto Press.

Magnet, Shoshana A. 2011. *When Biometrics Fail: Gender, Race, and the Technology of Identity*. Durham, NC: Duke University Press.

Manzo, Kate. 1991. "Modernist Discourse and the Crisis of Development Theory." *Studies in Comparative International Development* 26, 2: 3–36.

Marchand, Marianne H. 2008. "The Violence of Development and the Migration/Insecurities Nexus: Labour Migration in a North American Context." *Third World Quarterly* 29, 7: 1375–88.

Marchand, Marianne H., and Jane Parpart. 1995. *Feminism, Postmodernism, Development*. New York: Routledge.

Marchand, Marianne, and Anne Runyan. 2011. *Gender and Global Restructuring: Sightings, Sites, and Resistances*. 2nd ed. New York: Routledge.

Mason, Corinne L. 2012. "Men, HIV/AIDS, and Culture: An Analysis of the World Bank's The Other Half of Gender—Men's Issues in Development." *International Feminist Journal of Politics* 14, 2: 247–66.

———. 2016. "Race, Media, and Surveillance: Sex-Selective Abortions in Canada." In *Expanding the Gaze: Gender and the Politics of Surveillance*, edited by Emily van der Meulen and Robert Heynen, 135–55. Toronto: University of Toronto Press.

Massumi, Brian. 2000. "Translator's Foreword: Pleasures of Philosophy." In *A Thousand Plateaus*, by Gilles Deleuze and Félix Guattari, ix–xvi. Minneapolis: University of Minnesota Press.

———. 2002. *Parables for the Virtual: Movement, Affect, Sensation.* Durham, NC: Duke University Press.

Mbembe, Achille. 2003. "Necropolitics." Translated by Libby Meintjes. *Public Culture* 15, 1: 11–40.

McClintock, Anne. 1995. *Imperial Leather: Race, Gender, and Sexuality in the Colonial Contest.* New York: Routledge.

McGreal, Chris. 2012. "U.S. Marines Accused of War Crimes: Video Posted Anonymously on YouTube Claims to Show American Troops in Afghanistan Urinating on Dead Bodies." *Guardian*, January 12. http://www.guardian.co.uk/world/2012/jan/12/american-marines-accused-war-crimes.

McRuer, Robert. 2006. *Crip Theory: Cultural Signs of Queerness and Disability.* New York: New York University Press.

———. 2010. "Disability Nationalism in Crip Times." *Journal of Literary and Cultural Disability Studies* 4, 2: 163–78.

———. 2012. "The Crip's Speech in an Age of Austerity: Composing Disability Transnationally." Keynote presentation at Carleton University, Ottawa, February 16.

Meekosha, Helen. 2011. "Decolonising Disability: Thinking and Acting Globally." *Disability and Society* 26, 6: 667–82.

Meyer-Emerick, Nancy. 2001. *The Violence against Women Act of 1994: An Analysis of Intent and Perception.* Westport, CT: Praeger.

Miles, Matthew B., and A. Michael Huberman. 1994. *Qualitative Data Analysis: An Expanded Source Book.* 2nd ed. Thousand Oaks, CA: Sage.

Miller, Carol, and Shahra Razavi. 1998. *Missionaries and Mandarins: Feminist Engagement with Development Institutions.* London: Intermediate Technology Publications.

Miller-Adams, Michelle. 1999. *The World Bank: New Agendas in a Changing World.* New York: Routledge.

Mills, Charles W. 1997. *The Racial Contract.* Ithaca, NY: Cornell University Press.

Moallem, Minoo. 2005. *Between Warrior Brother and Veiled Sister: Islamic Fundamentalism and the Politics of Patriarchy in Iran.* Berkeley: University of California Press.

Mohanty, Chandra Talpade. 1991. "Under Western Eyes: Feminist Scholarship and Colonial Discourses." In *Third World Women and the Politics of*

Feminism, edited by Chandra Talpade Mohanty, Lourdes Torres, and Ann Russo, 51–80. Bloomington: Indiana University Press.

———. 2003. *Feminism without Borders: Decolonizing Theory, Practicing Solidarity.* Durham, NC: Duke University Press.

Mohanty, Chandra Talpade, Minne Bruce Pratt, and Robin Lee Riley. 2008. *Feminism and War: Confronting U.S. Imperialism.* London: Zed Books.

Molyneux, Maxine, and Shahra Razavi. 2002. *Gender Justice, Development, and Rights.* Oxford: Oxford University Press.

———. 2006. "Beijing Plus 10: An Ambivalent Record on Gender Justice." United Nations Research Institute for Social Development Occasional Paper 15. http://www.unrisd.org/publications/opgp15.

Moser, Caroline, Annika Tornqvist, and Bernice van Bronkhorst. 1999. *Mainstreaming Gender and Development in the World Bank: Progress and Recommendations.* Washington, DC: World Bank.

Mosse, David. 2005. *Cultivating Development: An Ethnography of Aid Policy and Practice.* Ann Arbor, MI: Pluto Press.

Munck, Ronaldo. 1999. "Deconstructing Development Discourse: Of Impasses, Alternatives, and Politics." In *Critical Development Theory: Contributions to a New Paradigm*, edited by Ronaldo Munck and Denis O'Hearn, 196–210. New York: Zed Books.

Mwesigwa, Alon. 2016. "World Bank Cancels Funding for Uganda Road amid Sexual Assault Claims." *Guardian*, January 12. https://www.theguardian.com/global-development/2016/jan/12/world-bank-cancels-uganda-road-sexual-assault-claims.

Nagar, Richa, and Amanda Lock Swarr. 2010. *Critical Transnational Feminist Praxis.* Albany, NY: SUNY Press.

Narayan, Uma. 1997. *Dislocating Cultures: Identities, Traditions, and Third-World Feminism.* New York: Routledge.

———. 2000. "Essence of Culture and a Sense of History: A Feminist Critique of Cultural Essentialism." In *Decentering the Center: Philosophy for a Multicultural, Postcolonial, and Feminist World*, edited by Uma Narayan and Sandra Harding, 80–100. Bloomington: Indiana University Press.

Nguyen, Vinh-Kim. 2010. *The Republic of Therapy: Triage and Sovereignty in West Africa's Time of AIDS.* Durham, NC: Duke University Press.

Nussbaum, Martha C., and Jonathan Glover. 1995. *Women, Culture, and Development: A Study of Human Capabilities.* Oxford: Oxford University Press.

Obama, Barack. 2015. "Remarks by the President in State of the Union Address." January 20. http://www.whitehouse.gov/the-press-office/2015/01/20/remarks-president-state-union-address-january-20-2015.

Oliver, Michael. 1996. *Understanding Disability: From Theory to Practice*. New York: Palgrave Macmillan.

Ong, Aihwa. 1987. *Spirits of Resistance and Capitalist Discipline: Factory Women in Malaysia*. Albany, NY: SUNY Press.

Ostry, Jonathan D., Prakash Loungani, and Davide Furceri. 2016. "Neoliberalism: Oversold?" *Finance and Development* 53, 2. http://www.imf.org/external/pubs/ft/fandd/2016/06/ostry.htm.

Oxford English Dictionary. 2013a. "Telescopic." *Oxford English Dictionary*. http://oxforddictionaries.com/definition/english/telescopic.

———. 2013b. "Urgency." *Oxford English Dictionary*. http://oxforddictionaries.com/definition/english/urgency?q=urgency.

Parpart, Jane. 2010. "Masculinity, Gender, and the 'New Wars.'" *Nordic Journal for Masculinity Studies* 5, 2: 85–99.

Parpart, Jane, Shirin M. Rai, and Kathleen A. Staudt. 2002. "Rethinking Em(power)ment, Gender, and Development: An Introduction." In *Rethinking Empowerment: Gender and Development in a Global/Local World*, edited by Jane Parpart, Shirin M. Rai, and Kathleen A. Staudt, 3–21. New York: Routledge.

Pateman, Carole. 1988. *The Sexual Contract*. Stanford: Stanford University Press.

Peterson, V. Spike. 2007. "Thinking through Intersectionality and War." *Race, Gender, and Class* 14, 3–4: 10–28.

Pietilä, Hilkka, and Jeanne Vickers. 1996. *Making Women Matter: The Role of the United Nations*. London: Zed Books.

Poe, Ted. 2010. "QandA: Ted Poe Discusses His Effort to Curb Violence against Women." *Houston Chronicle*, February 1. http://blog.chron.com/txpotomac/2010/02/qa-ted-poe-disusses-his-effort-to-curb-violence-against-women/.

———. 2012. "U.S. Congressman, 2nd District of Texas." http://poe.house.gov/.

Poster, Winifred, and Zakia Salime. 2004. "The Limits of Microcredit: Transnational Feminism and USAID Activities in the United States and Morocco." In *Women's Activism and Globalization: Linking Local Struggles to Transnational Politics*, edited by Nancy Naples and Manisha Desai, 181–219. New York: Routledge.

Price, Lisa S. 2001. "Finding the Man in the Soldier-Rapist: Some Reflections on Comprehension and Accountability." *Women's Studies International Forum* 24, 2: 211–27.

Prügl, Elisabeth M. 1999. *The Global Construction of Gender: Home-Based Work in the Political Economy of the 20th Century*. New York: Columbia University Press.

———. 2015. "Neoliberalising Feminism." *New Political Economy* 20, 4: 614–31.

Puar, Jasbir K. 2004. "Abu Ghraib: Arguing against Exceptionalism." *Feminist Studies* 30, 2: 522–34.

———. 2007. *Terrorist Assemblages: Homonationalism in Queer Times*. Durham, NC: Duke University Press.

Quadrennial Diplomacy and Development Review (QDDR). 2010. "Leading through Civilian Power." U.S. Department of State and USAID. http://www.state.gov/documents/organization/153108.pdf.

Rahman, Aminur. 1999. "Microcredit Initiatives for Equitable and Sustainable Development: Who Pays?" *World Development* 27, 1: 67–82.

Ramamurthy, Priti. 2003. "Material Consumers, Fabricating Subjects: Perplexity, Global Connectivity Discourses, and Transnational Feminist Research." *Cultural Anthropology* 18, 4: 524–50.

Rao, Rahul. 2014. "Queer Questions." *International Feminist Journal of Politics* 16, 2: 199–217.

Razack, Sherene. 1998. *Looking White People in the Eye: Gender, Race, and Culture in Courtrooms and Classrooms*. Toronto: University of Toronto Press.

———. 2004. *Dark Threats and White Knights: The Somalia Affair, Peacekeeping, and the New Imperialism*. Toronto: University of Toronto Press.

———. 2005. "How Is White Supremacy Embodied? Sexualized Racial Violence at Abu Ghraib." *Canadian Journal of Women and the Law* 17, 2: 341–63.

———. 2007. "Stealing the Pain of Others: Reflections on Canadian Humanitarian Responses." *Review of Education, Pedagogy, and Cultural Studies* 29: 375–94.

———. 2008. *Casting Out: The Eviction of Muslims from Western Law and Politics*. Toronto: University of Toronto Press.

Reuters. 2011. "Clinton Says China Seeks to Outflank Exxon in Papua New Guinea." March 2. http://www.reuters.com/article/2011/03/02/us-china-usa-clinton-idUSTRE7215UV20110302.

Revolutionary Association of the Women of Afghanistan. 2013. http://www.rawa.org/rawa.html.

Rich, Adrienne. 1983. "Compulsory Heterosexuality and Lesbian Existence" In *Powers of Desire: The Politics of Sexuality*, edited by Ann Snitow, Christine Stansell, and Sharon Thompson, 177–205. New York: Monthly Review Press.

Ritchie, Andrea. 2006. "Law Enforcement Violence against Women of Color." In *Color of Violence: The INCITE! Anthology*, edited by INCITE! Women of Color against Violence, 138–56. New York: South End Press.

Rodney, Walter. 1972. *How Europe Underdeveloped Africa*. Washington, DC: Howard University Press.

Rogers, Carey. 2010. "Obama Administration Exports Neo-Marxist Ideology across the Globe." *Renew America*. http://www.renewamerica.com/columns/roberts/100408.

Royal Canadian Mounted Police (RCMP). 2014. "Missing and Murdered Aboriginal Women: A National Operational Overview." http://www.rcmp-grc.gc.ca/pubs/mmaw-faapd-eng.pdf.

Said, Edward. 1978. *Orientalism*. New York: Vintage Books.

Saint Louis, Catherine. 2010. "Creams Offering Lighter Skin May Bring Risks." *New York Times*, January 16. http://www.nytimes.com/2010/01/16/health/16skin.html?pagewanted=all.

Sankore, Rotimi. 2005. "Behind the Image: Poverty and 'Development Pornography.' *Pambazuka News*. http://pambazuka.org/en/category/features/27815.

Saunders, Kriemild. 2002. *Feminist Post-Development Thought: Rethinking Modernity, Post-Colonialism, and Representation*. New York: Zed Books.

Savage, Charlie, and Elisabeth Bumiller. 2012. "An Iraqi Massacre, a Light Sentence, and a Question of Military Justice." *New York Times*, January 28. http://www.nytimes.com/2012/01/28/us/an-iraqi-massacre-a-light-sentence-and-a-question-of-military-justice.html?_r=1.

Save Indian Family Foundation. 2010. "I-VAWA: A Failed Experiment." February 18. http://archive.is/sgc2j#selection-283.0-283.27.

Schissel, Bernard, and Carolyn Brooks. 2008. *Marginality and Condemnation: A Critical Introduction to Criminology*. 2nd ed. Halifax: Fernwood Publishing.

Schoenpflug, Karin. 2006. "World Bank Discourse and World Bank Policy in Engendering Development: A Comment." *Feminist Economics and the World Bank: History, Theory, and Policy*, edited by Edith Kuiper and Drucilla Barker, 117–24. New York: Routledge.

Sen, Amartya. 2006. "Foreword." In *Women, Development, and the UN: A Sixty-Year Quest for Equality and Justice*, edited by Devaki Jain, xvii–xix. Bloomington: Indiana University Press.

Sherry, Mark. 2007. "(Post)colonising Disability." *Wagadu: A Journal of Transnational Women and Gender Studies* 4: 10–22.

Shohat, Ella. 2002. "Area Studies, Gender Studies, and the Cartographies of Knowledge." *Social Text* 20, 3: 67–78.

Sjoberg, Laura. 2010. *Gender and International Security: Feminist Perspectives*. New York: Routledge.

Smith, Andrea. 2005. *Conquest: Sexual Violence and American Indian Genocide*. Massachusetts: South End Press.

———. 2010. "Indigeneity, Settler Colonialism, White Supremacy." *Global Dialogue* 12, 2. http://www.worlddialogue.org/content.php?id=488.

Smith, Malinda. 2010. "Terrorism Thinking: '9/11 Changed Everything.'" In *Securing Africa: Post-9/11 Discourses on Terrorism*, edited by Malinda Smith, 1–30. New York: Routledge.

Smith, Neil, and Cindi Katz. 1993. "Grounding Metaphor: Towards a Spatialized Politics." In *Place and the Politics of Identity*, edited by Michael Keith and Steve Pile, 66–81. New York: Routledge.

Smyth, Ines. 2010. "Talking of Gender: Words and Meanings in Development Organizations." In *Deconstructing Development Discourse: Buzzwords and Fuzzwords*, edited by Andrea Cornwall and Deborah Eade, 143–52. Oxford: Oxfam House Press.

Spade, Dean. 2011. *Normal Life: Administrative Violence, Critical Trans Politics, and the Limits of Law*. New York: South End Press.

Spivak, Gayatri. 1988. "Can the Subaltern Speak?" In *Marxism and Interpretation of Culture*, edited by Cary Nelson and Lawrence Grossberg, 271–313. Chicago: University of Illinois Press.

———. 2004. "Righting Wrongs." *South Atlantic Quarterly* 103, 2–3: 523–81.

Staudt, Kathleen. 2008. *Violence and Activism at the Border: Gender, Fear, and Everyday Life in Ciudad Juárez*. Austin: University of Texas Press.

Stoler, Ann. 1995. *Race and the Education of Desire: Foucault's History of Sexuality and the Colonial Order of Things*. Durham, NC: Duke University Press.

Talley, Ian. 2016. "World Bank Forms Task Force to Tackle Rape, Other Abuses at Its Projects." *Wall Street Journal*, August 11. http://www.wsj.com/articles/world-bank-forms-task-force-to-tackle-rape-other-abuses-at-its-projects-1470952840.

TED Blog. 2010. "TED Blog Exclusive: Hillary Rodham Clinton Speaks at TEDWomen." December 10. http://blog.ted.com/ted-blog-exclusive-hillary-rodham-clinton-at-tedwomen/.

Telegraph. 2011. "Hillary Clinton Says Egypt Is Failing Its Women." December 20. http://www.telegraph.co.uk/news/worldnews/africaandindianocean/egypt/8967424/Hillary-Clinton-says-Egypt-is-failing-its-women.html.

Thompson, Nissa. 2008. "Does the International Violence against Women Act Respond to Lessons from the Iraq War?" *Berkeley Journal of Gender, Law, and Justice* 23, 1: 2–17.

Thursdays in Black. 2015. http://www.thursdaysinblack.co.za.

Tickner, J. Ann. 1992. *Gender in International Relations: Feminist Perspectives on Achieving Global Security*. New York: Columbia University Press.

Titchkosky, Tanya, and Rod Michalko. 2009. *Rethinking Normalcy: A Disability Studies Reader*. Toronto: Canadian Scholars Press.

Tomkins, Silvan. 1963. *Affect, Imagery, Consciousness. Vol. II: The Negative Affects*. New York: Springer Publishing.

Treichler, Paula. 1999. *How to Have a Theory in an Epidemic: Cultural Chronicles of Aids*. Durham, NC: Duke University Press.

Tzemach Lemmon, Gayle. 2011. "The Hillary Doctrine." *Newsweek*, June 3. http://www.newsweek.com/hillary-doctrine-66105.

Uddin, Sohel. 2013. "Bangladesh Factory Collapse: Why Women Endure Danger to Make Clothes for the West." NBC News, May 26. http://worldnews.nbcnews.com/_news/2013/05/26/18447688-bangladesh-factory-collapse-why-women-endure-danger-to-make-clothes-for-the-west?lite.

United Nations. 1976. "Report of the World Conference of the International Women's Year." Mexico City, June 19–July 2, 1975. http://www.un.org/womenwatch/daw/beijing/otherconferences/Mexico/Mexico%20conference%20report%20optimized.pdf.

———. 1979. "Convention on the Elimination of All Forms of Discrimination against Women." http://www.un.org/womenwatch/daw/cedaw/cedaw.htm.

———. 1980. "Report of World Conference of the United Nations Decade for Women: Equality, Development, and Peace." Copenhagen, July 4–30, 1980. http://www.un.org/womenwatch/daw/beijing/otherconferences/Copenhagen/Copenhagen%20Full%20Optimized.pdf.

———. 1985. "Report of the World Conference to Review and Appraise the Achievements of the United Nations Decade for Women: Equality, Development, and Peace." Nairobi, July 15–26, 1985. http://www.un.org/womenwatch/daw/beijing/otherconferences/Nairobi/Nairobi%20Full%20Optimized.pdf.

———. 1993. "Declaration on the Elimination of Violence against Women." http://www.un.org/documents/ga/res/48/a48r104.htm.

———. 1995. "Beijing Declaration and Platform for Action." http://www.un.org/womenwatch/daw/beijing/platform/

———. 2004. "A More Secure World: Our Shared Responsibility." Report of the High-Level Panel on Threats, Challenges, and Change. http://www.un.org/en/peacebuilding/pdf/historical/hlp_more_secure_world.pdf.

———. 2006. "In-Depth Study on All Forms of Violence against Women: Report of the Secretary-General." http://daccess-dds-ny.un.org/doc/UNDOC/GEN/N06/419/74/PDF/N0641974.pdf?OpenElement.

———. 2011a. "Cambodia: Reclaiming Life after Acid Attacks." UNiTE Say No to Violence. http://saynotoviolence.org/around-world/news/cambodia-reclaiming-life-after-acid-attacks.

———. 2011b. "Guatemala: Young Mayan Women Shape the Future." http://www.unwomen.org/en/news/stories/2011/11/ guatemala-young-mayan-women-shape-the-future.

———. 2011c. "UN Issues First Report on Human Rights of Gay and Lesbian People." December 15. http://www.un.org/apps/news/story. asp?NewsID=40743#.UUyu8aVQqa4.

———. 2012a. "UNiTE to End Violence against Women." http://endviolence. un.org/.

———. 2012b. "The Situation." http://www.un.org/en/women/endviolence/pdf/ pressmaterials/unite_the_situation_en.pdf.

———. 2012c. "UNiTE Worldwide." http://www.un.org/en/women/endviolence/ world.shtml.

———. 2012d. "Say No—UNiTE to End Violence against Women." http:// saynotoviolence.org/.

———. 2012e. "The Secretary-General's Network of Men Leaders." http://www. un.org/en/women/endviolence/network.shtml.

———. 2012f. "What Is the United Nations Doing to End Violence against Women and Girls?" http://www.unis.unvienna.org/pdf/factsheets/ UNiTE_WhatWeDo_en.pdf.

UN Women. 2012. "Ending Violence against Women and Girls." http://www. pacificwomen.org/wp-content/uploads/UNwomen-EVAW-Brief.pdf.

———. 2014. "Facts and Figures: Ending Violence against Women." http:// www.unwomen.org/en/what-we-do/ending-violence-against-women/ facts-and-figures.

United States Senate Committee on Foreign Relations. 2010. "Members of House and Senate Stand in Support of Landmark Legislation to Combat Violence against Women." February 4. https://votesmart.org/ public-statement/482493/members-of-house-and-senate-stand-in- support-of-landmark-legislation-to-combat-violence-against-women#. V3_rnGPduCQ.

U.S. News. 2010. "Hillary Clinton Promotes Human Rights in Papua New Guinea." November 3. http://www.usnews.com/news/articles/2010/11/03/ clinton-promotes-human-rights-in-papua-new-guinea.

Visvanathan, Nalini. 1997. "Introduction." In *The Women, Gender, and Development Reader*, edited by Nalini Visvanathan, Lynn Duggan, Nan Wiegersma, and Laurie Nisonoff, 17–32. London: Zed Books.

Wallace, Robert Daniel. 2010. "Whither State? The Institutional Politics of American Nation-Building Policy." *Contemporary Security Policy* 31, 1: 114–33.

Watson, Amanda D., and Corinne L. Mason. 2015. "Mapping the SlutWalk Paradox: Challenges and Possibilities of Using Raunch in Transnational Feminist Politics." In *"This Is What a Feminist Slut Looks Like": Perspectives on the SlutWalk Movement*, edited by May Friedman, Alyssa Teekah, Erika Jane Scholz, and Andrea O'Reilly, 133–53. Brantford, ON: Demeter Press.

Watts, Michael. 1995. "'A New Deal in Emotions': Theory and Practice and the Crisis of Development." In *The Power of Development*, edited by Jonathan Crush, 44–62. New York: Routledge.

Weaver, C. 2010. "The Strategic Social Construction of the World Bank's Gender and Development Policy Norm." In *Owning Development: Creating Policy Norms in the IMF and World Bank*, edited by Susan Park and Antje Vetterlein, 70–90. Cambridge, UK: Cambridge University Press.

Wetherell, Margaret. 2012. *Affect and Emotion: A New Social Science Understanding*. London: Sage Publications.

Whitworth, Sandra. 2005. "Militarized Masculinities and the Politics of Peacekeeping: The Canadian Case." In *Critical Security Studies and World Politics*, edited by Ken Booth, 89–106. Boulder, CO: Lynne Rienner Publishers.

Williams, Gavin. 1995. "Modernizing Malthus: The World Bank, Population Control, and the African Environment." In *The Power of Development*, edited by Jonathan Crush, 158–75. New York: Routledge.

Willman, Alys. 2009. "Valuing the Impacts of Domestic Violence: A Review by Sector." In *The Costs of Violence*, by the World Bank, 57–70. Washington, DC: World Bank Group.

Wolf, Naomi. 1991. *The Beauty Myth: How Images of Beauty Are Used against Women*. London: Vintage.

Women Thrive Worldwide. 2010. "The International Violence against Women Act of 2010 (IVAWA)." http://www.womenthrive.org/index.php?option=com_contentandtask=viewandid=366andItemid=115.

World Bank. 1944. "Articles of Agreement." Amended June 27, 2012. http://siteresources.worldbank.org/BODINT/Resources/278027-1215526322295/IBRDArticlesOfAgreement_English.pdf.

———. 1993. *World Development Report 1993: Investing in Health*. New York: World Bank, Oxford University Press.

———. 2001. *Engendering Development: Through Gender Equality, Rights, Resources, and Voice*. Washington, DC: World Bank Group.

———. 2006. "Gender Equality as Smart Economics: A World Bank Group Action Plan." http://siteresources.worldbank.org/INTGENDER/Resources/GAPNov2.pdf.

———. 2009a. *The Cost of Violence*. Washington, DC: World Bank Group.

———. 2009b. *Gender Equality as Smart Economics: Gender Action Plan*. Newsletter, April 2009. http://siteresources.worldbank.org/EXTGENDER/ Resources/GAPNewsletterSpring09.pdf.

———. 2011a. "President Robert B. Zoellick Announces 6 New World Bank Group Commitments on Gender Equality." http://go.worldbank.org/ GY6U8JNS50.

———. 2011b. *The Members of the External Gender Consultative Group*. http:// go.worldbank.org/AWXA1P0120.

———. 2012. *World Development Report: Gender Equality and Development*. Washington, DC: World Bank Group.

———. 2015. "World Bank Statement on Cancellation of the Uganda Transport Sector Development Project (TSDP)." http:// www.worldbank.org/en/news/press-release/2015/12/21/ wb-statement-cancellation-uganda-transport-sector-development-project.

World Health Organization. 2008. *The Global Burden of Disease: 2004 Update*. Geneva: World Health Organization.

World Health Organization and World Bank. 2011. *World Report on Disability*. Geneva: World Health Organization.

Yeğenoğlu, Meyda. 1998. *Colonial Fantasies: Towards a Feminist Reading of Orientalism*. Cambridge, UK: Cambridge University Press.

Zangana, Haifa. 2007. *City of Widows: An Iraqi Woman's Account of War and Resistance*. New York: Seven Stories Press.

INDEX

||||||||||||||||||||||

preventing, 68, 71; to promote U.S. as global leader, 14, 48, 120, 185, 190–91, 194; responses to, 37, 60, 66, 69, 73–74, 78, 164, 196; and UN campaigns, 132–33, 135, 144, 150, 155, 160–64, 166–67; as urgent issue, 3, 6, 13, 16, 18–20, 23–24, 45, 65, 183, 187, 189

women, violence against, elimination of, 19, 75, 150, 152, 163, 184–85; to achieve development, 140–41; by aligning towards solidarity, 175, 192, 196; as efficient use of resources, 62; for national security reasons, 73, 78; through UN campaigns, 159, 169, 172–73, 181; using economic approaches, 81

Women and Development (WAD), 88

Women in Development (WID), 88

Women Thrive WorldWide, 34, 61

women's equality/inequality, 32, 34, 43–44, 52, 111, 136, 138, 141–42, 151, 175

women's rights, 31, 44, 47, 49, 75–76, 141–42, 151, 187, 194; and development and security, 77–78; as justifying war on terror, 45, 65; and national security concerns, 36–37, 43, 77–78; promotion of, 32, 64; through imperial acts, 61, 67, 73; as tied to development projects, 21, 33, 130, 185

World Bank, 20–23, 65, 81, 90, 142, 184, 187–88, 193–94; and ableism, 98; and beauty ideology, 122–24; and cost of violence, 62, 79, 93, 97; economic-focused work of, 85; External Gender Consultative Group, 88; focus on economic growth, 106–7, 109, 113, 118, 120, 130, 195; focus on gender, 22, 84, 87–91, 94, 103, 187, 886; as knowledge bank, 89, 105, 122; neo-liberal development models, 85, 89, 92, 95, 98, 104, 114, 125, 128–29; as normate figure in development industry, 85, 104–5, 116; rehabilitative logic of disability, 124; Social Development Group, 87; as using DALYs, 29, 80, 83–84, 96, 98, 100–102, 107–8, 112, 115–16, 120; and violence against women, 82, 114, 185

World Development Report 2012: Gender Equality and Development, 92, 118

World Health Organization, 26, 80, 95, 101

World Report on Disability, 101

World Survey on the Role of Women in Development, 139

Y

Yeğenoğlu, Meyda, 47

Yunus, Muhammad, 132

Z

Zanetti, John M., 58

Zangana, Haifa, 48, 67

zero tolerance policy, on abuse, 68

Ziering, Amy, 73

Zionism, 137–38

Zoellick, Robert B., 91